make it reality

make it reality

CREATE YOUR OPPORTUNITIES.
OWN YOUR SUCCESS.

CRIS ABREGO

with MIM EICHLER RIVAS

A CELEBRA BOOK

CELEBRA
Published by New American Library,
an imprint of Penguin Random House LLC
375 Hudson Street, New York, New York 10014

This book is an original publication of New American Library.

First Printing, May 2016

For more information about Penguin Random House, visit penguin.com.

LIBRARY OF CONGRESS CATALOGING-IN-PUBLICATION DATA:

Names: Abrego, Cris, author.
Title: Make it reality: create your opportunity, own your success/Cris Abrego.
Description: New York: Celebra, 2016.
Identifiers: LCCN 2015050418 (print) | LCCN 2016006940 (ebook) | ISBN 9781101990360 (hardback) | ISBN 9781101990391 (ebook) Subjects: LCSH: Abrego, Cris. | Success. | Success in business. | Self-realization. | Television producers and directors—United States. | BISAC: BIOGRAPHY & AUTOBIOGRAPHY/ Business. | BIOGRAPHY & AUTOBIOGRAPHY/ Personal Memoirs. | PERFORMING ARTS/Television/ General. Classification: LCC BJ1611.2 .A23 2016 (print) | LCC BJ1611.2 (ebook) | DDC 650.1—dc23
LC record available at http://lccn.loc.gov/2015050418

Printed in the United States of America
10 9 8 7 6 5 4 3 2 1

Designed by Tiffany Estreicher

Penguin
Random
House

contents

To the next generation of visionaries, I can't wait to see what you do next . . . and don't forget to pass it on.

And to all my fellow Martians, may you have the courage to embrace your differences and pursue your dreams!

— In loving memory of Carlos Hernandez Jr.

It is not enough to teach our young people to be successful . . . so they can realize their ambitions, so they can earn good livings, so they can accumulate the material things that this society bestows. Those are worthwhile goals. But it is not enough to progress as individuals while our friends and neighbors are left behind.

—César Chávez

foreword

by Armando Christian Perez (Pitbull)

Dale! If you know anything about me and my approach to dreams, goals, and success, you probably know that's the word I use to power up, to get you hyped to go for it, to do it, to live it, and to do it now! There's no exact translation but I promise once you've read *Make It Reality*, that's what you'll be ready to do.

It was late 2007 when I first met Cris Abrego—one night in Miami after being introduced by a mutual friend. As "Mr. 305" back in those days, I was learning a lot about making dreams happen. My career was definitely going places and Cris—co-creator and executive producer of hit shows like *Flavor of Love*—was fast becoming the name to know in television. He was somebody, I had heard, who was in the business of turning his own and other people's dreams into reality. In fact, the friend who introduced us was Miami's own Josh Gallander/aka Whiteboy—who had been a local pawnshop owner when Cris discovered him and made him a huge star on the hysterical reality series *I Love New York*.

So Whiteboy and Cris come walking into the club and head over to the corner of the bar—where I'm sitting with some friends. Whiteboy says, "You two should meet." His point was that Cris and I had both overcome obstacles and had found early success by turning the negative into positive.

From the moment Cris and I started to talk, we clicked. Not only did we have similar stories and come from similar backgrounds—one of us Cuban-American from Miami and the other Mexican-American from Los Angeles—but also as two young, hungry guys, we were on a similar path working tirelessly to take our game to the next level.

Cris was so positive and supportive, telling me, "Hey, man, good luck. I'll be watching." And I told him the same.

Even though our paths didn't cross again for almost seven years, I always remembered that conversation and how that night at the bar Cris Abrego predicted that I had a brand that could lead to global business success—beyond music. His belief in me and what was possible was that real, and I never forgot it.

And well, you know how it goes—timing can be everything. By early 2014, when we did reconnect in the hopes of finding a way to work together on some projects, the timing was perfect. I was proudly representing my hometown of Miami as Mr. Worldwide and Cris, still that same down-to-earth guy from El Monte, was Mr. International himself as co-CEO of Endemol Shine North America, a division of the global TV giant.

We met for hours to kick around some ideas, and as the night got later and later, I decided to drive Cris to the airport for a five a.m. flight back to L.A. It must have been about three in the morning when I took him on a driving tour of Miami's Bayfront Park—a favorite waterfront destination with shops and restaurants near American Airlines Stadium, where the Heat play. As we drove, I found myself telling Cris the story of how, as a kid, I used to come to Bayfront every New Year's Eve to watch the fireworks and how I dreamed of one day hosting my own show on New Year's—in my hometown.

That's where we left it. And true to form as an enterprising doer, Cris came back to me just weeks later and made it a reality. He sold the show to FOX, and that very next year we started airing *Pitbull's New Year's Revolution* live from Bayfront Park. It's been everything I could have asked for and more.

It's also an amazing experience to watch Cris work. We speak the same language and heartily embrace the truth that sometimes we have to make something out of nothing. So there is never a limit on what's possible. There is never a "no" where there is intention, belief, and vision. His ability to inspire others is at a level I've rarely seen in my life. He is a reminder to all that your past or your background doesn't have to hold you back from creating your reality. His philosophy echoes my own—that as you look at the world, you can choose to believe that there is nothing you can't do, so go after your dream and truly own that success.

Don't just take it from me. Read this book to be inspired by Cris's story of victory and hard-won success, and learn how to write your own. *Make It Reality* should be required reading for everyone who is preparing to go into unchartered waters in their careers and their lives, for everyone who wants to shake up the status quo or who wants to empower and lift up others.

So why dream when you can wake up and live it? Now go make it reality! *Dale!*

Why I Chose Reality

Over the past few years, I've batted around the idea of writing a book like this one. But it was only recently—as I was about to deliver a speech to the graduating class of my alma mater, Mountain View High School in El Monte, California—that *Make It Reality* was actually conceived.

When I was first invited to give the commencement address, I accepted the honor on the spot. *Wow*, I remember thinking as I put down the phone, *now I know what it really means to make it!* Even as a successful executive, entrepreneur, and philanthropist—and as a public speaker comfortable addressing a range of topics and audiences—I confess to being daunted by the prospect of returning to the place that had launched my journey and talking about what I'd learned.

Of course, it's always a little surreal to make the trek back to my hometown, and especially to relive all the memories of the people and events that shaped what once seemed to be my crazy plans for the future. It's true. I was that guy—the one with the big dreams and goals. As a high school grad, my ultimate dream—after earning my degree at Cal State Fullerton, where I was headed on a four-year wrestling scholarship—was to go on to have an impressive career in the television industry. At the time, it didn't seem so crazy to me because I didn't know any better!

But I can tell you now that back when I graduated from Mountain View, class of 1990 (damn, I know that's gotta sound *old*!), I didn't have a clue about how to make my dream a reality. I didn't even know where to begin. There I was, so close to the entertainment industry that I could almost see the Hollywood sign from my backyard. Yet I knew next to nothing about the television business . . . except for how to watch it.

In the days leading up to giving this graduation speech, I thought about the fact that most of the graduates who came from where I did were probably where I was twenty-some years earlier—with great hopes for their lives ahead but little knowledge about how to overcome the many roadblocks that would no doubt arise. After all, could the world have changed that much in the years since I walked the halls of Mountain View, a proud and victorious Viking? By the way, in case you're wondering how an ancient Scandinavian warrior became the mascot of a nearly all-Latino high school, the answer is—who knows? What I do know was that in El Monte, then as now, you learned to make the most of what you had. Where other, more affluent LA suburbs had the more iconic In-N-Out Burger, back in my day we had the lesser-known low-frills version—EZ Take Out.

Obviously, many things had changed since 1990. But not totally. When my friends and I graduated, the hit songs on the radio were Madonna's "Vogue" and MC Hammer's "U Can't Touch This." Cut to: Present Day. One of those celebrities is still on top, and the other returned from obscurity ten years ago when he landed a part on a reality show. As for the most popular TV shows with our graduating class, we watched *Beverly Hills 90210* and *The Fresh Prince of Bel-Air*. Will Smith's career worked out pretty well for him, and there was also a happy ending for the actors of *90210* when the entire cast wound up on various reality TV shows.

Now, if you had told me that part of this history would in some way be connected to me, I wouldn't have believed you for a second. Not if you told the high-school-graduate version of me, or even the college-graduate version, or the barely employed newlywed at age twenty-four—just married to the love of my life, who had graduated the same year as I did from Mountain View (although I didn't even know her until later). That scenario would have seemed especially out of reach to me at age thirty when my first reality TV production company took a nosedive around the same time that my wife and I, both unemployed, became expectant parents to the first of our three amazing children. But at that stage of my career, once I'd gained an understanding of the power of great ideas brought to life with skilled execution, I actually *would* have believed what happened next: I cocreated a reality show that was to become *The Surreal Life*, the same show that I was able to convince MC Hammer to appear on under the banner of a new company co-owned by me and my partner, Mark Cronin. And, as a pioneer of what would soon be dubbed "Celebreality," I could also take a bit of credit for the subsequent emergence of a genre that has been most welcoming to an astonishing variety of iconic figures from across the entertainment and pop culture spectrum—including some of those stars from *90210*.

Even with all my big dreams, I could never have envisioned how the reality that unfolded could be so much better than the fantasy. Nor could I have envisioned being invited back to my high school to hopefully offer meaningful and empowering advice to the seventeen- and eighteen-year-olds getting ready to pursue their dreams. That too was surreal. During a handful of visits that I'd already made to the high school, I couldn't help thinking how unbelievably young the seniors looked for their age. Could I have ever looked that young? No way. But I could recall the same sense of excitement and accomplishment that I knew they had to be feeling as graduation day approached. When I thought about this idea of coming full circle and speaking to a crowd with so many brown faces—like mine, just like most of us back in 1990—I found myself becoming emotional about giving them advice that could really make a difference as they prepared to leave home for college and the real world.

Believe it or not, once upon a time, before I left El Monte for college and the real world, I used to think everybody who wasn't on TV or famous had to be Mexican or at least Latino in some form or fashion. After all, that's what my community looked like. Imagine my culture shock when I started to ascend the ladder of the television business and I'd walk into offices to hold my own with heavy hitters only to realize that my brown face put me in a minority of one.

Those realities were in my mind on the day of the graduation ceremony as I pulled off the 10 Freeway a good hour before I had to show up at Mountain View. Although it's only about thirty miles due east from my Sunset Boulevard office—where, for the past two years I have been at the helm as co-CEO of the North America division of Endemol Shine, the largest television company in the world— El Monte might as well be on the other side of the country. Maybe that's why, whenever I go home, whether it's to speak to youth or to business leaders or to visit relatives who never left, I always make a point of going early to drive the neighborhood, just to cruise the streets I used to run with my friends and roll past the old places that remind me where I come from.

For all intents and purposes, El Monte was the barrio. We weren't exactly the urban barrio. We had modest houses, well-kept lawns, and small backyards for the expansive family gatherings of the multiple generations who moved in but never left. Yet we still faced many of the challenges of living in the barrio: poverty, drugs, and gangs, along with rougher neighborhoods that you learned to avoid.

Without a doubt, the house where I grew up on Redstone, a cul-de-sac off Parkway, was a safe haven, where my mother and father not only raised me and my older brother but also provided a second home to many of our friends—whose own parents weren't together anymore or just weren't around. Though it took me a while to appreciate all the lessons that my parents used *every* opportunity to teach us, that house—where they no longer live—was my first school, run by my earliest and most important teachers.

Home was also where I fell in love with television. I watched a lot of it, preparing for a career I didn't yet know I wanted. We're talking every kind of show that a kid growing up in the late seventies and eighties could have watched: Sitcom, variety, drama, you name it. One of my all-time favorites was a show called *That's Incredible*, arguably one of the early forerunners of reality television and of formats with celebrity anchors or panels like you see on *America's Got Talent*. To an eleven-year-old like me, that TV show was proof that incredible people with incredible abilities and stories could exist anywhere and everywhere. Even El Monte.

There was something about El Monte that made it seem lost in time, as if the city belonged in the past—back in the glory days of lowriders (which were still ruling the streets when I was a kid), full of *cholos* and *cholitas*, music blaring and engines grinding. We still had roots in the fifties and sixties, when rock 'n' roll was countercultural, when you could hear anyone from Ritchie Valens to the Grateful Dead at the El Monte Legion Stadium and when DJ Art Laboe hosted the famous Friday night dances there, as immortalized in the 1963 doo-wop hit "Memories of El Monte."

For me and my circle of friends, that was our anthem, so much so that a bunch of us later got tattoos inspired by the title and the images we each chose not to forget. So what if that record was released a decade before most of us were born?

We wore those lyrics on our skin, like a badge of belonging, at the same time that we mapped out our futures away from El Monte. I wasn't the only crazy dreamer. There was one friend who planned to go into TV too and another couple of the guys who would rise up in the ranks of law enforcement. And then there was one of my best friends, Carlos—"Ghost" as I had nicknamed him because he was so small and quick he reminded me of that line "You can't hit what you can't see" from *Everybody's All-American* with Dennis Quaid. A kid who had been through more than his share of instability but who never stopped smiling and who was always up for an adventure, Carlos had opted to play football at a local junior college and then planned on transferring to one of the California state universities with a higher-ranked program. After that, you never knew. At the least, we figured he could join one of my other best friends, Danny "Dog," who wanted to go into business, and the two would come work for me . . . that is, once I'd landed a foothold in TV.

The point is simple—there are no guarantees but we gave ourselves permission to dream. It didn't matter that we didn't grow up in the lap of luxury. We grew up in the lap of reality. Weirdly, even when there were no tangible reasons to have a lot of hope, something about being from El Monte gave you a sense of pride. What's more, El Monte made you tough. And that toughness has a way of fueling your pride and feeding your dreams.

As was my ritual whenever I went back home, I made one last stop before meeting my parents, who planned on attending the graduation to hear me speak. In that final slow drive down Parkway, instead of continuing on at the intersection of Fineview, I pulled up to the curb, let the engine idle, and remembered everything that had happened before, during, and after the accident that took place there on May 6, 1991.

The story of that afternoon is one I haven't ever wanted to tell, for many reasons, not the least of which is the sincere desire to spare everyone the pain—myself included. As a matter of fact, other than a few brief conversations to share the memory behind my tattoo, I couldn't remember talking to anyone about it over the years since it happened, not publicly and not even privately. On a gut level, I knew as I sat in the idling car that there had to be someone out there in the world who would be helped by hearing this story. But, damn, I argued with myself, to tell it right, I would have to go back and relive it all, everything that until now I have kept locked away, packed up in a box. Literally.

A decision, long delayed, was at hand. Not immediately, but soon, the time had come for me to take down the box from the shelf, to go through its contents, to review the accident report and the trial transcripts, to take out the shorts I was wearing, still bloodied, and to reread the journal entries in the notebook that I had kept for over a year, unbeknownst to anyone but me. Avoiding the subject, I now believe, would be a disservice to the memory of my best friend, Carlos "Ghost" Hernandez Jr.

As I try to give you a sense of that day, I'll start by saying that there was nothing ominous or threatening in the vibe. Not at all. I was nineteen, enjoying my freshman year at Cal State Fullerton, doing well on the wrestling team, and happy when practice was canceled that afternoon. I got a call from Danny "Dog," who said, "Hey, come on up to 'Monte and we'll hang out."

Good excuse to see the guys and maybe to go say hello to Adriana, a beautiful girl I'd just met (and would later marry). So I hopped in my Honda Accord and met up with the guys at the local Tastee Freez, one of our hangouts. Carlos was there, along with the rest of the regular group, and when I asked Danny if I could take his motorcycle to run a few errands, Carlos asked if he could ride with me. For me, the more the merrier—except, as I later realized, the bike wasn't designed well for more than one rider. But everything was cool. Danny took my Honda and we planned to meet at his place later on. In the meantime, Carlos and I drove the bike to get haircuts, this being in the prehelmet days, then stopped by Adriana's, and continued cruising around El Monte—driving familiar streets that we knew every bump and rut of, taking the same curves and turns I'd driven a thousand times in cars and on other motorcycles.

At four or so in the afternoon, we were closing in on Danny's house, maybe five blocks to go at the most, when I came around the curve on Parkway and tapped the brake to slow down. Whether the motorcycle recoiled and lurched on its own because of the pressure on the brake or it hit the edge of a gutter and catapulted up—I don't know. All I knew was that as I lost control of the bike, it went up in the air, flipping and sliding out from under us and throwing us in the direct path of a cement light pole. I was thrown but missed the cement pole and went flying onto the street, tumbling and smashing the back of my head on the asphalt. Carlos hit the pole and screamed so loud, I thought I saw his horror-stricken face. But I couldn't have seen him. It was only how I imagined he must have looked by the sound of his scream. For less than a minute, I passed out from loss of blood but regained enough awareness to crawl over to Carlos—who lay on the street in what appeared to be the most peaceful sleep that he would soon awaken from. Yet I knew he would never wake up. Helplessly, I cradled him in my arms, waiting for the arrival of paramedics.

When I opened my eyes after that, I was in the hospital, handcuffed to the bed. A police officer was at my side. He told me that the good news was that my blood work came back clean—no alcohol or drugs in it—and there would be no criminal charges. The bad news?

"Your friend is dead." Carlos was nineteen years old. Now he was gone.

Inside my head, I was screaming—*Why Carlos? Why didn't I die?* But there was no one to answer. After that, I would replay the accident time and time again, recalculating the trajectories so that I was the one who hit the pole and Carlos the one who lived.

As he uncuffed me, the police officer asked, "Do you believe in God?"

I nodded yes, not sure why he was asking.

"Well," he said, just before leaving the room, "then you should thank Him that you're still alive because it was not your turn. He must have plans for you."

I didn't understand what he meant. Not then. Later, however, during the trial—after the prosecutor went ahead and filed charges of felony vehicular manslaughter after all—the officer's words helped me through a dark time.

For a short period, I believed that my life, as I had once dreamed it, was over. Nothing would or could ever be the same. But then came the shocker: Life went on. Dad laid down the law that I go back to college two days after the accident. My professors wanted to know where my papers were, and instead of telling them what had happened, I accepted the markdown to my grades. They knew nothing of the tragedy. It was another example of the fact that life goes on—in spite of the loss of someone so important.

That was when, at one of the most critical crossroads of my life, I chose reality. Sure, I could go into denial, as others seemed to do. I wrote in my journal, "Carlos knew I loved him but that doesn't make it all right to put him behind me. God help me." Or I could give in to depression, or drinking and drugs, or give up on my dreams and decide my life was over. I remember thinking that people would say, "Yeah, well, there was the accident," and they would give me a pass. I would have that excuse. But I didn't want an excuse to go numb, to be a loser or a victim. Days after Carlos died, I wrote, "Everything I do reminds me of Carlos. We went to so many places together and did so many things that everywhere I go reminds me of him." My greatest fear was that I would forget Carlos just to go on. I hoped to God that I wouldn't.

I didn't want an excuse to stop living. And I made up my mind that I was not going to waste another second. I was not ever going to take life or the opportunity to do something with my life for granted. I was going to carry some of the Ghost with me for the rest of my life, and I pledged that somehow my success would let him live through my achievements and adventures. That was when I made the decision to go and to go hard, to wake up every day and go get it.

In remembrance of Carlos's dreams, a few years ago I was able to set up the Carlos Hernandez Jr. Memorial Scholarship at Mountain View High School—awarding college athletic scholarships to two seniors each year, one male and one female. These students are so remarkable and so inspiring, maintaining 4.0 GPAs with full academic loads, proving themselves on the athletic fields, and many coping with incredibly difficult challenges at home.

So all of this may give you a sense of the mix of memory and emotion inside of me as I was sitting up on the stage at Mountain View High School with the other commencement speakers, waiting to be called to the podium and watching the procession of seniors in caps and gowns as they filed in to take their seats. In an almost out-of-body experience, I heard my name being called, rose from my seat, and crossed the stage to stand and look out at all those younger versions of myself.

This was the moment when I made the decision to open up the box that I had tried for so long to keep closed. That, in turn, lit the fire in me to write this book. One of the important messages I hope to share—and a key discovery that I made after the accident, much further down the road, was the power of acting without fear. Of course, it's true that when the worst thing you can imagine has happened, you have a habit of not being afraid of very much. In Hollywood, a town that runs on fear, having a lack of it seems to have served me well. And it turns out that getting past your fear is an essential stepping-stone to making your dreams and goals a reality.

When the framework for this book was first conceived—at Mountain View High School, as I was thinking, *Boy, those young grads don't even have an inkling of the roller coaster ahead*—I wanted to share everything that I know now and wish like hell I had known then. I will tell you right up front that reality TV was not the genre that I set out to conquer. But I love it all the more for having let me create opportunities that weren't open to me elsewhere. I love reality because, as its title proves, it holds up a mirror to something that is REAL. The power of an unscripted show, especially in the early days of the genre, was that the people in the shows are playing themselves. They're not characters saying words they wouldn't normally say. The reality show stars—"real" people and celebs alike—engage us and elevate us by holding up a mirror to our everyday hopes and fears. If aliens visited our planet to study us, they would be very confused by most of our scripted entertainment. But reality would teach them everything they'd need to know about being human. And that's why I chose reality.

This is a book I hope will be meaningful to the dreamers in all communities—kids going off to college or entering the working world and college grads on the job hunt or struggling entrepreneurs or anyone struggling to break into a field like Hollywood or business executives hoping to raise their game or anyone returning to the workforce. I hope that it can be useful to employers and educators about how to recognize the reality makers of the future.

Before I get to the principles of success that have proven most effective for me, I want to reinforce a key lesson that was held in that box all this time—that you have a choice. You can let obstacles—loss, tragedy, limitations, lack of opportunity—overwhelm you. Or you can choose to be the creator and generator of the opportunities that will lead you to the reality of the success you seek to own. You can choose to move toward your goals every day and make every second count. Above all, you can choose to believe in what's possible.

And that is everything.

one

Bet on Yourself: *Would You Take the $200 Million Job?*

It isn't enough to just know your full potential; you have to get your ass out on the battlefield and reach your potential, with balls-to-the-wall action.

—Richard Marcinko,
Leadership Secrets of the Rogue Warrior

Now that you have chosen to *believe* in what's possible, the next step—no easy challenge whatsoever—is to put yourself in charge of making it happen. Though it may sound simple, turning dreams into reality begins to happen the moment you choose and commit to becoming the architect of your own destiny. How do you do that? By following my most valued business principle of *betting on yourself*.

As I recall the main turning points in my journey to success, the biggest strides were the direct result of a willingness to bet on myself—both on a daily basis and over the long haul. The first bet happened once I found what I loved to do and chose to do it at the highest possible level. And today, that dream I bet on is now my reality, one I never take for granted.

It's a reality that I get to savor every morning when I drive into work, either coming from an early workout at the gym or from a nearby breakfast meeting. No matter what, I can't hold back the rush of adrenaline that kicks in every time I cruise past the legendary Beverly Hills Hotel, moments before hitting the Sunset Strip—home to a vast network of talent agencies, management and production companies, exclusive restaurants, rock 'n' roll clubs, and a multitude of other businesses somehow connected to the Wild Wild West of the Hollywood entertainment world. Sometimes I honestly can't believe this is where I work!

Of course, I get over that disbelief once I'm riding up the elevator to the offices of Endemol Shine and stepping into our main lobby, as I gear up for an action-packed agenda. On any given day, I could find myself starting with a presentation I'm giving in our conference room with Ashton Kutcher and his people, then moving onto a phone call with Pitbull and his manager, followed by a sit-down with my co-CEO, Charlie Corwin, and our COO, Ben Samek—a long-time business partner who personifies my practice of not being afraid to hire executives who are smarter than I am. Our agenda might include finalizing a deal for shooting a new TV series in Israel and a chat about the next strategic planning session we're hosting with our global partners. Then I'm on to another conference call, this time with Jay Z and his team, all before I have to make a dash across town to help pitch a manhunt-themed show to the top execs at CBS.

Rarely is there a spare minute in the day to muse about my unlikely journey—or just how much stranger than fiction my reality has become. Still, every now and then, when I cross the threshold into the corner office that has my name on it, I have to stop and feel amazed to be here.

My success wasn't guaranteed. Far from it. And there were a few moments along the way when I thought failure was imminent. Like in the early 2000s, when circumstances in the economy and my industry shifted abruptly, causing the business I'd built to implode. This was at a time when *Survivor* and *The Amazing Race* had emerged as the two behemoths at the top of the genre of reality TV. In general, the practice for all reality—unscripted—shows was to cast contestants or participants (as in the case of shows like MTV's *Real World*) who were *real people*—not actors, not celebrities. The standard format was to put these real-life characters into a specific setting—like a tropical island or a mansion somewhere—and let their different personalities react to outrageous challenges and changing situations as they interacted authentically. At its inception, the genre had been fresh and new and thrilling. But eventually as reality started to explode as a genre, many of the shows would become harder to distinguish from others. The freshness was definitely starting to fade.

So in the midst of my business crisis I was sitting at home one day watching TV (aka doing research) and, at the suggestion of a UTA agent, was checking out a commercial for a product called Lipton Sizzle & Stir. In it, Loni Anderson is at the stove cooking up dinner with seasoning from the package as Mr. T. helps, along with Mary Lou Retton, who's stirring something up too, while George Hamilton sits in an adjoining room playing video games. There's a whole family story line with Mr. T. affectionately telling Loni what all those spices do to him and Mary Lou answering the phone as she teases George that it's for him and "It's a girl!" This commercial was the second in a series for Lipton Sizzle & Stir, and I had loved the first one too. In it, we meet the Woolerys, a family who consists of Sally Jessy Raphael at the stove with game show host Chuck Woolery checking out the appetizing meal while character actor Pat Morita sets the table and Little Richard tries to sneak down the stairs without having to help. Too late, Sally calls to him to pitch in, and the next thing we see is a pouting Little Richard smacking down a fork, saying, "There! I helped!" with Pat Morita growling at him. Sally gets the last line though, as she quips: "C'mon, guys. Can't we have one nice meal together?"

The tagline for both commercials? "When you cook, you're a family."

My first thought was how hysterical it would be if the commercial was conceived as a spoof of what would happen if all these crazy personalities lived together and loved easy-to-make dinners they could cook together as a family. My second thought was to take it a step further—*Wait! What if a group of celebrities really lived together? How crazy would that be?* The next thought was one of those lightbulb-going-off eureka! moments where I saw a new kind of show that I wanted to executive produce. The pitch could be something like "Imagine these celebrities together, *living* together. Imagine that they're a family." In kind of a blend from the commercials, I thought of every family-member archetype that could be cast—the Mom, the Dad, the crazy Uncle, the young, sassy Daughter, the cool Brother, or the troublemaking Brother . . . and so on.

Crazy as it was, I had the choice to play by the rules of the marketplace and come up with something more traditional or to go against the grain—and bet on myself, as well as my own instincts. The next thing that happened, after meeting and teaming up with comedy writer/producer Mark Cronin at the suggestion of the same UTA agent, the idea was born for the show that became *The Surreal Life*, an approach that was to become the new standard—Celebreality, as it was eventually named.

Even with the phenomenal success that resulted from betting on that crazy idea that had never been tried before, I know it's still a long shot that I'm here today. As a business executive, coming from a nontraditional background as I do—and considering the odds—I'm probably not supposed to be sitting up in this rarefied air at all. There are even moments when I feel like someone's going to show up and say, "Hey, man, you don't belong here! What's the deal?" I'll have to respond, "OK, it's over. I got it. You're finally onto me!"

Well, good thing, so far that hasn't happened. But I do frequently pick up on a level of disbelief from colleagues and even family members when they ask: *How is this possible? How in twenty years did you climb this mountain—from having no access to building your company from nothing and selling it for a hefty amount, only to be asked to co-run the same corporation that bought the company?*

Actually, the more direct question I'm usually asked is: *How did you get so lucky?*

I have to correct their assumptions. Again, having an impressive title and getting to sit at the head of the conference table doesn't make me lucky. Where I am lucky is that I love what I do. To me, getting to do what I love makes me the luckiest. But that too was a choice, as was the belief that I could make a living at it. To clarify, the money has never been my main motivation. Not at any stage. My main motivation has always been the quest to do what I love—television—and to continually create opportunities that challenge me to grow. That's success in my terms.

To answer the question of how I got here and how you can get to where you'd love to be, I come back to the powerful lesson that you can put to use right now: When you really choose to bet on yourself—rather than counting on luck or connections or benefactors who will champion your cause—you give yourself permission to create the opportunities that lead to success. The dimensions of that success, that reality, are totally up to you.

PLAY THE LONG GAME

You might be wondering why this powerful business principle is often overlooked. There are two explanations. First of all, betting on yourself—and not on a proven path—requires a lot of risk without any guarantees. Second, betting on yourself usually requires that you invest years of hard work, time, focus, passion, energy, and sacrifice into an undertaking that you may lose interest in. In other words, in order to achieve the reality you seek, you'll have to learn to play the long game. Forget overnight success. Forget fairy-tale thinking or expecting opportunities to be put in front of you like bread crumbs leading you to where you should go. Somebody else already got there first—trust me on this. Don't look for promises or predictable ways for this dream to materialize. Do embrace your own crazy dream. In my book, the crazier, the better.

If you don't know whether or not you've found your lane yet and aren't sure where to start, my advice is just to start. Set out on a path and bet on your instincts to guide you to where you can go and grow. If you have connections that can offer help, you'll have a leg up that many of us don't have. But don't take them for granted. And don't bet on them. Bet only on yourself.

Avoid following someone else's playbook. Look to write your own, although you can adapt moves from the principles and examples offered ahead—and from anyone else's success playbook—as long as you do the work required.

Playing the long game was the result of major lessons I learned in the wake of business disappointments and tough challenges. As an example, I'll never forget how difficult it was to approach celebrities and pop culture icons about being on *The Surreal Life*. When my partner, Mark Cronin, and I couldn't get agents or managers to return our calls, we resorted to showing up at hairdressers or coffee shops to pitch our ideas in person. At one point, we flew ourselves to New York City in the hopes of casting a big media personality, and after countless phone calls, we *finally* were given a face-to-face meeting with the one and only Reverend Al Sharpton. The hitch? With only a few hours' notice, we had to meet him at the legendary Four Seasons Restaurant—only one of the fanciest, most high-end places to meet and dine anywhere in the world. Opened in 1959 and designed by architects Philip Johnson and Mies van der Rohe, it has long been recognized for being home to the ultimate power lunch—where, I should add, a suit and tie were the absolute requirements to even step foot in the restaurant. Shocking as it may sound, in those days, I didn't even own a suit, much less have one with me. For one thing, I lived and worked in the (at least superficially) more laid-back LA. And for another, as a producer you typically avoided the stuffy-suit look. Clearly, if I wanted to pitch Reverend Al on why doing *Surreal Life* would bring him fantastic exposure, not to mention financial rewards, I had to get a damn suit. And fast.

So, I jog across town in sweltering New York City heat to Hugo Boss to buy a suit off the rack. Incidentally, being 175 pounds and a really broad-shouldered ex-wrestler—where being shorter and stronger than my opponent gave me an edge—doesn't in turn make me an easy fit for buying a suit off the rack. But, being from El Monte, where you make the most of what you have, I manage to find a suit that will get me in the door at the Four Seasons—despite the fact that the pant legs are way too long and the jacket arms too short. No sooner do I begin my race back across town to the meeting, now dressed in this ill-fitting suit and sweating like crazy, than I realize that the alarm tag on the bottom of one of the pants legs is still attached!

Excuse my language, but all I can think is—*Shit!* Not only does the suit *not* look like it is mine, but with the alarm tag stuck on it, everybody at the Four Seasons will think I friggin' knocked off a Hugo Boss store. There is nothing I can do but try to hide the leg with the alarm tag behind the other leg, which gives me this weird pimp walk as my partner (who is shooting me dirty looks) and I make it to the table with Reverend Al—where he and his associates have already begun ordering.

Needless to say, this didn't bode well for the desired outcome of the meeting. But we'd already made a substantial investment in creating this opportunity, so the last thing I wanted to do was give up without delivering the best possible pitch that I could. Embarrassing alarm tag on my pants and all.

However, the moment we sat down, Reverend Al's uninterest made it clear that he was never going to seriously consider being on *The Surreal Life*. I figured he only took the meeting so we could buy him and his cohorts a super-pricey lunch. Celebrities are used to being wined and dined, after all.

In any event, once we finished ordering all the wine and the crab cakes and jumbo shrimp and steak and lobster entrées, we finally got down to business. Mark Cronin, a master of comedic timing, broke the ice and cued me up to begin the pitch. We took turns describing our show and our respective successes in the industry—enough to get a nod or two from Reverend Al before he interrupted to say, "Guys, get to the end."

By then he was having coffee and dessert. Not a good sign. Apparently, we had just spent five hundred dollars on lunch for nothing. Not to mention that I would have to return my suit to Hugo Boss.

We were almost at the big close of our presentation when, again, Al interrupted. "Guys," he said, "I'm just gonna be honest with you. I'm never gonna do this show. There's a chance that I could decide to run for president. And I can't have anything disrupt that."

If you could have read my mind about then, it would have been full of four-letter words, trust me. But instead of cursing out loud, I said, "Well, I'm gonna be honest with you. Reverend Sharpton, I don't mean any disrespect, but you're never going to be president."

Mark Cronin nearly choked as he shot me a look that said—*Are you out of your mind?* Al and his friends appeared to be just as shocked.

Not stopping there, now that I had gone this far out on the limb, I decided to bet on myself and on another idea that might just change his mind. So I repeated, "You're never gonna be president," and went on, "But I tell you what I will do, and what you could do. And how you can be in the White House."

Nobody said a word.

I proceeded: "I will build you the White House on this set of our show. I will turn *The Surreal Life* house into the White House, with an Oval Office, with a full West Wing, a Blue Room, a Lincoln Room. The whole thing. And you will be the commander-in-chief, and it'll look like you're in the White House. On *The Surreal Life*."

A deafening silence followed. Finally, Al said, "I love that idea. Tell me more."

No turning back, I was literally spit-balling more ways to develop this idea, proposing, "You would be the president of the house. We would change the format where everyone else would be in your cabinet, and you'd be POTUS and you and your team would go out and implement policy that makes a difference in the local community. You would be acting presidential, from the Oval Office, on television."

He loved it. We all loved it. Reverend Al wrapped up lunch by saying, "OK. Let's do it."

The deal eventually fell apart before we got the show made. But guess what. The idea had been born and was still mine to develop into an entirely different hit show, one that might soon be coming to a TV platform near you. After twelve years, a lot of people would have given up. But good ideas really do have staying power if you're willing to be patient. And the truth is that in many other ways my career has been a testament to the opportunity and empowerment that flow from choosing to play the long game.

YOUR TWENTY-YEAR PLAN

Whenever I talk about the importance of creating a plan for doing what you love for a living, I hear a common misconception: *Oh, so if it's what you love, then it's NOT work?* The answer is plainly *NO*. Turning a crazy dream into reality is an unbelievable amount of work. Loving what you do doesn't mean that it's any less work. Nor does it mean you get to kick back as you gain more success. In each phase of the game, my focus on short- and long-term goals has become more highly tuned. And my commitment to the success of every aspect of what I'm doing is all-consuming. That's no exaggeration. Outside of family, I have no hobbies, nothing to distract me. As fate would have it, I'm a terrible golfer.

The value of hard work is not a secret in any business. And yet it can be the ace up your sleeve—especially when you're not the most likely candidate for making it to the top of an industry. A lot of people were highly skeptical when I sold my production company and was first hired to run it for a while and then was asked to be co-CEO of a division of our multinational parent corporation—without any corporate executive experience, no MBA, and no background in finance per se. How have I been able to make it work? By developing a plan, a playbook, that served me at the earlier stages of my career—with the same strategies that helped me get my foot in the Hollywood door and later start my own company (because no one else would hire me for the job I did want). And these are the same strategies that can be applied by anyone who hopes to reach further than just what is expected of you.

Yes, it was a major leap to go from the equivalent of having my own small corner "mom-and-pop" grocery store to running an international supermarket chain—the biggest in the world, owned by a multibillion-dollar corporation. But as it turns out, when it comes to the bottom line, this big global corporation runs on the exact same gas that a small company does, which, in my business, is ideas. *Good* ideas. And, by extension, hit television shows.

Because my long-term plan was to one day work at a high level in the television business, my job early on was to learn the ins and outs of the industry and to become skilled at creating, making, and selling TV shows. Part of my acceleration stems from betting on my instincts as to what ideas will or won't work. Hit shows are our lifeblood. Even with the five hundred or so employees who work in our division of Endemol Shine, none of us can do our jobs successfully if we don't start with a hit. No matter how talented and skillful our executives and sales and marketing people are, we can't do anything— whether it's to sell the ancillaries or do publicity and branding or negotiate licensing or build our international distribution—*unless* we have a project that audiences want to watch. The challenge, then, goes back to making sure there is a strong and robust supply of good ideas and compelling stories that are essential to hit television shows.

Not surprisingly, a lot of betting goes on in the effort to evaluate the potential of an idea or a story when it first comes to us. And you may be curious to know what metrics we use to predict what is going to be a hit or not. Well, as I used to joke—*Hey, if I had the formula for guaranteeing a hit, I'd be rich.*

A recent response I got to that was—*Yeah, but you are rich.*

My comeback to that—*If I knew the answer, I'd be writing this book from my own private island.*

The poorly kept secret in Hollywood is that there is no playbook for coming up with the goods each and every time. Let me take that a step further. If your ultimate dream is to make it in any aspect of show business, there are no hard-and-fast rules; there is no real set path. But there are multiple barriers. So learning to trust your instincts and cultivating a drive that won't let up are mandatory. Those are essentials for getting past even the first few rounds, when the objective is to surpass everybody and anybody who might be just as driven as you. After that, you'll need something more, something different, something unique, that puts you ahead of the competition and lets you stand out. Again, as a business that's the Wild Wild West, there are no certifications, no degrees, no qualifications.

Don't get me wrong. Just as in many other professional fields, you can find a job in Hollywood without special skills. If you want to join the rank and file, if all you have is breathing and standing and a driver's license, you can work in the entertainment business. But if you have ambitions to go further than that, it's not easy. And that's why the long game leads to the greatest rewards; it's why you need a plan of your own for going the distance.

My feeling is that what happens in Hollywood occurs to varying degrees for everyone in the working world. In many arenas, you will never be shown a tried-and-true avenue for getting past that first stop you make because as much as you want to chase your dream, you have to pay the bills. Right?

Granted, if your passion is to become a doctor, you'll usually study premed, then apply to med school, do your internship, ascend to a residency in your area of specialization, and then find job openings. If you want to be a lawyer, there is a demanding structure to follow, along with choices for what kind of law you want to practice, and then a rigorous series of hurdles to pass before you can go out and land a position. But even with professional aspirations that offer opportunity, the ebb and flow of the marketplace and a changing global economy are factors that make it tough to guarantee success beyond a paycheck.

The challenge, should you choose to accept it, is to make a commitment, here and now, to betting on yourself and your dream. Wherever you might be—on your path, thinking about it, looking for motivation, regaining your footing—it doesn't matter. The issue is *commitment*. Let's put it to the test. What if I were to offer you a job for $200 million? What would you say? Before you answer, we should discuss the fine print.

Usually when I make this offer to new grads—high school or college or graduate school—it draws attention. Who doesn't need to get out there and start on the path to making money? Likewise, for anyone who's been at the grind for a while and feels stuck or undervalued or stretched too thin or not where they once dreamed of being, isn't the offer of a job for $200 million a no-brainer? But here's the catch: The main payout won't happen until you've been working for twenty years straight, and during that time, you would be required to make this quest your absolute priority. You will be given jobs along the way; you will be overworked and underpaid. There will be no vacations, no time off, no time-outs. You'll miss your friends' weddings and relatives' funerals. An important family reunion or the need to take a break to see your brother on leave from the military? Not if it takes time away from the commitment you've made.

My point? It's not a pretend commitment or a half-assed commitment or a wishful-thinking commitment. It's a mind-set that requires you to sacrifice and to make tough decisions. You will not miss work or skip class because you don't feel up to par. You've made a commitment to your top priority in life, right? It's up to you. This is the $200 million job offer. There will be no special perks or even acknowledgments to reward you for your efforts. No matter how many obstacles you face—external or internal—you will be required to overcome them on your own. Additionally, to qualify for this position, you will need to devote some of your time to identifying your dream and constantly educating yourself in every aspect of it. A college degree will be required. (Because I'm the son of two educators, that's nonnegotiable.) You may need to add on time to expand your studies and learn the lay of the land you intend to conquer. During your twenty years, you will need to continually fine-tune your dream by setting short- and long-term goals that are actionable. And last but not least, you will never, ever be allowed to QUIT, even on the days when you doubt yourself and when you feel like you just can't go on another second.

If you could do all that for twenty years, then and only then would you qualify for the salary of $200 million. Now ask yourself if I offered you that job, what would you say?

Well, I hope you would say yes. Not because I am in a position to actually offer you that job, but because if you are willing to bet on yourself and play the long game, without any guarantees or promises that you can do everything required of you, it means you have already begun the journey to making your dream a reality.

It's also important for me to let you know in advance that the twenty-year plan is by no means a straight uphill climb. You'll find that there are natural breaks that occur over time—where you come to various turning points as you choose to fine-tune your dream or adapt your goals as you reach them or reroute as you encounter obstacles and unexpected challenges. At those turning points, you'll continue to refine your plan to build on what you've already achieved or on what you've learned. Generally, if you're starting at an entry level, you can figure that those breaks will occur every five years or so. Or, if you prefer, you might want to look at your twenty-year plan in four phases:

- **Phase 1** is about learning to navigate in whatever field you've chosen.

- **Phase 2** is where you take that knowledge and transfer it to paving a road that's yours to own.

- **Phase 3** is where you take everything you've learned, especially from what didn't work, and you become the master of your lane.

- **Phase 4** is where you take that up to the next level to expand and grow your dream.

Again, I know that not everyone has a sense of what his or her dream really is. Hey, if you are in that category, let me reassure you that it's never too late to discover what it is that truly engages your passion. Don't dismiss what you think might be too small or inapplicable to be worthy of your passion. It's what you go to sleep thinking about and what you wake up thinking about it. You might want to ask yourself, first, what you would do if "reality" wasn't an obstacle. Give yourself permission to have that crazy dream and then begin to evaluate what resources you would need to create your reality. Why not research how others have turned their dreams into viable paths for themselves? Ask them! Use your natural curiosity to get their take on success. In so doing, you may find that someone else's passion fires up yours. Sometimes your passion finds you. The key is then choosing to own it.

For those who already know what your dream is, well, you're about five years ahead of the curve. And, next, just as important as knowing what you want to do, is then being willing to get out of your comfort zone to achieve it, time and time again.

Before I get to the lessons that I had to learn in order to win at the reality game, let me give you an overview of the main principles that you can use in your planning and in your execution of that plan, no matter what your aspiration:

- Bet on yourself
- Find what you love to do and choose to do it for a living
- Employ vision (see what no one else can)
- Cultivate an unstoppable work ethic
- Prepare for each and every shot by training like a professional athlete
- Embrace your passion and your purpose
- Create opportunities for yourself because no one hands them to you
- Write your own rules for success
- Be willing to change the game
- Believe in a mission that's bigger than yourself
- Above all, take on the mantle of leadership

In the chapters that follow, I'll point out how these various principles were vital in my journey and offer suggestions for how they can be helpful in yours. Along with the importance of believing in what's possible and choosing to bet on yourself, coming up next in CHAPTER 2 (*See Beyond the End of Your Street*), I'll draw from my personal story to talk about how to employ vision to find your path, even when you're going against the odds. The value of a relentless work ethic for overcoming obstacles and getting past fear will be explored in CHAPTER 3 (*Seize the Moment*). In CHAPTER 4 (*A Brief History of Reality*), I'll offer some background on my field and give you my take on why you have to do your homework in every aspect of your area of interest—as you prepare for every shot with the discipline of a pro athlete. CHAPTER 5 (*Make It Happen*) will address how to embrace your passion and your purpose as you develop expertise in your field by learning from the best. We'll continue in CHAPTER 6 (*Everything I Know Now That I Wish I Knew Then*) as we focus on ways to create opportunities for yourself while avoiding the common pitfalls of launching your own company or carving out your own niche. In the next three chapters (*Surreal Life, Celebreality,* and *Every Day I'm Hustling*), I'll be talking about how to own your turf by writing your own rules, by using marketing and storytelling skills to take on the competition, and even by betting on your ability to change the game. Finally, in the last two chapters (*Know When and When Not to Leave Money on the Table* and *Live Your Full-Court Life*)—we'll conclude with the power of embracing what makes you different as you take on a mission that's bigger than you, along with other leadership principles that have helped to guide me in recent years.

As a storyteller, I share my stories with you much as I recall them and relive their lessons and takeaways on a regular basis. I hope that those lessons will be relevant as you look to the future and get started on the journey to living your dreams. We both know that there are no guarantees of $200 million payouts twenty years down the road. But reality begins when you choose to bet on the possibility of what you see beyond where you are in this moment and when you promise yourself to never, ever quit.

two

See Beyond the End of Your Street: *Vision*

If I could go back to those days of the past,
I'd show you a love . . . a love that would last.

Oh, I remember those wonderful dances.
In El Monte . . . in El Monte—

—FRANK ZAPPA and RAY COLLINS,
"Memories of El Monte" (Recorded by the Penguins, 1963)

As a student of the field of motivation and empowerment, I'm always fascinated by the great success stories of our time. In my quest over the years to research the main business principles that have been applied by famous individuals who were able to transform their dreams into reality, I've discovered what I believe is the key hallmark of successful, iconic leaders from across the spectrum of industries. Very simply, that hallmark is the ability to *employ vision—to see what no one else can.*

This is a business principle that I follow on a daily basis. Without vision, how can you create an opportunity for yourself or for others and then take action in a focused, determined manner to make the most of that opportunity? Without vision that reflects what your life lessons have taught you, as well as what you've learned from your formal education and training, how do you differentiate yourself from everyone else competing for those opportunities? Vision is essential to leadership, for motivating yourself and others, and for seeing the big picture, rather than getting stuck in the current view. Vision allows you to focus on your purpose, rather than being overcome by fear, failure, and the challenges of life.

We tend to think that being a visionary puts you way out there on a lofty peak with prophets or eccentric inventors who predict the future far ahead of the curve. But I like to think of a visionary more as someone who can make sense of the present and see into the future by learning from the past. That's why I place the highest premium on the value of life lessons I was taught growing up in El Monte and in the Abrego household—where I first learned to see possibilities for myself and then was encouraged to believe in them.

Those lessons are with me every day, especially when I'm heading into an intense meeting with more seasoned negotiators or any of the strong personalities and power brokers who operate in my industry. By employing vision and summoning the strength gained from overcoming challenges in my earlier years, I'm able to see solutions, opportunity, and purpose beyond the discomfort or limitations of the moment.

About four years ago, as a case in point, I saw an opportunity that others had apparently dismissed but that required me to get past the obstacles and intimidation of entering a federal prison in Arkansas. In previous months, practically everyone in the entertainment industry had been pursuing hip-hop superstar T.I. (aka "Tip," aka Clifford Joseph Harris Jr.)—the Atlanta-based rapper/actor/mogul who was becoming known as the Jay Z of the South. But before I could get a meeting, news surfaced that T.I. and his manager were about to close a deal for a feature film with one of the hottest movie producers in town, along with setting up a major television series. As far as I could tell, I had missed the chance.

But then, in a reversal of fortune for T.I., he was arrested for parole violation, some sort of drug possession, and because of a prior offense was sentenced to a year in federal prison—in Forrest City, Arkansas. His pending Hollywood deals were instantly put on hold. Serving time in prison wasn't going to hurt T.I. and his credibility with his hip-hop fans. But to the entertainment industry, getting busted is viewed as an insurance risk to producers. So the show business wait-and-see approach was not a surprise. To me, though, it was shortsighted.

The opportunity was now mine to make happen. But how? Well, I'd have to meet him on his turf, in this case, prison. When the idea first arose, making it happen was a long shot. But why not try? The logistics were challenging. Before I could travel to Arkansas and officially enter the facility, I had to first submit all kinds of documentation to prove—who knows?—maybe that I wasn't planning a prison break.

Though I had never visited a penitentiary, I was no stranger to the issue of the growing, disproportionate incarceration rates for young men and women of color in this country, often for nonviolent crimes. In the San Gabriel Valley, where I grew up, prison-run gangs were prevalent. Mostly controlled by the Mexican mafia, also known as *La EME* (*M* in Spanish), the list included the homegrown EMF— *El Monte Flores*. As a result, many of us knew someone who had gone to prison or who had a family member who had served time and maybe was still behind bars.

Despite this background, I was not prepared for the red tape involved in visiting an inmate in a federal prison. While waiting, I went ahead and flew to Atlanta to meet T.I.'s wife, Tiny—Grammy-winning R&B singer/songwriter Tameka Cottle, nicknamed Tiny on account of being 4'11"—and the brood of kids they were raising together. Amazingly, in spite of the challenges of the media glare, Tiny had this super-cheerful attitude that gave their household an atmosphere of normalcy. She gave me her vote of confidence in my idea. Between Tiny and T.I.'s manager, the only real advice I got was "He likes candy, so be sure to bring lots of change for the vending machines."

Nobody warned me about the humiliating treatment received by prison visitors. Even with the official authorization—proving that I was an upstanding citizen and not a threat to security—the armed prison guards treated me like a five-year-old.

First, they're barking orders that you turn over everything (phone, keys, wallet, backpacks, briefcase, pencils, pens, paper), leaving you only with the clothes and shoes you're wearing and, thankfully, change for the vending machines. Next, I have to follow a yellow line on the floor down a hall while guards watch my every move.

"This way?"

"Read the sign!"

I stop, read the sign that says, "Please follow the yellow line as you proceed," and continue, although maybe I'm not exactly on top of the line but about a foot or two off it.

"Hey! You! Did you read the sign?"

Me (respectfully): "Yes."

Guard: "What's it say?"

Me: "Follow the yellow line."

Guard: "It means walk on the line! Go back!"

So I go back to the beginning and walk exactly on top of the yellow line, with my stomach churning. In the most intense of situations, I can just about always handle discomfort and I do know how to keep my cool. But I can't stand humiliation. It's not about fear; it's about being made to feel powerless. Then again, I have my vision for why this meeting needs to happen; it is my mission. So I hold my tongue and do as ordered.

When I am seated in the visiting room, T.I. is accompanied in to meet me. As planned, I buy him coffee and candy, and then, with the clock ticking, in this cold and barren prison visiting room, I move into a pitch—letting him know why I am the best person to work with him upon his release and how I see the show we could create together.

I told T.I. about El Monte and about myself, that I'd never been in prison but that I knew people who had, how I came up from the bottom in my field, and how passionate I felt about helping him to tell his story. There was no reason for me to talk about his case or the legalities behind his troubles. That would have been the more showbiz approach. Not my thing. My approach is more down-to-earth and draws from the power of respect—maybe because of how I grew up.

Where I come from, we don't judge. Not everybody had the same stable household. Not everybody had options for the future. We were a community of proud, hardworking folks who wanted a better life for themselves and their families. The unwritten code was that you didn't make yourself superior to someone else; you didn't sit there and judge one another as better or worse.

T.I. said little as he listened to my journey in television. Finally, he spoke up, still guarded, to ask what my concept was for a show with him.

"Imagine a family," I began, referencing classic family sitcoms, and describing what I saw as an urban *Cosby* series (still regarded then as the ultimate crossover TV success). "But instead of two doctors, the husband is a hip-hop icon and the wife is R&B royalty, and they're living in Atlanta as a young family with little kids, and the episodes would show us what it's like to teach those kids the rules of the road in terms of the family business of being a hip-hop impresario." We could tell their family story to date, the truth of it all.

T.I. saw the vision I had and assured me that he would bring his highest values to the show: God, family, and hustle. We shook hands and we made a deal for what became *T.I. & Tiny: The Family Hustle*.

At this writing, more than one hundred highly rated episodes later, the show has become a phenomenal success for VH1, as well as for Endemol Shine. None of that would have happened, obviously, if I had never gotten past the prison gatekeepers. And, more important, none of it would have happened without the ability to see an opportunity to tell a great story that hadn't been told.

In looking at how you can do more to employ vision for seeing opportunities ahead, I recommend that you take the time to review your past and the life lessons that shaped your ability to see beyond the end of your street. You may be surprised at how empowering it is to go back and revisit memories of your story, your family, your mentors, and your community. By remembering the influences that helped or hindered your dreams, you may even reclaim parts of yourself you thought you'd forgotten but are only waiting to be found again.

LEARNING TO DREAM

The Abrego family hustle, which could have been its own TV series starring my parents, Sy and Tina—or Dr. Silas H. Abrego and Mrs. Florentina Carrasco Abrego—was where I was first challenged to employ vision. Though I didn't appreciate it at the time, my parents handed me a set of road rules for life that, later on, I was smart enough not to forget. For both my big brother, Steve (two years my senior), and me, my parents placed an emphasis on hard work and education as fundamental to success.

My mother, born in Mexico, had come to the United States as a teenager and had worked her way through school, eventually earning her bachelor of arts and master's degrees and both her teaching and administrative credentials, extending her career in education for thirty years as a teacher and administrator. My father, born here, the son of a Mexican seasonal farmworker, grew up in Pomona on the streets—fighting to survive every day of his life. As tough as they come, he served in the military in the Vietnam War era before pursuing his postsecondary education. Because of his background at a high school that did little to encourage Chicanos to attend college, my father became passionately involved in the Chicano Student Movement of the 1960s and 1970s. Though his degree was in industrial arts, he went on to attain his master's and doctorate at USC in higher education and eventually, he would become Vice President for Student Affairs at California State University at Fullerton. In the wake of my father's recent retirement from CSUF, Governor Jerry Brown appointed him to the Board of Trustees for the California State University system.

Very different in style, my parents were both visionary. They were also both tough and equally relentless in creating teachable moments of all kinds—especially the lessons intended to motivate us to dream and find the path to attaining those dreams. The earliest, most pivotal lesson came from my mother. Though I've had many teachers in life and in my career, Florentina Carrasco Abrego remains to this day my number one mentor. Because of her, I believed that what I visualized was possible and could become reality.

As fair and honest as anyone I've ever met, my mother is always the first person I call for advice, whether it has to do with opportunities or when the path forward is not clear or when I stumble. She's strong, no-nonsense, yet emotional, as I can also be, **and someone** who will always tell me how it is, even when I don't want to hear it. No matter how busy I am, rarely does a day go by that I don't manage a phone call to her.

When I was about ten years old, my mother had an occasion to offer wisdom about *how passion can reveal the path to your dream*—that I'll call *Motivation Lesson #1*—after I announced, "When I grow up, I'm gonna be a dentist!"

Why? I have no clue. It's not like I personally knew a dentist or that I even liked going to the dentist. I just had it in my head that being a dentist was the height of success.

"*Mijo,*" she said carefully, "you know that being a dentist is like being a doctor. Not really the same but similar. You sure you don't want to be a doctor?"

"Nope, I want to be a dentist."

"Just so you know, *mijo*, you will have to work just as hard to become a dentist. The same as if you were to become a doctor. You know that?"

That was news to me but that didn't change my resolve. I was going to be a dentist. We had this back-and-forth a few more times. Then, finally, my mother relented. "If you really want to be a dentist and that's what you really, really want, then go for it!" This seemed to be the end of the conversation until she added sharply, "But make sure you *love* it!"

We had variations of this conversation several times over the next couple of years. As puberty set in, I did start to wonder if I knew what she meant by making sure that being a dentist was what I really loved. The only things I loved for sure were sports—mainly football and wrestling—and, above all, watching TV. I wasn't yet able to envision how to turn my television obsession into a career. But my mother's message got through, and I soon lost interest in being a dentist. That left my future as uncertain as anyone else's—until my true dream came along somewhat later.

The counterpart to that lesson in dreaming came from my father, our resident reality expert, who had his own brand of vision. As a leader in the Latino community who devoted himself to creating opportunities for kids like me to go to college, he exemplified the value of having focus. Whereas my mother could make her point with *cariño*—caring, affection—my father did not. Not his style. When he gave advice, it was handed down as the gospel. You listened and you paid attention. His regular sermon to me was "If you want to move up in life, you will always have to outwork the competition. You will always come across people who are smarter than you. . . ."

Jeez, Dad, I'd be thinking to myself, *I get the hard-work part but why can't I be smarter too?*

He'd go on. "You will always meet people who come from more affluent backgrounds, people with family connections who've traveled and seen the world while you have not. But none of that means anything if you can outwork them."

Call this *Motivation Lesson #2*—that *with focus you can achieve your goals, that is, as long as you have the stamina to outwork, outhustle, and outdeliver everyone else.* This was a theme repeated over and over. Harsh as it sounded, I knew he was right about how to confront the competition. For better and for worse, I was bred to be a work machine.

When I say that both my parents were relentless about looking for teachable moments, I mean they went beyond advocating that I work hard in school, sports, extracurricular activities, and daily chores. They were also big on self-education—getting me into reading newspapers at a young age, as well as encouraging me to research topics I'd shown an interest in. And this was before the Internet and Google and information always at our fingertips. As usual, my parents were well ahead of their time.

The question I've asked myself over the years is whether I was able to see beyond the end of the street from an early age because that was just in my hard wiring or because that was how I was raised. Probably it was a combination of the two. All children have the capacity to dream and fantasize about the future—perhaps to varying degrees— and those visions, if you will, can be harnessed as an internal motivator that some call drive or ambition. As I've come to better understand that force, I realize how important it is to have parents and teachers who recognize and encourage it. My parents did all they could to egg me on. They would often cut out articles and leave them outside my bedroom door—like the story of some kids in Santa Cruz who launched the Odwalla company selling fresh juice out of the back of a VW, plus lots of other accounts of young entrepreneurs and successful individuals who came from humble beginnings to do something impressive.

That's one way to *employ vision—simply by finding examples of others like you who achieved their dreams.* Basic and useful, that was *Motivation Lesson #3.* The articles were so influential that I began to imagine how proud I'd be if one day there would be a story about me in the *Los Angeles Times*—the paper I knew my mother and father loved to read. My plan was not to tell them in advance. I'd be motivated just imagining the excitement my parents would feel opening up their paper on Sunday and seeing my picture there.

Clearly, the articles were meant to feed my imagination about what was possible. By the way, they never stopped trying to do that. Instead of leaving newspaper stories by my door, nowadays my father forwards me news items from his iPad that he thinks I should read. Even after the success of *T.I. & Tiny*—the show I developed—Dad recommended I read a piece on the influence of the FOX series *Empire*, noting that I should not overlook the importance of hip-hop on television. Just keeping me on my toes.

There was always a method to the madness. Much of their approach was developed by necessity as both my mother and father worked full-time while continuing their education for advanced degrees, plus raising us two kids. For example, in order to keep us out of trouble and keep an eye on us, whenever Steve and I asked to hang out and socialize with our friends, they'd say yes—but with a hitch. Everybody had to come to our house. We were not allowed to hang out at other people's houses. That way, they also got to know our friends. Of course, whoever wanted to come over would be subjected to our house rules—homework, chores around the house, and, hey, if you slept over on a Friday night, you'd be up early on Saturday doing yardwork. Every week we'd be out there pulling weeds and running the mower.

Damn, I used to think, *how fast could lawns grow?*

Still, the chores went faster when there was a team doing them. Again, that was how we were motivated to work for what we wanted—without making it feel like punishment. This message was sent successfully because of something else I never fully appreciated until later: the gift of being raised by both parents—who consciously parented together. In El Monte that was definitely unusual. Out of my close circle of eight friends, 99 percent lived in households headed by single parents, mainly by their moms. Dad became a father figure to many of the guys, in some cases the only one they had. And to some friends, Mom was like a second mother, offering counsel and wisdom from her perspective as a parent and an educator.

Without naming it as such, my parents also both understood the need to *have vision to play the long game*—what I would have to categorize as *Motivation Lesson #4.*

My father was the mad scientist of that reality. Anything we wanted to do, he'd say yes and then put a massive obstacle in front of it. If, say, my brother and I wanted to go somewhere on a weekend with our friends, his first response was "Of course you can go." There would be a pause, and then he'd add, "The minute you get rid of all the junk in the garage and reorganize the workbench and clean everything off the shelves, then you are free to go." There was no way we could do all that without planning our time after school and getting it done together in advance.

The Dr. Silas H. Abrego approach was to let you determine how badly you wanted to do something by what you were willing to get through in order to do it. He never micromanaged the tasks we needed to accomplish on our way to getting what we wanted. We had to figure out the logistics.

Don't get me wrong. There was still a right way and a wrong way to get anything done. Whatever the subject matter, there were no shades of gray with Dad. His manner was stern, clear, and, again, concise. His lectures came in the form of Dos and Don'ts. No nuance, no niceties. Once we got into our teens, he would cut to the chase even more, as he headed out the door, saying things like, "Hey, if you go out tonight and you drink, don't 'f-ing' drive!" or "I saw you talking to that girl. You know that if you two have sex, you know to wear a condom, right?"

Really, Dad, just "wear a condom"? No coddling, no "Let's sit down and talk about the birds and the bees." Obviously, I listened and his blunt approach was effective. But it was not always fun when you were being told how something was "this" or wasn't "that."

To make the Dr. Abrego approach more complicated, he was also down-to-earth, almost humble or just not someone to show off his many achievements, yet dignified in the formal way he carried himself. Instead of hugging or high-fiving us as kids, he would greet us by shaking our hands—as he does with me to this day. His stern demeanor could also make him overly critical and blunt.

Sometimes his criticism was used as a way of making us tough like him, as if preparing us for the long game and the challenges to come. And he knew how to get under our skin, as he questioned our strengths and weaknesses. If you were good at something, why not be better? If you had a weakness, work even harder to improve. He knew, for instance, how much I hated being embarrassed in public. If, say, I hadn't done my homework or had slacked off because I was busy doing something else, instead of standing over me and making me do it, he'd say nothing as I went to school without the homework and then the teacher would call me out in front of the whole class—which *sucked*! I rarely made the same mistake twice.

Or my father might embarrass me on purpose, taking me to task in front of others for failing to do something that I didn't know how to do. Whenever my cousins and uncles were over and wanted to see how our latest automotive project in the garage was coming along, Dad would test my knowledge of what tool was needed to perform a certain job for fixing the engine. I'd have all the tools lying there and he'd shoot questions at me rapid-fire, asking me to bring him the right tool for that mechanical problem. I never knew which one, and I'd grab something totally wrong and then run over to him and he'd just shake his head, so I'd run back and grab another tool—only to be wrong again. With all my relatives standing there, I got even more flustered. Eventually, I taught myself what each tool did and would line them up like medical instruments at the ready.

This lesson was not really about identifying tools. It was more about learning how to keep my cool under fire. Guess what. It worked. And the ability to remain unflustered when somebody else has gone off has certainly been a valuable asset in the business world.

No matter how much my father tried to get me to improve when it came to my understanding of mechanics, I never really did. Steve wasn't the best student in school, but he was an auto mechanic child prodigy. Truly gifted, he and Dad bonded over everything automotive. Meanwhile, I had other strengths but not fixing cars.

I can vividly recall my father watching me toil over an oil change, telling me, "Man, I hope you work hard on your education and on getting a good job so you can pay someone to do this for you." Better yet, as he'd say to both me and Steve, why not really go out and make something of ourselves, so, who knows, we could lease brand-new cars and never have to change the oil or the brakes for ourselves?

The point wasn't just about cars. He wanted us to see beyond the end of our street. He was teaching us about setting ambitious goals: "You think it's fun making eight dollars an hour? You think it will be fun when you're single at thirty? Hey, if you want fun, try making a hundred thousand dollars a year. That's fun!"

The motivational message got through. Later on, after my brother served in the Marines, he was the guy I put in charge of running the video-equipment rental company that I would launch in time. Today, it's one of the top video-equipment rental businesses of its kind in Hollywood—and to his credit, my brother bought the company from me a couple of years ago, and it's thriving.

Whether you do or don't come from a background that gave you lessons in seeing beyond the limitations of the moment, all that matters is that you give yourself permission to dream starting now—and see where your vision takes you from here.

WHAT CAN YOU DO?

When you consider what your eventual path might be, there are two obvious lines of questioning that may be helpful. First, what kind of interests and influences are you most passionate about? Second, do you have any particular skills or is there anything that you're really good at? Thanks to prodding from both of my parents, those were questions I started to ask myself early in life.

Television and storytelling were always a part of my answers. Even before I decided to make working in television a goal, I knew that I was passionate about everything that had to do with the act of watching television, especially the experience of escaping into stories that felt real and added to my ability to daydream about my own exciting future—whatever it was going to be.

The added bonus was that watching TV was one of the few ways I could enjoy spending quality time with my father. He loved television almost as much as I did. The best time of day was after seven p.m. when he came home from work, changed out of his suit, got a bag of Lay's potato chips, and sprawled on the floor in front of the television set. As little guys, my brother and I would literally lie right on top of him. The three of us watched and loved every type of show, every genre, every channel. We were fans not only of shows with displays of unusual talents like *That's Incredible* but of all the many different variety shows. We watched reruns of *The Carol Burnett Show* and died laughing over the comedic antics of Tim Conway. *The Smothers Brothers* was must-see TV—hilarious, entertaining, and sometimes thought-provoking. There wasn't a sitcom of the seventies or eightiess that we didn't watch—from *The Jeffersons* and *Cheers* to *Three's Company* and *Who's the Boss?*—on top of reruns of all the classics like *I Love Lucy*. We were junkies for police and detective dramas of all stripes—*Rockford Files*, *Kojak*, *Cagney & Lacey*, and, of course, *Hill Street Blues*, the best!

Though my mother rarely joined us in front of the TV set, she didn't seem to mind us enjoying ourselves. Well, there was one night after dinner, when us guys jumped up from the table and hurried to watch a show and she gave my father an unhappy glance of "We'll talk later" as she trudged off to do several loads of laundry. Apparently she was no longer amused by our TV-watching habits, as we realized when she marched into the living room and dumped a basket of clean clothes onto the floor. She said nothing but we got the message: *Start folding!*

Nobody ever suggested television could be bad for our brains. But just in case, my father managed to invent learning exercises connected to TV shows. That's how I found out what a good TV watcher I was. If we were watching, say, *The Gong Show*, he would goad us into coming up with our own acts, asking us, "What can you guys do? What can you do?" He'd have us suggest crazy costume ideas and oddball talents that could get us onto the show and not get gonged immediately. Without intending it, my father started me thinking like a producer. Just thinking about what it was that I could do to stand out was a great exercise for leadership. Why follow the crowd and be like everyone else when being you could win the day?

Then there was this game we had for dramas. If we were watching *Hill Street Blues*, for example, as soon as one of the characters said something, if you could guess what the next line was and say it before the other character responded, you could claim that you wrote the whole episode. I was the champ, hands down. Still, the competition during these games was fierce—when friends were over or during family get-togethers. My friends loved to trash talk and make up crazy stuff. So did my uncles, Dad's brothers, who came up with some of the funniest lines ever.

Comedy was a staple of Abrego family get-togethers. We loved to share bits we'd seen of the great stand-ups like Richard Pryor and Eddie Murphy. When the jokes started to fly, you had to be fast with the comebacks, or you would be at the receiving end of the sarcastic put-downs that would get worse if you said something lame.

In that mix of family and friends, I learned early on to sharpen the very storytelling skills that I'd later use developing and pitching TV shows. I also learned a lot about making presentations from my father—who, as a leader in various educational and community organizations, was an in-demand public speaker. He taught these storytelling lessons both directly and by example. His main criticism of me was that I talked too much. In my defense, I was just an outgoing kid with a natural gift of gab—with lots to say on a range of subjects. But whenever I went on for too long, Dad would only have to glance over and I'd quickly wrap up.

This was Storytelling 101's top lesson: *Be concise, damn it.* So I learned to say more in a shorter amount of time, an essential for pitching ideas in Hollywood or in business, where time is money. Of course, sometimes I still get carried away and speed up to get all my points in. Eva Longoria, a colleague and very dear friend, is the first to tell me, "Cris, you talk too fast!"

"No," I have to remind Eva, "you listen too slow!"

The other critical lesson I learned from watching how my father developed his speeches: *Preparation, preparation, preparation.* Dad would start with a pile of books and articles as he researched his topic, making pages of notes on a yellow legal pad until he had written (and rewritten) the speech. He might practice it a few times in front of a mirror alone and then call me to come listen to him rehearse.

That was where I learned another huge lesson relevant to every form of communication: *Know your audience.* Knowing what the event was and who might be attending, I could hear how my father adapted his message, tone, enunciation, even his rhythm and accent to the intended audience. But no matter what the audience, I came to the conclusion early on that timing in delivery could make or break the presentation. Even more important was making sure that the jokes landed. For me, this was the takeaway that really came into play later on: *Comedy rules.*

I developed the habit of offering to punch up the jokes. My father took all my suggestions. The truth is, Dad might have been funny with his dry sarcastic sense of humor, but I was funnier. I loved to make him laugh. Eventually I figured out that he had put me to work without making it seem like work. More to the point, in challenging me to be better than him at something, he was helping me find something that I was good at, something that I could do.

What could I do? That was the question I'd been asking myself in thinking about my various passions and skills—"What can I do with all this?" Well, had it not been for a course offered at my high school, I might never have discovered that television could be the answer and a legitimate pursuit. But lo and behold, at age fourteen, at the start of my freshman year at Mountain View High School, I was filling out my schedule and needed an elective for the year. None of the listings appealed to me, until I read a description for an actual class called "Learn How to Make Television."

What? And no, it wasn't a technical class for learning how to build a television set. The course synopsis promised to cover the gamut: how to use cameras, how to master the basics of broadcast journalism like lighting, sound, editing, and even an introduction to script writing and directing. Within weeks, I knew that as much as I enjoyed watching television, I liked making it even more. Suddenly I could see the possibility of this as a career. I didn't know what it paid or anyone who had a job in the TV field or even if I could make a decent living doing it, but I knew one thing for sure: I *loved* it.

No bolt of lightning came down from the heavens to announce I'd found my calling. It just made sense. For starters I had a vast knowledge of television shows. And I was good at mastering the technology and the creativity required at the high school level.

But what if I wasn't up to par? That brings up an important moral to this part of the story. As a fan of the competition format of reality shows (like the early seasons of *American Idol*), I'm unfortunately aware that because you love something and it's your dream, that doesn't guarantee that you're any good at it or that you'll have what it takes to go the distance, no matter how vividly you can visualize your name in lights.

I'm not trying to rain on anyone's parade by pointing out that not all ambitions are created equal. But that's one of the challenges in shaping your vision for the future. When you explore your interests and narrow them down to the things that you can do, then ask yourself if you are ready to get out there and handle the competition.

YOUR COMPETITIVE EDGE

As focused as I eventually became in pursuing television, for the longest time I had no idea whether I could compete in that arena. But I did know a lot about how to compete, thanks to athletics—which allowed me to find my competitive edge, which would carry over into other pursuits. Sports of every kind were my passion. In particular football and wrestling offered a real proving ground for the competitor inside me.

It may come as a surprise that when I was young, I was not the most likely of candidates to emerge as a top high school athlete. In fact, my nickname for years was Gordo. Translated? I was the fat kid. Some in the neighborhood still call me that. Being called Gordo wasn't fun. Then again, that feeling may have fueled my motivation for the rigors of conditioning that were extreme by most standards. I also had to learn how to use what made me different—being shorter and broader—to my athletic advantage. By training like a maniac,

I'd eventually wind up at 175 pounds and 10 percent body fat. That level of discipline and focus began for me as early as nine and ten years old when I'd put myself through a grueling regimen—running three miles along a path by the LA River basin, draped in a big plastic bag to sweat the pounds away so as to be eligible to play Pop Warner football. The rule was that you could play with your age group or weight group. Since I was always heavier than my own age group, the only way I could play with kids up to two years older was to meet their weight limit—which often meant dropping seven or eight pounds by the start of the season. Learning the discipline necessary to do that only strengthened my resolve to excel on the actual playing field.

By high school, I had upped my training and skills not only to become a leader in varsity football as a captain and star player, but I'd also ascended the ranks in wrestling to become a team captain. Was it cool to feel the hometown pride whenever we won a game or I did well and then saw it covered in the local paper? Hell, yeah. Every kid should get to experience that feeling of being a local celebrity and of delivering on the hopes of others.

Being a winner on the field and on the mat was a thrill every time. But even better was sharing the victory with others, knowing that I had made my homeys proud, that I had represented El Monte with toughness and pride. The icing on the cake, of course, was having my family rooting for me. Incredibly, as busy as my father was with work, he managed to attend every one of my matches and games. He would even sometimes come to practice in the middle of the day. This was something of a double-edged sword. Though we strengthened our father-son bond around a shared interest in athletics, afterward Dad would never hold back from giving me his blunt criticism of my performance. The method to that madness was that it taught me not to get rattled by criticism and also to ask myself the question you should always feel free to ask yourself when you are criticized—was it true? If so, I could take it as constructive. If not, I could move on.

Nothing could mute my passion for athletics. Whatever season we were in, I was the super Mr. Jock of that sport, adding hours of training before and after our actual practice—the first to arrive and the last to leave. If we were done sparring in the gym or scrimmaging out on the football field, I'd go find our track team and run with them. I also attended special football camps and trained all summer when school was out. I read every issue of *Sports Illustrated* cover to cover and encouraged my friends to do so too. My football jersey number was 51, and I wrote it out constantly, big and bold, beside my name whenever I signed anything. Like a pro.

Did I fantasize about playing in the Super Bowl one day? I did. But I was realistic enough to know the odds weren't great for that in the long run. Still, I always played to win and wanted my fellow teammates to be as serious as me. Not everyone had my edge or my intensity. I remember one football game when the score was close, and I thought we were going to lose, so I decided to call different defensive plays—because I thought that I knew better than the coach. The instant I hit the sidelines, our head coach grabbed me by the face mask and blasted me, saying, "Hey, Abrego! Hey! There's fucking one coach here. *I'm* the coach." He paused and then added, "You're just a clown in my circus."

Point well-taken. Whether I was right or wrong—and we did lose that game—there can only be one coach. Later on, I saw what happened in production and in business when there were too many self-appointed coaches. In sports as in the real world, knowledge of your role on the team is a key to overall success. You have to check your ego and know there will be times when you are just a clown in somebody else's circus.

By the same token, when you're a leader, your competitive edge can be used to inspire the rest of your team and not let them down. True leaders in sports, I learned, don't have to be a captain or the star of the team, just as a leader in business doesn't necessarily head up the company or sit in the corner office. A true leader should lead by example, from the front, not from behind or after the fact. Leaders can always be spotted as those players who raise everyone else's game by giving their absolute all. Leadership is also about having vision and a strategy for winning that can be communicated to the rest of the team.

Coach Adam Delgado—who coached the wrestling team at Mountain View—encouraged me to employ vision whenever I was preparing for a match. Visual preparation let me imagine all the possible moves and countermoves in advance. The moment I met my opponent, I had a readiness that came from having already won in my mind! The result was a competitive edge that was as much mental as anything.

Just before a match I was never nervous but, weirdly, I always felt like I had to pee right before we started. When I told my coach, he told me not to worry.

"The day you feel like you don't have to pee, that's when you should worry. It means you're too relaxed, too confident." As the saying goes—there's a fine line between confidence and arrogance.

These days I still have that feeling of having to pee whenever I'm about to sit down to pitch a superstar or negotiate terms on a show. I don't mind. That's how I know that I've got my edge.

Wrestling really taught me the meaning of accountability. Coming from the team sport of football, I welcomed the one-on-one combat. Win or lose, you're 100 percent accountable. There's no one else but you to make it happen. You can't blame a missed opportunity on a teammate who dropped the ball or got sacked. It's on you.

Our wrestling program was tiny compared to many of the high

schools in the wealthier nearby suburbs. Coach Delgado was actually our full-time maintenance supervisor who was only helping out as a part-time wrestling coach. At matches, I'd look over in my opponent's corner and see multiple coaches, trainers, and lots of fans. In my corner? Our little team, a few parents, and Coach Delgado—whose highest level of wrestling was his own high school background. But what he did know was the greatest secret of all: that if I could go out there and for six minutes give the other guy hell, and if I came prepared and could outcondition and outwork my opponent, we could win!

Talk to most high school wrestlers, and they'll recite a litany of crazy moves and tricks. I had only two moves. One was a fireman's carry that was unbelievable, showstopping, and the other was an outside single leg, not fancy but it got the job done. So much so that in my last two seasons, I had a record of 105 wins and 7 losses, after which I became the first person from Mountain View High School to qualify to go to the state championship, where I finished fifth in the state. That was enough to send me to nationals, where I placed fifth.

More than anything, wrestling taught me how to raise my pain tolerance and how to handle discomfort. Everything about the sport is uncomfortable. You learn how not to give in to the intensifying discomfort and pain. You've got an opponent smashing your head into a mat and twisting your arm into a full torque behind your back. You endure prolonged pain. You suffer. You use the pain to work harder, to be smarter, and to wait for your moment. The patience required for wrestling feels superhuman. There is no high drama. The points aren't massive. If you win a match 3 to 1, that's major—you killed the guy. Those points happen when you're waiting for your moment, waiting for that opportunity, for that move that can shut it down. Your edge is about patience, stamina, and will.

So too is the TV production process. In later years, when I was on the road as a producer in the most unglamorous, uncomfortable settings—without food, without sleep—all of that felt easy. Wrestling also gave me a lasting reserve of patience and high-level pain tolerance to inoculate me against future deal fatigue in my career so that in negotiations I could wear others down long before I gave in. Patience is also good in the long run for avoiding the general stress that can be a handicap in typically stressful work environments.

Coach Delgado helped me relax my level of intensity in the aftermath of a loss. Instead of harping on mistakes, he would encourage me to move on and put my focus on the next match. "You will always have wins and losses. You can learn from both."

I've never forgotten that lesson. It's been indispensable, especially after the tougher losses that do happen—despite every effort, every intention, and even my best-laid plans. Failure should never be seen as final. What you learn from facing failure and disappointment is about the value of time. As you take time to reflect on what caused the fail and how to avoid repeating the same mistakes, you're then able to sharpen your focus on your goals. Obstacles to success can also give you a wealth of information about where you've chosen to go. The questions then become—*well, how badly do you want the reality of your goal, how fast can you pick yourself back up when you've fallen, and how hard are you willing to work to achieve a different outcome?*

VISION AND PURPOSE

It takes courage to dream and even more to share your vision with others. You don't have to tell anyone, by the way. What matters is only that you can see the possibility. That said, I think that when you make a declaration about everything that you can envision in your future, you make it more real. Many of my peers thought I was crazy whenever I talked about getting to travel around the world after attending Cal State Fullerton on a wresting scholarship. To me, travel was part of the success that I was going to achieve once I landed a job working in television. Even though the two weren't connected, part of my dream was getting to actually visit the places that I'd once seen only on TV. Everyone just thought wanting to travel anywhere far away was weird. It wasn't that they thought I was not capable of doing something ambitious; it was more like "Why would you want to leave here?"

Not everyone felt that way. All of my close friends had joined with me in making plans for the future. Even though senior year would be my last to play football, my best friend, Carlos "Ghost" Hernandez Jr., planned to stick with it at the local community college level with the hope of transferring to a junior college in Fullerton and then moving in as my roommate there.

Our friendship had begun freshman year of high school—when he'd join me in the gym or for a run after football practice. Though you would never have known it, the always fun-loving Carlos had been through really rough times in his upbringing. Our friendship—and football—gave him a focus for his life that I think had been missing. Ghost trained hard to use his quickness to become a major contributor to our team's success. This was the case even as the other players shot up and he remained 5'5" and 120 pounds, retaining the nickname I gave him in homage to the Grey Ghost from *Everybody's All-American*.

Everybody loved Ghost. He had such a huge personality for such a little guy. He was as chill as anyone you could meet, also comedic, and he had a passion for music. Me, I was a hip-hop and oldies fan, but Ghost was into punk and alt rock. He turned me on to the Smiths and Morrissey and even had his own band, which played around locally. They weren't great, but his charisma made them popular. He was bighearted, a good boyfriend to the girls he dated, and generous. He didn't have much, but whatever he did have, he'd share with you.

During off-seasons from football, he'd sometimes go off my radar. From what I knew, he had only one parent residing in El Monte; at a certain point, that parent apparently moved away too. If Ghost was bouncing around, staying under different roofs, I'd have to hunt him down to check up on him. But once it was time to train for football again, Ghost would reemerge, and we'd be right back on track.

In my last two years of high school, my parents moved up in the world and bought a bigger house about twenty minutes from El Monte. We decided that Carlos should come and live with us so he and I could commute to school together, go to practice, work out together afterward, and then drive home to our house.

During those drives, he'd talk about how football had become for him what working in television was for me. Carlos could see beyond the end of the street because he had found a sense of purpose. That got me to thinking about how important purpose was to vision. Maybe that was something I'd always understood because of the way my parents had raised us but had probably taken for granted. Carlos reminded me how special those lessons from my parents really were.

After every Friday night football game, everyone in the extended Abrego family would gather at Shakey's Pizza in downtown El Monte and cheer as Carlos and I and the rest of our teammates would hobble in, dressed in our street clothes, still bruised and bloody from the game. Dad bought pizza for everybody, but before I could eat, he would have to take me into a corner and review the entire game, critiquing what I did and didn't do that could have been better. His big criticism was "You know, every time, you have been getting beaten off the line . . ." I'd listen, using my best Zen master mind technique, and not defend myself. But even with my thick skin, it was one of the more humiliating experiences of those years.

After that, depending on his evaluation, he'd either give me twenty dollars or forty dollars, money to spend for going out later or on the weekend. It was bizarre. If he was pleased, he gave me the forty. If not, I'd get the twenty. But having to stand there, muscles throbbing, head ringing, listening to criticism, and then be humiliated by the difference between the two amounts, that was brutal.

The craziest thing of all? Carlos would observe all of this at a respectable distance, and then, when I got the money, he'd lean in and ask my father, "What about me? How'd I do?"

Carlos would ask for the same criticism. And Dad would give it.

"You're so lucky," Carlos would say to me after that. "You're so lucky."

"You're crazy, Ghost," I'd tell him. "You know that? You don't have to take that shit. I do."

"Nope," he'd reply, "you don't know how lucky you are."

For a long time, I never could understand how Carlos could say that. Years later I would finally understand. And more than being lucky to be loved and advised by parents, coaches, teachers, and best friends, I was even luckier to have paid attention when they were talking. My parents said it all: If you got an education, worked hard, and were willing to be different—to set yourself apart—you would find your direction.

What Carlos was trying to tell me was not to take those gifts for granted. I would say the same to anyone who feels you've hit a wall or an obstacle too big to overcome or that you've lost your way. When you focus on appreciating all that you have been given and on making the best possible use of those resources, you can reclaim your vision and you'll find your footing again—as some of us must learn from the toughest experiences.

WHEN SOMETHING MUST CHANGE

I was thirty years old when I got the tattoo of Carlos and the words "Memories of El Monte" inscribed underneath his face. When people asked me about the tattoo, I'd talk about the accident and about Carlos but not go into too much detail. The truth is, I felt haunted for years. The question I'd often ask myself was one that must be asked by many who go through similar unforeseen tragedies. How does life go back to normal? Trauma—disbelief, shock, powerlessness, guilt, and, above all, loss—how does it not scar you? How do you crawl out of the hole to face reality again? Nobody controls everything that happens to you or your loved ones, and you can die a thousand deaths in your mind trying to come up with if-only alternatives to accidents.

That was my thinking for a long time after Carlos and I took our last ride together on the borrowed motorcycle—running errands, getting haircuts, and, as usual, planning our futures. If only I hadn't borrowed the motorcycle . . . If only I had told Carlos not to come with me . . . If only I hadn't braked as I swung into the curve . . . If only there hadn't been a cement pole right there . . . If only I had died and not my best friend . . .

Life isn't fair, and terrible things happen that aren't our fault. We all fall. We all have loss. If I had all the answers, well, maybe I wouldn't strive so hard to continue to grow and understand more and to honor Carlos's memory. But as to how I dealt with the rabbit hole, as I call that dark place, the only place of solace I could find was the journal that I kept for more than a year after the accident.

The hospital released me late Monday night or early Tuesday morning. There was no skin on my back at all. My head had been shaved before the doctors put in the forty-seven staples to close up the hole in the back of my skull. Nothing seemed real, but I knew nothing would ever be the same again. Carlos was dead, and nothing would bring him back. Every time I closed my eyes, the accident would replay itself over and over.

My family tried to create normalcy. My mother cried her eyes out at the hospital, yet the next day she adopted a stoic expression, staying tough for me. My brother, who had been close to Carlos too, was openly emotional. Dad was the one who surprised me that Tuesday evening when he appeared to be covering his tears. I had never seen him cry before.

On Wednesday, Dad went out and bought me a hat, a ball cap. Later I understood why he required me to return to college the very next day, but I was miserable about the prospect of everyone staring at me or of losing my composure in front of strangers. However, the opposite happened. Nobody stared. Nobody cared. Campus was completely unchanged. The planet hadn't shifted on its axis for anyone but me. The one eerie thing that did occur that Thursday morning was that as I rode up on the bicycle I used for getting back and forth to class, a guy from the college newspaper decided, for no reason, to snap a picture of me. The photo wound up on the front page of the paper with a date stamp of that morning, May 9, 1991, freezing an image of me caught in the moment of truth—like a deer in the headlights—shocked by the reality that life goes on.

That was probably the true crossroads when it dawned on me that I could slip farther down into the rabbit hole and never find my way back, and everyone would say that I'd had an excuse—a right to abandon the dreams. I could use that excuse to blame this massive obstacle and sit back, not do anything, just coast, or be average. But that would betray the promise I had made to myself and to Carlos as he took his last breath. So the other option was to seize the opportunity, the gift of having my life spared. Whatever the reason was, and I would struggle to figure that out, the reality was that I was here—alive—and now that I saw how quickly it could be gone, I chose to double-down on life, to strive harder, to live as fully as possible—no matter how painful the road ahead.

The funeral services at the church were filled to overflowing. Because of the Frankenstein's monster stitch-up on the back of my head, I worried that everyone would know I had been in the accident, and so I chose to sit alone in the last row. Relatives of Carlos looked at me as if to say—how could you? I understood the desire to have someone to blame, to ease the grief. There was nothing I could do or say.

Right before the burial, when everyone was still arriving, a couple of *cholo*-type guys who knew Carlos came up and blocked my path. One of them pointed his finger and warned, "You better watch your back." I tried to go another way, and the other got in my face, saying, "Yeah, watch your back."

My brother and a cousin came running over, telling them, "It was an accident! It wasn't his fault." For a moment, I thought a fight would break out but the two guys walked away, still mouthing threats as they went. After the burial, I didn't see them, but when I had the chance to go up to the grave site and have time alone, I knew it wasn't safe.

All these events blurred in my mind—the wake, the funeral, the rosary. That last service was the toughest, as I wrote in the journal:

5-13-91. The Father said at the rosary not to ask why but to "put your faith in God and not in yourself" because it will tear you up inside. He also said that Carlos had completed his mission and it was time for him to go home—and that mission was to love and he did; that was why the church was so packed. The priest also said, "Carlos is not dead. He continues to live. He is only dead from this world."

Though I had faith and took comfort in the words of the priest, I couldn't wrap my head around the idea that Ghost had completed his mission.

In the months that followed, I felt myself changing. Wrestling started to become less about proving my athletic prowess and more about a means to an end. I had more losses than wins, and by senior year, I would only practice with the team but was no longer competing. My academics and work at the media center now took precedence. By winter of sophomore year, I'd come to the conclusion that not much could strike real fear in me. What did I have to lose, after all? When you have already had a loss, you begin to feel that your number has already come up. It's a common coping mechanism, I would learn, for accident survivors, along with what's known as "survivor guilt." In my struggle to make sense of Carlos's death, I sought out stories in magazines and newspapers about how other survivors climbed out of their rabbit holes.

A collection of letters to *Dear Abby* came from teenagers who had survived car accidents or had lost friends their own age in vehicle crashes. Abby recommended that instead of focusing on the guilt, they should focus on their survival and try to raise road-safety awareness. There was a lot in the news about states passing laws to require the use of motorcycle helmets. California's law would be passed on January 1, 1992. If our accident had happened seven months later, we would have been wearing helmets, and Ghost would have survived. An article that struck a chord with me was about Henry Rollins of Black Flag, a punk rock band I'd gotten to know through Carlos. In December 1991, Rollins had been outside his house with his best friend when the two were robbed at gunpoint. His best friend was fatally shot, but Rollins survived and was initially accused of having planned the robbery. Even after he was cleared, he felt responsible and traumatized, but as he said in the interview:

> *"I realized the other day that you only get one break in all this and that is that you get to go on. I get onstage for one reason, I write for one reason, I play music for one reason, 'cause I'm messed up and I write to get what's inside out."*

Around this time, I learned that despite having been told that I wouldn't be charged in Carlos's death, the local prosecutor was going to pursue felony manslaughter charges against me. The judge didn't want to take the case. The most upstanding members of the community—including my high school teachers and coaches—came forward to speak to the court about what an exemplary kid I was, how I'd never been in any trouble at all, and about my leadership and character.

The judge tried to shut the case down, telling the prosecutor, "Even if you win, I'm not sending this kid to jail. Do you still want to go ahead?"

The prosecutor went ahead. Every morning I put on a tie and went to court, wearing a stoic expression, feeling like I was in hell. My father's advice: "Don't let your feelings get involved."

Dad and I went to work to build supporting materials for our lawyer. We photographed the motorcycle and the cement pole, show-ing where Carlos had been thrown and where I'd landed. We had research about the numbers of accidents that occurred with this type of motorcycle. We photographed the irregular grade of the road where the gutter had a bump next to the curb. But the fact that I had taken the curve at close to 50 miles per hour was the problem. The jury deliberated briefly before finding me guilty of vehicular manslaughter and gross negligence. Instead of the felony offense sought by the prosecutor, my conviction was knocked down to a misdemeanor. Instead of one year in the county jail for a felony, I was sentenced to a crazy amount of community service hours working for Caltrans cleaning up the side of the freeways—usually assigned to hardened criminals who have made plea deals or were on worker-release programs.

When I showed up for my first day at Caltrans, imagine my shock as a twenty-year-old among all these cons and bangers who had gotten off on reduced sentences for assault or grand theft with thirty or forty hours. They'd ask how many hours I was in for—like in prison. When I told them four hundred hours, they were shocked, asking,— "Hey, man, what the hell did you *do*?"

Call it the El Monte homeboy in me, but I wore my Caltrans stint as a badge of honor. Fortunately, the following summer, I was able to switch my service hours over to working at a camp as a wrestling coach.

It's possible that the trial and its aftermath were helpful in ultimately pulling me out of the rabbit hole. During that ordeal, I was humbled by the outpouring of support from my community. My high school English teacher wrote to say how proud she was of me— not in spite of what happened or aside from the accident or because of it. She wanted to make sure that I didn't allow unwarranted feelings of guilt to stop me from attaining my goals. She reminded me of my vision to one day travel, and she hoped I wouldn't forget the value of what it meant to be the good person she knew me to be.

There was more to come for me, she said, and I shouldn't forget that everyone was counting on me to make that success happen.

Whenever anything happened to pull me back out of the hole, I'd want to tell Carlos about it, and I would go out to the cemetery in Montebello to talk to him. There was one visit early in this process, maybe a month after the accident, when I felt that he was trying to send me a message too.

Because of the warning from those two guys at his funeral about watching my back, whenever I went to the cemetery, I had to be careful.

I'd enter through a back gate, then park at the top of the hill where I could look down and see most of the cemetery. If it looked like there were people in the vicinity of Carlos's grave site, near a tree that was my marker, I'd wait until they left before I went down to visit. After the first few times I visited, I started to feel less concern, and on this one day, I saw that there was almost no one in the cemetery.

So I drove down the hill, parked, and made my way to where I thought he was buried. But when I got to that spot, I realized that, no, I was in the wrong section, near the wrong tree, so I walked to a nearby similar-looking patch of graves, many with newer headstones. No sign of Carlos's grave there. After several minutes, many loops around this corner of the cemetery, many attempts to triangulate and backtrack, I came to the conclusion that I was lost. At just that instant, out of nowhere, I saw these two *cholo* guys—all tatted up, I mean, serious gangbangers with tattoos on their necks—both drinking from forty-ounce beer cans in paper bags. They seemed to be just hanging out, not paying much attention to me but also checking me out.

I kept walking, glancing at the grave markers but keeping an eye on them. Back up the hill I went and looked down to see if they were gone. When I returned once more to find the grave site for Carlos, again, out of nowhere, the two of them stood up from behind a headstone. This time, they started over toward me.

"Hey, homes, whatcha looking for?"

"A grave site."

"Yeah, whose grave site?"

"A friend's."

The slightly older of the two asked, "When was the funeral?"

"A few weeks ago." The less information I gave, the better.

"Ah, no, brother, you know it takes a few months to get a headstone made. Where do you think your friend is buried?"

I pointed to about where I thought Carlos was buried.

The younger one pointed to a spot a bit farther. He said, "Well, yeah, there was a kid over there who got killed in a motorcycle accident." They knew about it, telling me it was a bad, messed-up deal. That gave me pause.

When I asked if they knew him or something, they said, "Nah," and pointed to another gravestone, saying, "That's our brother over there, our *carnal*."

I could see now that these two were brothers. Their younger brother had been shot in a gang shooting. The three had all been in the gang, but when he was killed, they realized that if they continued down that path, he would have died in vain.

"Some people die because things need to change," said the older brother. They believed that if things didn't change, that person would have died for no reason. Because of their brother's death, they chose to change by deciding they were no longer going to gangbang.

As these two *cholos* told me their story, they spoke with the wisdom of pain and of loss. They explained that their belief was that when some people die because things need to change among the living, that change could be different for every person. But their message was about taking steps to make sure that the one who was killed didn't die in vain.

That was when I felt comfortable enough to tell these two that not only was Carlos my best friend but that I was driving the motorcycle.

"No shit?" said the younger brother. "Yeah, we heard something about that."

"Maybe," said the older one, "it could be you. Maybe there's something you're doing that needs to change. Or it's something he was doing that you can change."

When I drove away that afternoon, I no longer carried the same level of fear that I was going to be assaulted by whoever had made those threats at the funeral because they blamed me for the accident. On the contrary, I felt strangely supported by these two former gang-banger brothers, who talked so profoundly, in their own way, about life and death and people not dying in vain. The strangest thing of all was that in all the years that followed, and in all the visits that I made to the cemetery to visit Carlos, I never saw those guys again. And as many times as I went to look for their brother's gravestone, I never found it.

But I never forgot a word they said. And as the weeks and months went on after that encounter, I thought often of their message and did find myself changing. Where before I had waited for everything to go back to normal, I accepted that for me, it would never be.

All this time I had been trying to understand the reason that Carlos had to die. There was no one answer for everyone that made any sense. But if by his dying I could commit to being, above all, a good person and even to becoming a better man and make that part of the reality I was trying to create, that would be a success that could truly honor his memory and let him live on through me.

We all have obstacles that cloud our vision and stand in the way of our dreams. As I've learned through my own journey and in mentoring others over the years, sometimes the hardest obstacle you will ever have to overcome is you. Whether it's your fear of failing, your belief that you don't deserve success, or your inner doubts that you won't measure up because you're different or somehow not good enough, I can testify that those deterrents don't have to define you. Obstacles can be overcome. They are only as powerful as you allow them to be.

Maybe that was the message that Carlos wanted me to hear and pass on to you.

three

Seize the Moment: *Overcoming Obstacles, Getting Past Fear*

Reach for the stars, and if you don't grab them,
at least you'll fall on top of the world.

—Pitbull,
"Give Me Everything"

There is some dispute as to whether Thomas Edison actually coined the phrase "There is no substitute for hard work"—although the original attribution remains unknown. All I can say is that whoever first said it was right. Likewise, there is no substitute in business for the principle of *cultivating a relentless work ethic.* As obvious and well-worn as this principle may be, it's a clincher for turning dreams into reality. Your relentless work ethic is the determining factor of whether you not only find what you love to do but also get to do it for a living. When it's time to take action on your goals of landing that job or getting your big break, your work ethic is what gets you past the very real obstacles and your own fears.

THE JOB OF GETTING A JOB

Not long ago I read a startling article in *USA Today* about the challenges of finding employment in any field. One of the top myths about looking for work, the article said, was that most people believe they can find their next job by applying online—but, in fact, only 15 percent of positions are actually filled from public listings. These days, the majority of jobs come from personal referrals or they are filled internally. The takeaway that grabbed my attention: "More than 70 percent of people land jobs through networking." Or, as I've heard from experts in the headhunting business, qualified candidates should stop looking for the right job and start looking for the right person.

Welcome to reality. If only I had known what networking even meant back in the summer of 1994 after I graduated from Cal State Fullerton when I began to apply for any and every job that was even remotely connected to television. My résumé, complete with four years of paid part-time TV production work at my university's media center, was impressive. At least I thought so! On top of that, I had strong internal motivation, and though I had never been in the working world, my background forced me to have nerve or—for lack of a better word—*cojones*. For years, I had known what it was that I was going to do one day, and now, finally, it was time to go out, claim my prize, and conquer the world.

True, as I envisioned my future career, I had never been very specific about what I actually saw myself doing in my chosen field. But, in my view, that wasn't a bad thing because I could be all the more open to the opportunities that came along.

Months flew by as I did everything and anything to get hired. But all roads—not just to getting the right job but to getting any job—turned out to be dead ends. Newspaper classified listings were our equivalent of the online job boards of today. I would go to the companies or studios where I'd read they were looking for a production assistant or video camera operator, but nothing came of that. Then I started cold-calling, dropping in at production houses, large and small, just asking if I could fill out an application. Nothing again. Every morning I'd drive into LA to hit the pavement and spend the day handing out copies of my résumé like newspapers, all in the hopes that I'd get it to someone who knew someone who could steer me in the right direction to a paying TV job.

If this sounds like an experience you've had before, you probably know how intimidating it can be to navigate unfamiliar turf where everybody appears to be an insider holding the keys to the kingdom you're trying to break into. No matter how confident you might be, it can be intimidating to get past those gatekeepers—who are sometimes paid to keep you out.

At my wit's end, I even contemplated going to law school, going so far as to take the LSAT. When I told my mother that maybe a path into entertainment law would open up doors for me in television, she pointed out that now was the time to pursue my dream with all of my being. Besides, in her opinion, "Law school will always be there later on. If working in television is your goal, don't go on a detour."

So I went back to the job of finding a job.

Unbeknownst to me, that in itself taught me a fundamental of Entrepreneurship 101—the idea that even when you're looking for a job, you can be both boss and employee in this business of finding that employer. Take charge of the process as much as you can by presenting yourself and your materials in the best light. The age-old tips still apply:

- Proofread and perfect your résumé and any testimonials or recommendations in the event of an interview.

- Develop a brief cover letter to introduce yourself to a potential employer. Be on point and add a touch of humor without being heavy-handed. That same pitch can be used when you leave phone messages as well. Of course, follow up all e-mails and interviews with thank-yous.

- Present yourself professionally, in appropriate business attire, and if you're not sure what that might be, ask for input from someone who does.

- Needless to say, you should be on time for interviews and meetings.

You can't go wrong by following steps that are just common sense. But those guidelines aren't necessarily going to get you past the gatekeepers or help you walk through doors with the confidence that can make or break an opportunity. My advice, based on my experience struggling in those early days to even get my name in front of an employer, is to go deeper in your preparation. A key to your job hunt can be *focus*, just as my mother advised me. Forget getting your dream job but focus instead on getting into your dream arena. Spend time *doing inventory of your strengths and weaknesses.* Be honest with yourself. Figure out *who your competition is.* Rather than being defeated, ask yourself *what you have to offer that makes you different*—not only from your academic or work experience but also from what you've drawn from your life lessons and obstacles you've overcome already. Make sure before you apply for a job that it *engages your enthusiasm, curiosity, and vision.* You may not even have all the qualifications needed, but if you walk in with passion and a desire to learn, you will better your chances of getting someone's attention—

especially if you can see the potential opportunity even when that may mean starting at the bottom to prove yourself up ahead.

All of those points can help you seize the moment and make the most of it—when it comes. What happens though, when it doesn't, when you can't seem to even get your foot in the door, much less get past the gatekeepers? That's when you have to change your game. How? By choosing to *widen your search* and *go out of your comfort zone.*

By widening your search, you may need to cast a wider geographical net or expand the kinds of openings that won't take you too far off your focus. By going out of your comfort zone, you may have to risk being seen as pushy or annoying by not letting the gatekeepers intimidate you. You can be funny; you can be charming. You don't have to apologize for being hungry to work. Pump yourself up. This is your dream, where the rubber meets the road—just go for it.

The decision to widen my search and get out of my comfort zone led me to a listing about two hours away in Palm Springs. KMIR, an NBC news affiliate, had an opening for a part-time sports editor. As a plus, I did have solid editing experience. Part-time and out-of-town were not ideal. But at that point, I was not ruling out anything. Although a mailing address with a PO box was included in the listing, I knew by now that the odds were slim to none that whoever opened the mail would even look at my résumé, let alone pass it on to the news director doing the hiring. Then I thought—why not go there in person to drop it off and maybe be taken more seriously? But that was like a cold call and wouldn't guarantee I'd get an interview.

That was when I picked up the phone, called the news station first thing that same morning, and was able to speak directly to the assignment editor in charge of hiring—who obviously was pressed for time and wanted to get off the phone the minute I introduced myself.

Good thing I can talk fast! All I said was: "Hey, if I come out there, will you give me ten minutes of your time? I just want to drop off my résumé."

"Of course," she said.

And with that, I put gas in my car and headed out to the desert, arriving at the smallish TV station of KMIR by about noon. The news director granted me the interview. At first, I thought she was just being nice as she sat down to look over the various skills that I'd gained working at the media center. Though I'd been paid, it was only a college job, and I had no professional television experience. She had no issue with that. In fact, we had a great conversation, mainly about my lifelong passion for television. She wrapped up by saying, "You're terrific, Cris, and you know how to edit—"

Before I reached over to shake her hand and thank her for taking the time to see me, she interrupted, "You know what? The person you need to meet comes in at five o'clock for the six o'clock news, and I'd love for him to take a look and talk to you. Can you hang out?"

But of course. After biding my time at the mall for five hours, I return to the station to find that their sports anchor has called in sick and won't be back until the next day. The news director apologizes and asks if I wouldn't mind coming back the next day. Before I can answer, the weather man runs in, interrupts us, and says to me, "Hey, I heard you know how to edit. Do you want to stick around and watch the newscast and possibly help me edit?"

How crazy is this? Next thing I know, I am helping the team. The system used by the station was an older editing system that I knew well. That gave me the ability to jump right in and help them cut the highlights to the sports. Everything moved like clockwork, and before I knew it, they were calling for quiet in the studio for the taping while directing me out to the lobby to watch. As I walked down the hall, I could hear the weather anchor (subbing for the sports anchor), announcing an update on the Dodgers game coming up next, and as I ran to the monitor in the lobby, I watched the footage I had just edited as it was broadcast out over the air on the TV!

A chill came over me as I realized that what I had worked on was now transmitting into people's homes all over the Coachella Valley. All the sports fans and news followers were sitting in their living rooms in front of their TV sets, enjoying the piece that I had put together.

In that moment, I had the best first taste of reality of my life. No longer was I a crazy dreamer. A new understanding began to dawn on me that I had something to offer that was needed, that audiences cared about. And I also knew, finally, that whatever was going to happen next, television could really be a possible path for me.

Making the break happen for myself was an instance of an old-school success strategy of *carpe diem*. When you have an idea that could lead to an opportunity, that takes you out of your comfort zone, that may mean widening your search, don't put it up on a shelf and think about it for a while. Go for it. Seize the day, seize the moment.

That night I realized something else about running my business of getting a job. I had to stop thinking that someone was going to roll out a red carpet and tell me that I was everything they'd been waiting for. Big news flash, especially when you've just come from getting your education—when there are resources that are in place for you to do well. In the real world, that benevolence pretty much ends. Employers, on the whole, are looking to fill a need. Rather than assume the TV industry was going to empower me because I had this dream, I had to have something to offer to the industry. Passion is contagious, but it may not overcome the question "What have you done lately and how does that help our bottom line?" I had everything to learn.

Still, I hoped my help that evening would be enough to land me the next interview. But there would be no second interview. Before I left that night, the news director stopped me and said, "I've never done this before and I may be wrong, but you can start tomorrow. Just come in."

I started work the very next day as the assistant sports editor and would spend the next two years rising up through the ranks of KMIR. My television adventure had begun.

But wait. Now that I was in—albeit at the entry level—I was met with a somewhat rude awakening. Turns out that the news business has its own rules that are different from the entertainment-driven arenas of the television business. Since I was new to the real working world anyway, I was somewhat naive to the politics that goes on in most fields. Broadcast news has a distinct culture unto itself that revolves around a specific game that's played by everyone from the cameramen or camerawomen to the directors to the reporters and anchors and everybody in between. The premise of the game is that these affiliate stations in smaller markets are like the minor leagues for players in the news business to hone their craft in order to get to the better jobs in the bigger markets—and then get paid. Though KMIR was low on the totem pole, the advantage of being in Palm Springs was that it was two hours away from Los Angeles, the number two market in the country. If the goal was to advance in TV news, that meant using weekends or off days to network in Los Angeles by freelancing for our NBC station there, KNBC.

The hitch for a newcomer like me was that because there was a lot of turnover, there weren't many mentors offering to show me the ropes or guide me along. Fortunately, I didn't care. All I wanted to do was learn everything that I could, bottom to top. So I began a practice that was the equivalent of working a job and a half—excelling at my job, the one that I had been hired to do, and then, when I was finished, I'd offer to help or sit in at another desk with someone else, and learn what that position entailed.

The takeaway? Even when you get a job, if you have vision and higher goals beyond that starting place, you're still in the business of getting a job. The difference is that you are now being paid not just to provide a service but also to take advantage of the opportunity to gather the skills and experience that can open you up to other opportunities. How? By upping your relentless work ethic.

EMBRACE THE OPPORTUNITY OF HARD WORK

One of the most common complaints for many of us with big dreams is that when you actually get your first shot, the job is nowhere near as glamorous as you thought it would be. That doesn't mean you should throw up your hands and walk away. If it's really not for you, take note. But be sure before you quit that you've learned everything you can even when it's not exactly what you want to do. See the job that you don't love as a training ground for generating enthusiasm about working hard. I truly believe that everything you learn at the start can give you an edge later on—even when your journey takes you in a different direction.

From the get-go, as an assistant sports editor at KMIR, I was able to hone my storytelling skills. Usually what happens in sports news is that a story person will write the script for the broadcast and the editor cuts highlights toward the script. Because we were so busy and there weren't many of us, the main sports editor would let me cut the highlights first, with a script in my mind as to how we would tell the story. What piece goes first? What clips should we use? What game score should we feature? Once I'd put the clips together, I'd take them to the anchor and we'd write the actual script together. With live news running three times a night—at five p.m., six p.m., and eleven p.m.—the time constraints were crazy. If the sports anchor was in the middle of the broadcast and the Angels game was in late innings, I'd edit on the fly and change the script to be read on air as it was happening in real time. So in addition to sharpening my story skills, the news was a crash course in learning how to work at breakneck speed. For good reason, we all referred to our environment as "the pressure cooker."

During my two years at KMIR I was promoted from part-time sports editor to full-time sports editor to managing newsroom editor (for lack of an official title) to assistant director of the news to, finally, director of the news in charge of directing live newscasts three shows a night. The intensity increased with each step up. Every morning at every level, the job began with me getting up and reading three to four newspapers just to know what was trending. It was the classic quest to get the scoop and analyze it from the local angle. Of course, by the mid- to late nineties, we had to scour the Internet too, making sure we weren't missing any national or global stories that would be breaking. The process taught me how to tell stories not just quickly but also dramatically—how to lead with the most attention-grabbing piece of the news item and then how to follow and conclude.

My experience working in the field put all these new skills to the test. As news editor, I would travel out into the area with a camera and a microphone, sometimes with a reporter and sometimes without. The task was to shoot the pieces, starting with the stand-up—a reporter talking to the camera—or through direct interviews, and then shoot b-roll, which is the common term for the secondary footage that supplements the direct interview of the reporter or the main witness or source for the story. The term dates back to the way editing worked in the old days—when the principle footage was on the "A" machine, secondary footage was on the "B" machine, and then both a-roll and b-roll were fed at different intervals and cuts into a third machine to put the story together. Though technology had advanced, you still had to know in advance how you might put principal and secondary footage together once you got back to the studio.

So thinking on your feet took on new meaning. We'd show up on the scene and tell the story. It might be as simple as reporting the news of a local high school where somebody had stolen the computers, capturing the right visuals for the b-roll to convey how it happened, along with a stand-up of a reporter narrating the events that had taken place. Then I'd get back to the station, edit the footage, and put it on the air.

Nothing could have been more instructive for my pitching and producing abilities later on than learning to tell news stories in a very small amount of time. Occasionally, I'd have the luxury of telling a story in two minutes. But more often it was thirty seconds. In this crash course in Advanced Storytelling, I saw how important it was to open with a big lead. This was where I came to understand the saying "If it bleeds, it leads." We'd search for the most graphic visual that we could find and put it up front. It was how to hook the audience and hook 'em for good.

This was about more than storytelling; it was also about marketing. Let it not be forgotten that the news is still a major revenue producer for the television networks. A big lead gets eyeballs and advertisers spend their ad dollars on national and local outlets that show compelling news.

It was in Palm Springs—well-known for star-studded golf and tennis tournaments—where I had my first taste of meeting and interviewing celebrities. Some of these pieces that we'd air locally would actually be transmitted to NBC for national broadcast. Such was the case when I did a story on Andre Agassi—with the assignment from NBC to pull out all the stops.

Agassi was a top sports superstar of the 1990s, and his arrival in the desert to play tennis, after winning the gold medal in men's tennis at the Olympics, was newsworthy. Starting at the airport, I shot the landing of his private jet—Air Agassi—and then I led our TV crew onto the plane, where we interviewed him as if he was entertaining us in his living room. Wow! No sooner had I gotten back to the station and edited the footage for broadcast with our anchor than we transmitted everything over to NBC in LA, with enough time for me to call my parents and tell them to watch.

That moment felt like such a validation of everything that I'd been working toward. In spite of setbacks early on and insane hours and little pay, my dream to work in television was taking form in reality.

During my tenure at KMIR, I had a chance to wear every hat in the newsroom, including the job of jumping in at the last minute to sub for our sports anchor during a New Year's Day broadcast. Did I seize the day? You bet. But guess what. If I was ever tempted to pursue an on-air path, that one newscast put a stop to that thought. There was no way. I was bad. Seriously. And I have the tape to prove it.

After being promoted to news editor responsible for making sure we got the scoop on breaking stories, I relied heavily on the police scanner we had in the newsroom and, when I was in the field, the one in my van. On the way back to the station one day, I got a call from the news director to get to the scene of a freeway accident. When I arrived, emergency services hadn't shown up yet. A fifty-passenger church bus had somehow lost control and rolled. None of the passengers had been wearing seat belts, and when the bus rolled, everyone except for two passengers had been thrown from the vehicle.

The scene was a nightmare: mangled bodies all over the freeway, some dead, some knocked unconscious. Because I was working as a newsman, my job was to shoot the footage; but because the paramedics and ambulances weren't there yet, I had to make a decision whether to shoot first or to help the survivors. Without hesitation, I left the camera in the van and started helping victims who could be helped. The hero of the day was a Marine who had come from the nearby base, complete with landing sticks to guide the emergency helicopter onto the freeway—just as the fire engines arrived, bringing a team of paramedics who spread out among the wounded, making life-and-death decisions as to who needed what. There were stretchers to help carry, blankets to bring to victims. There was something I could do, even if it was small, and that was all that mattered.

Although I was promoted shortly afterward to assistant director of news and then to director of news, that devastating accident was a turning point in my tenure at KMIR. When I put the camera down on the freeway that day, I knew deep down that this was not the kind of TV I wanted to be making. Maybe the news might have been too real. I'm not sure if this decision had anything to do with the fact that I was a survivor of a life-and-death accident. The main reason was that deep down I knew that what I most wanted was to be in the world of entertainment that had inspired me in the first place.

When, after two years, I finally made the decision to leave the news in mid-1997, I was still making less than what I had made at the media center at Cal State Fullerton. The job was ideal for my ambitious coworkers ready to leapfrog to the bigger news markets. But because that was not the direction I wanted to go in, it was time for me to move on. Without a doubt, everything that I'd learned would be immeasurably valuable at every stage up ahead.

When you get to the point where you know that it's time to look for another job that's more in line with your goals, it's an uncomfortable if not scary place to be. What-ifs can raise your fear level. What if there's nothing out there? What if you leave and fail to build on the success you've established in your current job? What if you get a new job that turns out to be a step backward? Those are real concerns. But fear is not your friend. If you genuinely feel you've learned everything you can from where you're at, get past the fear, once again, by pushing yourself outside your comfort zone. Embrace the process. You can even choose to make it fun. What's more, I believe that once you're committed to your path, there is no such thing as backward.

BASIC NETWORKING

The crazy story of how I got my break in Hollywood may not apply to everyone's search for opportunity, but it came about because I was willing to turn over each and every stone in the hopes of making a connection. That's Networking 101. It's preferable to use your energy following up on leads that can actually do something for you. But, after exhausting most avenues, I didn't have any leads like that. So when my mother offered to make a phone call, I welcomed her help. The point is that you never know.

Even though my mother didn't know anything about television or the entertainment industry, she had a close friend named Pilar, who was also in education and whose daughter worked in marketing at ABC. Pilar said, "Tina, I can't get involved. I make it a rule not to recommend people to my daughter because she gets asked all the time."

Instead of giving up, my mother found an opportunity to introduce me to Pilar when the two of them happened to be attending a teaching conference in Palm Springs. The plan was for me to join them at dinner and that they would first stop by to meet me at KMIR. When they arrived, I took a moment to show them around the station and give them a sense of everything that I did there. At dinner, I went on to tell Pilar how excited I was to now pursue options in the entertainment side of TV. And, sure enough, after winning her over, she had enough belief in my potential to introduce me to her daughter, Lisa—who, when we met a short time later, couldn't offer me much by way of advice.

But then, as I stood up and thanked Lisa for meeting with me, she said, "There's a friend of mine who's working as an assistant director on a show right now. I'm not making any promises, but she might have five minutes to talk to you."

A week or so later, I found myself making the drive from Palm Springs for another meeting. This was the One, I felt certain, that was going to change my life. For one thing, the meeting was to take place at her house in Malibu, where all the power players in Hollywood lived—or so I was convinced. For another, I assumed that my accomplished rise to directing the news at KMIR made me a prime candidate for leapfrogging over to a spot doing some kind of assistant directing on a daytime or prime-time entertainment show. Besides, now that I was twenty-four years old, soon to be married and getting ready to settle down, this just felt like I'd paid my dues and it was time for the hard work to start paying off.

My résumé was stacked with vivid descriptions of the filming, editing, and writing that I'd been doing, plus all of the TV technology I'd mastered at KMIR. A folder with freshly printed résumé copies lay on the seat next to me as I drove my 1986 two-door red Toyota pickup truck from Palm Springs on the 10 Freeway. Wow, was I stoked, playing my hip-hop mixtapes on my cassette player all the way to Malibu. I'll never forget that drive up the PCH and how blue the ocean looked as a backdrop to the beach mansions that lined the highway as far as the eye could see. Clearly, every TV executive in Hollywood had to live somewhere in Malibu.

When I made it to the producer's house, she began with a confession. "Look," she said, "I only agreed to this meeting because you were recommended by a dear friend of mine. We've been best friends for years. But that's the only reason I agreed to meet you." She didn't give me a beat to answer before she added, "Let me see your résumé."

Well, I thought, handing it to her, this will change her mind. But no. In fact, as she looked it over and I quickly ran down my four years of experience at my college media center and how I'd worn every hat in production at KMIR, and the skills and positions I'd attained over the last two years, I watched her face register disapproval. Then, with a baffled tone, she asked, "Have you not worked in LA?"

"No, I . . ." I began, trying for a longer answer, but decided to answer in brief: "I just drove from Palm Springs."

"Oh, well, I'm sorry, but until you've worked in Los Angeles, then you haven't worked in this business."

And that was it. None of my experience counted. Despite the sinking feeling of "Holy crap, this was just a waste of time!" I decided to hang a bit longer and have a polite conversation. Besides telling her a little about growing up as I did with my lifelong passion for television, I was able to ask a few questions about what her job as an assistant director on a game show was like. After that, I headed back to Palm Springs, sadly watching the sun as it set on the Malibu horizon. No one had warned me about the Hollywood catch-22 that said you couldn't get a job in LA without experience in LA. Did that mean I was all the way back at square one, where I'd been two years before when I took the job in Palm Springs? It was starting to appear so.

Before returning to the desert, I swung by my parents' house in Pomona to say a quick hello. My mother greeted me with a hug and a phone message she had just taken from the Malibu TV director, who had called asking to speak with me. Weird. Except my parents' phone number was on my résumé, so, without any delay, I picked up the phone to return the call.

She got down to business. "Look," she said, "I can see you're serious about wanting to work in this business. So here's what I'm going to do . . ." She took a breath that I assumed meant she was going to refer me to someone else who might be able to help me. Instead, she went on. "I'm going to give you the worst job I can give you." What was it? The job of low-level postproduction assistant on *Big Deal*, a new game show that she was assistant directing for FOX. Not only was she offering me the worst job she could, but, as she emphasized, "That's the best I can do for you."

Translated: The favor she was offering was not to do me any favor. Eighteen years later, I use that same line myself whenever the chance comes up to do something for someone without experience but who seems promising. Why give them the worst job? Because that person can then make it or break it on his or her own merit without the favor hanging over their head.

She was not kidding about this post-PA spot being a less-than-desirable job. But, for more than a few reasons, I accepted her offer on the phone, with the job sight unseen, and didn't even ask how much the position paid. Turned out, as a runner (aka a gofer), assistant, and all-around grunt who would be working sixty-five hours a week, the weekly salary was four hundred eighty dollars, no overtime, which was less than my KMIR salary—which was already less than what I had been making at my college media center. By most measures it was a step backward. Who goes from a TV news gig where you're directing everything that happens in the control room to being a glorified errand boy on a game show? Well, if I had learned one thing from my experience in Palm Springs, it was that with a relentless work ethic, you could create other opportunities in fairly rapid succession. The business principle of finding what you love to do and doing it for a living will always be amplified by the principle of making the pain of hard work your best friend.

That's how I got my first gig in reality TV.

Remember, as I had to learn, you don't have to get your whole foot in the door of where you want to be, as long as you can get your little toe in there. All you need, actually, is a crack in the door or just a sliver of light to give you a sense of what lies beyond. That was what working this entry-level job would be for me—a chance to learn the lay of the land on the entertainment side of television production. How was I ever going to set realistic goals for myself without the experience of working on the inside? The more I thought about it, the more I accepted that starting at the bottom was ideal. My instincts told me that I was going to learn a lot in a short amount of time, so just to take the ball and run with it.

That would not be the first or last time that I was forced to go with my gut. Call it another variation of betting on yourself. Whether you are at the early stages of staking out your reality or if parameters within your industry have shifted and you're moving in a different direction as you seek out new possibilities, I believe your instincts are there to guide you toward your authentic path. So I listened when mine told me that I was on the right track and that this was no step backward at all.

The mission that I chose for myself, just as I had before, was to kill it so much at every level of this new job that I could advance quickly up the ladder.

AMBITION GETS YOU NOTICED

So you've made it to the big time, right? You've gotten past your fear; you've gotten hired in the field of your dreams. Or you may have a rude awakening, as I did, that even once you've gotten your toe in the door, this is where the hard work and competition really set in. If you are committed to advancing to the reality of your dreams, you'll need to engage your passion even more and not be intimidated by the higher level of competition you'll usually face. I learned first-hand that ambition is not a four-letter word—as long as you can back it up with the work to be a standout.

That's what happened as I began my Hollywood career. As a lowly PA on *Big Deal*, a game show that was shot live to tape and produced for FOX by a company called Stone Stanley, I became a bona fide working member of the entertainment industry rat race. One of my first special assignments followed the question: "Hey, Abrego, do you have AC in your truck?"

When I answered that my truck did have air-conditioning, I was assigned the role of company chauffeur—driving the host, Mark DeCarlo, to and from the set—as one of my many daily duties. Why they couldn't spring for a town car was not my place to ask. Hey, cool by me, except that my truck was a two-door with an open bed in back.

Mark DeCarlo was a former stand-up, funny and likable, and a really engaging host; he didn't seem to mind about my truck. Prior to *Big Deal*, he had been the host of *Studs*, the dating game show. After a few days of sharing the small space of my truck's cab, he asked, "What about you? What are your plans?"

I'm sure he was just being a good host by asking, but I didn't hold back. I told him that working in television had always been my dream. What exactly did I want to do in TV? Well, now that I'd been behind the scenes for all of a week or so, I knew exactly what I wanted to do and what I was absolutely going to do. "Executive producer," I announced with total assurance.

"Nothing like going for the gold," he laughed. In fact, in later years when I'd achieved that goal, we'd run into each other, and he'd remind me how impressed he was by my confidence in attaining so lofty a goal.

That was an eye-opener—one that reinforces the lesson that there is no penalty for the willingness to declare your dreams and goals out loud to others. I'm not talking about passing fancies or generic wishful thinking. What I mean is that once you have a clear focus that helps you ignite your own internal motivator—your drive, your passion, your sense of purpose—there is nothing wrong with declaring your intention to others.

Will people think you are overly ambitious? Maybe. But so what? Again, that's part of embracing what makes you different and what sets you apart. Ambition gets you noticed. In a competitive field, that's highly important. Granted, you can't be all talk. You have to back it up with action and a demonstrable ability to outwork and outhustle the competition.

During my five months at Stone Stanley, I approached every menial task with that same Johnny-on-the-spot attitude, going above and beyond my requirements. Even if I was just running to make a bank deposit for my boss or, yeah, getting coffee for a contestant, I did it in half the time others would and then added more to-do items to the list. Pretty soon, thanks to the editing and technical skills I'd already mastered, I was able to pitch in and help more directly in production.

When everyone else was heading home for the night, I'd work several more hours on my own in the editing bay, teaching myself how to use Avid, the new technology that was changing the game for editors in postproduction. Instead of the more linear methods of cutting videotape in sequence—taking from the a-roll, b-roll, and so on—Avid made it possible to employ a more nonlinear editing approach, allowing you to digitize footage so you could lift up a piece from a number five spot and put it back in the number two spot or move sections of tape around without having to start again from scratch.

In the matter of a couple months, thanks to late nights and teaching myself Avid, I became an integral part of the production of *Big Deal*. So much so that even when FOX canceled the show, the powers that be at Stone Stanley chose to keep me on staff for their upcoming productions. But then, in a stroke of seriously good timing, another job possibility turned up—in what was the very new genre of reality television.

I knew almost nothing about this new kind of unscripted TV series. No one did! But if my short time in Hollywood had taught me anything at that stage, it was the importance of seizing the moment. My well-tested advice is that if you sense that you have created an opportunity to pursue your reality, there is only one thing to do—run, don't walk.

four

A Brief History of Reality:
Ideas and Execution

*First comes the thought; then organization of that thought into
ideas and plans; then transformation of those plans into reality.
The beginning, as you will observe, is in your imagination.*

—NAPOLEON HILL,
Author, *Think and Grow Rich*

On a good day without too much crosstown traffic, the drive is
only about fifteen minutes from the Beverly Hills corporate
headquarters of Endemol Shine North America to our Hollywood-
based production offices. Whenever I hustle over from one office
to the other, I take the time to value the transformational power of
*learning to prepare for each and every shot by training like a professional
athlete*—a business principle too often overlooked.

This principle is on full display at the idea factory of our Hollywood offices. This otherwise unassuming three-story brick building—
what used to be a secret outpost for the FBI—houses a world of
expertise, all members of a team who have trained to be the best at
what they do. In no time, I can go from one of the wings where I
hear the latest from our marketing and licensing team to the next
stop, upstairs, for a casting discussion with our production heads, to

cruising down the hall and checking in with our master production chief whose wall-sized whiteboard shows where we are on every single current project (including unscripted and scripted series, as well as Web content and live events). During a coffee break, I might head down to the first floor to catch up with producers whose companies have overall deals with us—including creative execs for Randy Jackson, Pitbull, and Ryan Seacrest's company. Whether it's hearing what's new from a group we call the Think Tank (brilliant up-and-coming content creators who work in secrecy in a rooftop office suite) or reviewing online materials from the talented troops in our digital development department, there is no denying the level of imagination, passion, and productivity that is just infectious.

Even though I could probably conduct most of my work as co-CEO at the corporate office, I try to get to Hollywood at least two, if not three, days out of the week. In my view, it's important for everyone in the company to feel valued as integral to the whole. I want all of our employees to feel they have my ear. More than that, like an athlete who doesn't want to get out of shape, I don't want to lose touch with the fundamentals that were the building blocks of my career. Plus, whenever I get to go work at the Hollywood offices, I am able to marvel that this is my reality—something I couldn't have even dreamed up this perfectly.

One of those fundamentals has to do with recognizing the importance of both imagination and execution. Yes, while it's true that ideas are the fuel that Hollywood runs on, I learned early in the process that without execution—the flame needed to light the fire—those ideas never go anywhere. That balance of strong ideas and fresh stories mixed with artful execution is the engine of the show business industry, regardless of genre. Similarly, most businesses and organizations require a balance of great ideas and skillful execution.

The challenge is to develop your strengths and understanding with respect to both ideas and execution, again with the tenacity and focus of training like a professional athlete. How do you do that? Well, for starters, by taking the time to really get to know the arena or business that you're entering. Like a pro, before you step onto the playing field, you should command an expertise of the game and how it has been played. You should read everything you can about recent changes in the industry you've chosen and, when you've started work with a new company, about its track record. As you review that background, look for the ways that both ideas and execution have been important to the success of that company.

The other side of understanding ideas and execution is to consider where your strengths lie. Maybe you are more of an idea person. Or maybe you prefer taking the lead in implementing ideas. These strengths are important to identify as you look for opportunities to stand out in your field. And if you have the tenacity of a pro athlete to improve on the expertise you lack, you will make yourself that much more valuable.

While I knew many of these pointers about being prepared and that it would be helpful to do research about the arena of reality television that I was hoping to enter, there wasn't actually much information to be found. Still, I could have definitely been more prepared. Even so, the timing could not have been more opportune.

In the late 1990s, at the time when I thought there was a job with my name on a new reality TV show—which turned out to be more complicated than walking in with a strong recommendation—the field of reality TV was at ground zero for developments that would shape the future of media and popular culture. So this was a classic instance of hopefully being at *the right place at the right time.*

To give you some context of what this possible job opening would mean for my career, I'd like to first offer a brief history of reality TV in the late 1990s, when its future was as unpredictable as my own.

REALITY AS ENTERTAINMENT

No matter how dominant and lucrative reality television has managed to become in the current media landscape, it is still basically regarded as the unwanted stepchild equivalent of show business genres. Needless to say, as a practitioner in the field, I'm constantly scratching my head that we are not taken more seriously—especially now that reality has become a staple of every thriving media outlet. Still, in the hierarchy of entertainment offerings, we remain at the bargain-basement level. At the top, of course, would be feature films, the most revered, and just below that would be the scripted TV dramas, with scripted TV sitcoms a step below, then TV variety and specials under that, and on the lowest level would be reality TV.

Aside from the negative connotations, there are also other widely held misconceptions out there about how reality TV works. For example, not anyone can come in and pitch a crazy idea for a reality show that can then magically turn into a hit. Not so. You have to come in with the skills to execute your idea.

Many assume that storytelling rules for scripted entertainment do not apply to an unscripted show. On the contrary, we adhere to the same rules as scripted shows, whether it's a classic theme like *boy meets girl/boy loses girl/boy gets girl back* or a new twist on a fish-out-of-water tale or reality versions of ghost stories or crime procedurals. The expertise required to take a premise all the way to a successful reality series can include everything from knowing game theory to a deep understanding of human psychology. But above all, you can't make reality TV without real knowledge of entertainment—how characters and stories touch audiences to create suspense, humor, pathos, drama, and meaning. Why? Because this poor stepchild of a genre that we're talking about is really a distant cousin of genres that existed long before it ever came into being.

Let me add that, in its purest from, early reality TV was more documentarian than anything. Later, as it accelerated and grew into the behemoth it has become, the entertainment values made for much more polished products. Mark Burnett, the reality mogul who burst on the scene in 2000 with *Survivor* (the American version of a Swedish import) and boasted a season one finale of fifty million viewers, is often credited as the father of reality TV. That's not the case. The true parents of modern reality TV are Mary-Ellis Bunim and Jon Murray, who pushed the boundaries of technology helmed by Bertram van Munster—a producer of *COPS*, the crime docuseries that first aired in 1989 and is still going strong, as well as the executive producer of *Amazing Race*, which has reigned at the top of the reality heap since first airing in 2001.

The origins of reality TV are often traced back to 1948 when Allen Funt launched his soon-to-be-iconic *Candid Camera*. Using hidden cameras and mics, the series allowed ordinary people in everyday settings to react to out-of-the-ordinary characters or situations in highly entertaining ways. Then, in the mid-1950s, on *Queen for a Day*, the competition format added to reality's DNA by borrowing from the *Cinderella* story structure. After four contestants—real-life housewives—tearfully confessed their wishes that might improve their lives, the studio audience would vote by applause to determine who would be crowned Queen for the Day. Today, unscripted shows continue to use confessional soul-baring. Hard-luck backstories can improve the odds for winning a competition, especially when audiences witness a contestant's transformation.

The tipping point for reality, before it was called that, came in 1973 with the premiere of *An American Family*, a PBS docuseries that chronicled the lives of an ordinary California household—those of Bill and Pat Loud and their five kids. Anthropologist Margaret Mead soon described *An American Family* as a new art form that was going to be as "significant as the invention of drama or the novel."

The 1980s saw an update to the reality genre that focused on music and variety—many dating back to TV's earliest days—plus talk show formats, talent competitions, and newsmagazine exposés, all of which were primarily unscripted. Shows like *That's Incredible* and *America's Funniest Home Videos* proved, in different ways, that real people doing amazing or ridiculous things could capture the public imagination. Likewise, a docudrama that could bring a murderer to justice, such as *America's Most Wanted*, which gave viewers a phone number to call with information that might help law enforcement, turned the act of watching television into a less passive, more interactive experience. As cameras became smaller, lighter, and more portable, the visuals improved, making it possible for *COPS* to be shot as a true documentary. As a producer, Bertram van Munster advanced the art form on *COPS*, without intruding on the reality. He brought in better lighting, varied angles, and editing that put the cops front and center while also giving the show a more dramatic pace.

In 1992, it took the genius of Mary-Ellis Bunim and Jonathan Murray to conceive of a domestic docuseries that was as cutting-edge as *An American Family* had been two decades earlier, as dramatically yet authentically shot and edited as *COPS*, but that drew from a casting pool of real people that had been untapped until then. I'm talking, of course, about young adults who were connected to youth culture and coming of age as the MTV generation.

My people! I will never forget watching the third or fourth episode of the first season of *Real World* when I was finishing up my sophomore year at Cal State Fullerton. Everyone I knew had been talking about it. As a couple of friends and I sat in front of the TV, I was mesmerized by the voice-over that told us this was the true story of seven strangers who were picked to live and work together and have their lives videotaped to find out "what happens when people stop being polite . . . and start getting real. . . ."

Wow! *Real World* had us glued to the television. We hadn't seen anything like it before. Ever. Yes, we were connoisseurs of music videos, and we liked a lot of the entertainment media behind-the-scenes coverage. But to see real people who looked like us, who were our age and from diverse backgrounds, in their natural-seeming habitat—as they were getting out of bed, brushing their teeth, arguing with one another, talking about everything that we did—and then shot with cinema verité techniques of roaming and handheld cameras, that was crazy.

For most of the nineties, Bunim-Murray owned and ran the reality space with *Real World* and a second series, *Road Rules*—both on MTV. When Mark Burnett came along in 2000, he changed the game in terms of how reality was shot, adding scale and a more dramatic, different way of storytelling. For *Real World*, Bunim-Murray would typically use three to four cameras to cover seven characters. The realistic look of one cameraman with a handheld camera, shooting cutaways or over-the-shoulder shots, intentionally or not, could come across as too choppy and could even (as my father complained) give you a sense of motion sickness.

Mark Burnett basically said, "Forget that. People are watching dramas." So instead of shooting a cast of seven people with three cameras, with *Survivor*, he decided to use eighteen cameras. Unheard-of! This new approach made reality look like high-end polished drama, less gritty and sometimes more staged.

That's not to say that the more guerrilla style of shooting reality is done without the conscious intention of spurring dramatic moments. Most producers, regardless of approach, don't go as far as giving lines to cast members. But you might happen to shoot an exchange where it's clear that one of the women is angry with one of the men. You might suggest during a camera break that she let him know she'll talk to him later and then walk out. That doesn't take away from the emotion being real. Still, as reality TV has evolved, it has adapted in the service of entertainment.

No matter how rapidly the reality shows have reproduced and populated the airwaves, there really are only three main formats that can be traced back to the forerunners we've talked about so far.

The classic, of course, is the docuseries. That is, any reality show that just follows the lives of certain people in a certain culture or subculture or environment. On *COPS* the show followed policemen at work, so similar docuseries might follow firemen at work, guys living on the final frontier, girls surfing in remote settings, fishermen fishing for the big catch in forbidding waters, outdoorsmen and -women riding trucks on icy roads. A docuseries could document an individual or group of individuals, telling their stories in their natural habitat or special cultural environment, like *Real World* or, more recently, say, *Real Housewives of Atlanta*.

Reality TV has an endless use of the competition format. On *Survivor*, the competition involves taking eighteen contestants, putting them on an island and dividing them into two tribes and giving them challenges as they compete until one of them wins a million dollars. Competition-format reality shows include *Amazing Race*, *The Bachelor*, *MasterChef*, *Biggest Loser*, *The Apprentice*, *American Idol*, *The Voice*, and so on. In fact, as I would learn in depth, *Road Rules* was a competition format.

The third kind of reality show, what later became a mainstay for me, is known as a soft format—which is often a way of referring to comedy-based storytelling or quirky twists on other, harder formats like procedurals. Later on, when we came up with the idea of using celebrities as themselves, instead of it being a traditional docuseries, the focus lent itself more to a soft format.

Not all reality shows are created equally. That's where the combination of ideas and execution makes all the difference. The best examples of that balance can be seen on shows that have made me a devoted fan and that make me proud of our genre. *Survivor* set the bar in ways too numerous to list. I was also a huge fan of a show called *Whale Wars* on Animal Planet, a docuseries. *American Idol* was just addictive and undeniably influential across the field. I still watch *America's Got Talent*. And *MasterChef* never disappoints. Chef Gordon Ramsay is a reality superstar, as evidenced on my favorite show of his, *Kitchen Nightmares*.

Not all the criticisms of reality TV are created equally either. Some regard it as the fast food of television—not legit, made cheaply and without craft. That's straight up wrong. The craft required has to do with the fact that reality is a producer's medium. Where features are a director's medium, and TV dramas are a writer's medium, and TV sitcoms are a writing team's medium, reality TV is uniquely a producer's medium. As producer you have to act as writer/storyteller and dictate the overall vision to everyone on the set as a director would and also capture action and sequence as an editor would. The reality producer has to be all of these things in one. Anyone who has worked in our field can attest that there is real craft in reality TV, where you may encounter some of the most talented, creative practitioners in entertainment.

Some of the criticism that has been leveled at unscripted shows in recent years is valid. The editing process can be manipulative and can reveal cast members saying and doing things they wish they hadn't. But it's funny to me that some of the reality stars who complain loudest about how they were portrayed unfairly are also the ones who are cashing in the biggest—landing other TV shows, book and endorsement deals, living the celebrity good life.

The fact is that great storytelling doesn't require forcing the narrative. My feeling is that the strongest storytelling is when you run with a story as it is happening, without artifice. It's true and real and makes the best show.

STEPPING FOOT IN A NEW FRONTIER

Obviously, I wasn't an authority on the history of the genre or on any of these nuances back in 1997 when I arrived at the unexplored frontier of reality TV. I did, however, try to do as much homework as I could before showing up on that doorstep, hoping to be let in.

There are a few other reasons I should mention about why you should always prepare diligently to meet anyone who might be your future employer or anyone you'd like to invest in your dreams and goals. First, by taking the time to learn everything you can about the history of their company or their background, you demonstrate respect for their enterprise as well as a level of discipline that is valued in most workplaces. Second, by doing your own research about the field you're attempting to enter, you'll have a better sense, ahead of time, if this is the opportunity you want to create for yourself.

What do you do when there isn't much information to be found when you are entering a new frontier or looking to get started with a new company? You can still be ready to talk about your interests and ideas that might be related in some general way. Future employers or investors are impressed with ideas and probably even more so when you have a track record in executing those ideas. If you have neither, prepare questions that show your passion that connects to this new enterprise—or about their command of ideas and execution.

When you combine preparation with optimal timing, the result can be a game changer. That's how big a deal it was when I arranged to go interview for a job that would potentially get my foot in the door of reality TV. It was one of those things that happened because a coworker of mine at Stone Stanley, the second producer on the *Big Deal*, and I decided we'd use our rare nights off to bring our significant others and go enjoy a double date. My coworker's boyfriend was employed at the time as a postproduction supervisor at Bunim-Murray Productions, which was in full gear with both of their MTV shows, *Real World* and *Road Rules*. On one of our double dates, my coworker's boyfriend casually asked if I'd be interested in maybe coming over to Bunim-Murray as a postproduction coordinator on *Road Rules*. A step-up for sure from post-PA, the post coordinator who works underneath the post supervisor, this job seemed like a great opportunity to advance in my career and to learn more about another genre of television. But there was a hitch. Before anyone could hire me for the job, I had to first go interview with one of the company's owners, Mary-Ellis Bunim, to see if I passed muster. And that, as I was going to learn, was no small feat.

Atlhough I didn't know the full extent of their influence at the time, in context of the entire field of reality TV, Mary-Ellis Bunim and Jon Murray should be held in the highest esteem. What gives the art form its significance was fully on display in *Real World*'s earlier days. Yes, the lines were being blurred between reality and entertainment, but the format was still as close to *An American Family* as any other show has been.

For the first five years of *Real World*, at least, there was a wall between cast members and crew. Camera people were told not to laugh at any banter, not to say good morning, just to let reality play. That was why it worked, why it held up a mirror to real life, because the cameras were there like anthropologists studying an underreported subculture—holding up a mirror to youth everywhere, including me at the time. We could relate, on the one hand, but also escape into the lives of the characters and be entertained and allow ourselves to suspend disbelief as we got lost in their foibles and personal soap operas.

Back in 1997, looking at the medium in this new frontier from the outside as I prepared for the interview, I might have assumed that it would be easy to come up with an idea for a reality show and then slap it up against a wall like spaghetti to see if it stuck. Unfortunately, that's a recurring misconception about the entertainment business in general. You can write a rap, for example, and maybe you can rhyme and have a feel for street poetry and you can move around a stage, waving your hand. But without fresh beats or a hot track you laid down in the recording studio, without a delivery system for promoting yourself and your rap, you ain't got nothing. You need flow and hustle.

That goes for turning dreams into reality. Allow your imagination and your ideas to provide you with the fuel you need. Then light it up with skillful, knowledge-based execution—if you really want to make it happen, which is the focus of our next chapter.

five

Make It Happen: *Road Rules for the Real World*

Reality should not be excluded from this golden age of television, because it contributes plenty of gold to the equation, and there's art and magic to producing these shows. The best of this kind of programming makes you feel like you can't believe you have an eye into these worlds, populated by real people, doing extraordinary things that still tie back to your own experience, the human experience.

—MARC JURIS,
President WE tv

Rarely does a day go by at the office when I don't hear myself echoing the lessons learned from my parents and later reinforced in the working world—especially by my mentors, Jonathan Murray and the late Mary-Ellis Bunim. For that reason, I place stock in the principle of opting to *embrace your passion and your purpose*, especially as you *identify experts in your field and learn all you can from them*. In so doing, you'll probably be given not just inspiration but practical guidance for improvement, i.e., criticism, for how you can approach your project or undertake it in a way that's better and/or different. You'll also be challenged to see if you are ready for the very opportunities you seek and whether you have used all your resources in the process.

YOUR CHALLENGE, SHOULD YOU CHOOSE TO ACCEPT IT

As a mentor, I frequently challenge members of my team, often in order to make sure they're ready for an opportunity. Like the morning not long ago when I had to slow down one of our producers after he sent me a pumped-up e-mail saying he'd arranged a meeting with a TV network for the next day.

Why slow it down? Well, that's the same question I hear from my producer/developer after I get him on the phone. Before answering, I listen to him as he argues that the project he wants to pitch to CBS should be a no-brainer. It's a format already owned by Endemol Shine—a spelling bee with fresh game show elements that was created and has become a big hit in Australia—and that's ripe for selling to the US market. The network doesn't know what we have, so he wants to go in and give them the first shot, hoping they'll bite on the spot.

In my leadership capacity, I certainly don't want to discourage enthusiasm. But, then again, as I go on to say, I'm not seeing the level of preparation required for truly capitalizing on what could well be an easy sale.

This shouldn't come as a surprise to anyone on my team. They may have done some legwork in preparation, sure. But can it be better? Call me an overpreparer. I don't send an e-mail that I haven't proofread twice. I don't go to a meeting or a business dinner without first doing my research to know who's going to be there and what they do, where they come from, and how our interests might intersect. Or not. More importantly, if I'm going to the network to sell a show, even if it feels like a slam dunk and I think they can order twenty-two episodes in the room, I'm damn well not walking in there empty-handed.

My guy says, "I've got the promo from the Australian group to pitch the show."

That's not enough, I point out. When he asks what else we need to prepare, I say, "Well, we need to look at the last times that any other spelling bee formats aired here and what the ratings were. Let's know why they worked and why they didn't work, right?" He agrees and starts to hang up until I add, "Also, we need to be aware of the key differences in TV programming in Australia versus the US. So let's get stats on that."

I'm sure he must be thinking—*Really? I gotta do all that extra work?* That's natural for all of us at times, myself included. Most of us who sell (in one form or another) can also relate to those situations when you are on your game and you can show up and dazzle. But you know what? When you have only one opportunity to make your case—whether it's for getting hired or selling your big idea to potential investors or offering a solution that can make a difference in the everyday operations where you already work—why not do your due diligence in advance? If you're in good shape, can you be better?

You can give yourself an edge by anticipating pushback and knowing what kinds of resistance to anticipate. Or so I remind my guy by pointing out that the network might be interested but the first thing they'll do is downplay a format that's done well in Australia— a relatively tiny market compared to the United States. He'll need to be ready for that.

There is another part of the pitch that can be improved as we both consider a major question: "What about a host?" After all, a surefire way to up the ante with buyers is to have a celebrity host attached. We throw a couple of names back and forth and come up with an ideal fit—Michael Strahan. But can we get him? A couple of phone calls later, I hear from my casting executive that Strahan is available to host, but only exclusive to ABC networks. So now we know we can pitch Strahan as a host only to ABC but will have to come up with alternate hosts to pitch to the other networks. And to build excitement for these meetings, instead of generically saying we have a project to pitch, I suggest that my producer "leak" it to the buyer in advance by mentioning, "Hey, I don't know if you heard, but we have a hit on our hands in Australia, and before we go out on the block to everyone for North American rights, I think we can get it to you."

The only concern for my producer is the timing and whether he can put it all together to pull it off within the week.

All I have left to say to him is "Make it happen," before signing off.

If there's one thing I've come to expect from my team and from myself, it's the resourcefulness that comes along with getting the job done, no matter how daunting. "Make it happen" is not just a phrase used to tell someone else—or yourself—to take on a task without being shown the ropes; it's also a mind-set that comes along with reaching for any goal that's already hard to reach.

Make it happen is such a mantra for me, you would think I invented the expression. Nope, but I've never been shy about using it.

YOU LEARN FROM EVERYONE

Needless to say, I did not invent the saying "Make it happen" or the mentality. In fact, I'd never heard anyone use that expression until I started working as a post-PA at Stone Stanley on *Big Deal* for FOX. And everyone had his or her own signature way of saying it. One production coordinator used to say it in an upbeat way—like he didn't have time to explain how to do it but was counting on me and confident I'd make it happen. Then there was a supervisor who would say it in a mean way every time she asked me to do a task she wasn't going to do and wasn't going to tell me how. That was the same producer who also later told me, "You'll never work in this town again," for what she thought was my having gone around her to the executive producer.

This was someone who would page me in the middle of the night, an hour after I'd finally gone home and hit the bed, to tell me, say, they were done with a late-night edit session and to come clean up the bay and organize the tapes for the next day. Before I could sleepily ask any specifics, she'd say, "We're done here," and sign off with "Make it happen."

Regardless of tone, in the early days the subtext was always "I'm not doing this. It needs to get done. I don't want to have to explain it to you. You make it happen."

Not every business runs this way. Thankfully, medical interns aren't tossed into the operating room and told, "Hey, this guy needs a heart transplant. Make it happen!" Rookie firefighters aren't thrown a hose and sent to the front lines to put out a fire by making it happen. In most fields, there are well-established protocols for training and testing expertise.

In the production world of Hollywood, you learn on the fly. So if you're asked to clear a set from the soundstage within the hour without being told where everything goes, you learn to be resourceful and get the job done. And even if you haven't finished and you're told to have all the mic cords brought into the studio in a specific order within the next twenty minutes, you also find a way to make it happen. In effect, this was an unspoken filtering process whereby those who proved they could make things happen were the ones who would then move up the chain of command.

At higher levels, the demands would change. When you are a producer, for instance, and you've sold a show to the network and they want to see a revision of the format and no one knows how to execute that new idea, they'll still tell you to make it happen—to take their vision and bring it to life successfully. They want more than good execution. They want it to be a hit.

A can-do attitude, no matter what, is a winning trait. In my view, the *make-it-happen* mind-set is a requirement for anyone who wants to achieve the reality of their dreams.

How do you learn to be resourceful when it's new to you or there are no precedents? My feeling is that you can learn by watching, listening, and checking out who around you knows what they're doing. You can learn from everyone around you, even if that means observing the wrong way to go about making something happen.

DIRECTION IS MORE IMPORTANT THAN SPEED

In many ways, the strongest appeal of *Road Rules* had to do with how cast members learned to become resourceful when given challenges they had never undertaken before. Likewise, the producers were forging a road into a new frontier of reality TV, literally making it happen. The MTV series had launched in 1995, three years into the groundbreaking success of *Real World*, basically as a spin-off. Instead of a docuseries that followed a diverse group of kids living together in a house setting somewhere, this show took all of that to the next level—out onto the open road. The concept was a scavenger hunt that chronicled the adventures of six (originally five) cast members between the ages of eighteen and twenty-four, as they traveled across the country and beyond in a Winnebago—with a mission to complete challenging tasks or work odd jobs in order to earn money for survival, all the while learning life lessons about living and competing together.

The voice-over beckoned you to watch:

"Welcome to the ride of your life. Your destination? Anywhere. Your money? Gone. Your mission: survive. And then you'll be rewarded . . . handsomely. Throw out your rules. These are road rules."

That voice-over could have been the teaser for the next leg of my journey, almost from the moment when I first stepped foot in the offices of Bunim-Murray Productions. Far from the heart of Hollywood, BMP headquarters were in a nondescript area deep in the San Fernando Valley. If I hadn't known the office was there, I would have missed it. But thanks to the efforts of my coworker's boyfriend, who had all but gotten me the job as a postproduction coordinator, I found the address and arrived early enough to check it out.

Over the years, as I've reflected on the question of why I went into reality TV, I've often wondered where my path might have taken me—if it hadn't been for that 1997 interview with Mary-Ellis Bunim. Why didn't I go into scripted television? Why not dramas? Why not sitcoms? The answer is that I might have gone in those directions. But those weren't avenues that opened up to me. So, either by random circumstance or divine intervention—via the process of trying to make it happen for myself in the field of television—I wound up on the doorstep of reality TV.

Again, timing can be everything. Reality was still fresh and new but about to emerge as a booming genre. That put me at the forefront of it. As the rule goes for many successful businesses, part of winning is about being first to market. Perhaps, because I am a storyteller and have a background as a documentarian, reality allowed me to excel and quickly proved to be a good fit. And I was in tune with the demographics—young and diverse. Plus, I was ready to grow, and reality TV was too.

I was excited about the interview. In fact, because the opening seemed to be the ideal next step for me, I didn't wait to give my notice at Stone Stanley. They were sorry to see me go but wished me well. And here I was, grateful for the previous five months of learning and superconfident that my dues-paying days were behind me.

The whole atmosphere at BMP buzzed with a level of energy that was like nothing I'd seen before—other than in my fantasies! Everyone was dialed in to whatever their job happened to be, with a kind of focus that told me they loved what they were doing and would rather be at work than anywhere else. The vibe was unbelievably cool. Even though most of the employees were in jeans and T-shirts, they carried themselves with the importance of high-level executives or lab researchers about to make big discoveries. Imagine you've just arrived at a party where only the smart, creative, TV-savvy people have been invited. And now you're in! In my mind, this, at last, was where television was happening—my dream come true.

But wait. If there were sound effects playing in the background of our actual reality, I would have heard the screeching of brakes the minute I was led into the spacious office of Mary-Ellis Bunim. Apparently, I was wrong to think this interview was more of a formality. Somehow my friend had failed to warn me just how tough she could be. He also forgot to mention that there would be other candidates for the interview that would be conducted much like an audition. Looking around the office, I saw that there was a group of us, all apparently waiting to meet with Ms. Bunim for what turned out to be an interview pool—for various jobs.

Then Mary-Ellis strode into her office and closed the door. She had a strong presence as she stood there dressed in a pantsuit and a set of pearls—her uniform of choice that probably would have been a better fit in a Fortune 500 corporate setting than at a production company that made shows for the MTV market. She commanded the room with a serious frown, speaking in a highbrow Northeastern accent (she was originally from Massachusetts), as she asked for our résumés. As Mary-Ellis took a seat and reviewed them, she asked questions of each of us, now and then jotting down notes.

Mary-Ellis Bunim had originally made a name for herself in daytime TV. As the executive producer of such soaps as *Search for Tomorrow* and *As the World Turns*, she broke the glass ceiling as the youngest female to executive-produce a daytime series. In the early 1990s, Mary-Ellis was originally asked to develop a scripted night-time soap for MTV, along with Jonathan Murray, who was a documentarian with a background in TV news and cable programming. As the story went, Mary-Ellis and Jon soon realized that the series would be too expensive to make for cable, so they decided to try an unscripted format. And five years later the rest—as I sat in her office, hoping to pass muster for the postproduction coordinator job—was history.

As I recall, at barely twenty-five years old, I was possibly the youngest applicant in the interview pool that day. The other candidates, some of whom were already with the company, were visibly nervous. Strangely enough, I wasn't intimidated. Yes, Mary-Ellis was tough and the interview was grueling, but I knew something about putting up with discomfort.

Then came the writing test. What? Yep, it was important, she said, that we be able to communicate well—to get our ideas onto the page succinctly with proper grammar and correct spelling. We were all college graduates and had all worked in some capacity in production. Nonetheless, we all had to take the same writing test. Afterward, Mary-Ellis printed the tests out, marked them up, and reviewed them with us as a group.

Crazy, huh? But I had to trust there was a method to the madness. Fortunately for me, I survived this first challenge and met with Ms. Bunim's approval.

Unfortunately for me—and the friend who had opened this door for me, hoping I could step in as post coordinator once he was promoted to post supervisor—Mary-Ellis decided against promoting him, filling his spot instead with one of the candidates from the interview pool. So that left me without a job. After I'd already given notice at Stone Stanley. In hindsight, I guess it was cavalier of me to leave one job before officially securing the next job. But the truth is that I was ready to move on. Sometimes you have to risk pushing yourself out of your comfort zone, even if it means finding yourself unemployed.

The good news was Mary-Ellis went ahead and hired me, although not as a post coordinator. Instead, she told the post supervisor to hire me as a logger—that is, logging video footage for *Road Rules*, then starting its third season. Even though it was a lesser job, this still meant I would be moving ahead with my dream and working in television at Bunim-Murray Productions. As the saying goes, direction is more important than speed. True, the going rate for loggers in those days was not much more than three hundred fifty dollars a week; as a newlywed, I had to be responsible, as finances were already stretched thin for me and Adriana—who was then working at an accounting firm and taking classes to become a CPA. But luckily, the guy who had brought me over to the company managed to let me start at what I would have made as a post coordinator, which was a modest increase from what I'd been making before.

And so, without further ado, I joined the BMP family and began to earn a graduate degree in a TV genre being pioneered by Mary-Ellis Bunim and Jon Murray, two extraordinary and life-changing mentors. Very much like parents or coaches, they mentored together, sharing the same higher goals, but each with his or her own distinct approach. Like good cop/bad cop—with Jon as the more empowering, uplifting cop and Mary-Ellis as the tougher, more demanding one. They each reinforced lessons my parents had first instilled in me.

My mother's belief in the importance of finding your work passion was personified in Jon Murray. He had so much passion for television and the process of making it, you naturally wanted to match his level of enthusiasm. Jon, a good-looking guy of average height and build, somehow always seemed younger than he was and, to this day, looks about the same as he did eighteen years ago. Along with that youthful energy, however, he also had an older, Jedi level of wisdom that he used in teaching the patience and deep thought needed for artful storytelling. In so doing, he made us all feel that our contribution to the process mattered—including mine as a low-level logger.

To some, starting out at a ground-floor job can seem like a step back, especially when you've come from having more responsibility elsewhere. But as I learned at Bunim-Murray, there are advantages that come with starting out at the bottom. Rather than rushing your advancement, by taking the time to learn everything about day-to-day logistics, you better understand the workings of the whole operation—an executive trait. As long as your low-level position allows you to gain resources that matter toward your ultimate direction, that's more important than rapid advancement.

Tape logging was not glamorous. The drill involved sitting down in front of a computer, popping in an hour-long tape, watching the footage, typing in keywords for context, and transcribing everything that was said and by whom. Once you logged seven tapes, the daily quota, you could go home. Raised in the school of outworking/ outhustling, I quickly became the heavyweight champ of logging, to the point that I could log ten tapes in the time that it usually took to log the quota. Then, instead of going home, I'd go to the editing bay and learn from the editors as they brought up footage from our logs to fit in their edits.

Whenever Jon Murray held a meeting on the edit, I would drop everything to be able to sit in and hear him give a master class in Advanced Storytelling. He was keenly interested in behavior and motivation. So, as you watched hours of video taken of real people reacting with unscripted words and actions to real situations in real time, he was on the constant lookout for the *why* of the reaction. If we noticed that one of the males was acting weird around one of the females, Jon would question that: "Why is he behaving that way toward her?" If the answer was because he liked her, then he would follow, "Why do you think he likes her?" That was a cue to either reinterview the characters—possibly with a technique using a "confession cam" that was honed on *Real World* and that became a staple of reality as well as mock-reality series like *The Office*—or for editors to sift through footage that might answer his questions, perhaps where those feelings might be articulated by a character.

Jon also pushed us as a team to connect the emotional dots in visual storytelling. For example, a recurring inner conflict for our characters on *Road Rules* was how to deal with the girlfriends and boyfriends they left at home at the same time that they were flirting and becoming close to other cast members. Jon would challenge us to show that conflict, for instance, of the sensitive guy—we'll call him Billy—who really wanted to make a move on the fun-loving girl—we'll call her Jane—but had promised to go back to his girlfriend at home after the show wrapped.

That prompt was a chance for me, a logger, to say, "Oh, I have footage of him on a balcony, writing in his journal and looking out at the sunset."

We would then have the team on the ground reinterview Billy and then lay his voice-over on top of the footage of him watching the sunset. The result was an emotional moment that added to the suspense. What was going to happen next?

The more that Jon challenged the producers to think about the stories they wanted to tell, the more I began to look for those story possibilities in the logging process. That way, if I was in the editing bay and an editor mentioned, "Man, I would love a scene where this guy looks angry," I knew exactly where to find that footage.

I quickly became the editors' go-to logger—not just a machine for logging but a contributor with interesting ideas for how to put the pieces together. Eventually, that reputation would help me advance through the ranks, although not as immediately as I would have liked. Later on, I was grateful for not moving too fast because it allowed me to benefit from the influence of both Jon and Mary-Ellis.

As far as toughness, authority, and directness, Mary-Ellis Bunim was almost a female version of Dr. Silas H. Abrego. She too strove for excellence in herself and in others and simply didn't have the time or inclination to coddle. Mary-Ellis ran a tight ship that involved various challenges. We learned to meet them or fall by the wayside. She was so fastidious with spelling, grammar, and sentence structure that if you were so thoughtless as to send her an e-mail without proofing it, she would print it out, mark the errors with a red pen, and drop it off at your desk, with a stern "Look at all these mistakes. Improve on that the next time you send an e-mail. Writing is representative of who you are."

Thanks to those instances, I developed not just a thick skin when it came to handling criticism but a practical way to respond that has served me in good stead ever since. For starters, it's normal to feel a little bad when a superior—or client or partner—gives you feedback of any sort that is not a pat on the back. *My first step is to allow those feelings to happen.* I acknowledge them but also try not to react defensively. The *next step is to sit on the criticism,* giving it time to no longer sting but possibly be of value. The *step after that is to ask myself whether it's true or not.* If it has some truth, *the last step is to incorporate the constructive aspects.* If it's not true, yet one more step may come into play—either to *let it go and not get bogged down* by it, or *respond reasonably by saying you've thought about it but don't agree.* Ultimately, the watchword is not to be thrown by criticism. View it as an opportunity to learn.

Mary-Ellis used criticism strategically, choosing otherwise to put protocols in place to prevent the need for it. Putting the same emphasis on punctuality as she did on punctuation, she trained everyone to be on time. We didn't have to punch a clock, but she would assign someone on staff to log down the times when we arrived and when we left. For anyone who has worked in Hollywood, that is almost unheard-of. We all complained, some more loudly than others. But as the year wore on and I began to pay some attention to the business part of the equation, everything she did made sense.

As a woman in a leadership role, Mary-Ellis may have needed that kind of sternness. That's what it took to get the two shows done. Besides the creative and production aspects of crafting an entertainment success, BMP had to be on top of every detail of logistics of managing operations that involved six months of chronicling every move of a group of young adults in a house in a different location each season, along with another group of young adults traveling together around the world.

At one point, we accumulated a large amount of Coleman camping equipment and other outdoor gear that had been donated to *Road*

Rules for use by the cast members. There was so much stuff that had been lightly used, if at all, that we would just house it at the office. Funny thing how these expensive mountain bikes and state-of-the-art tents and sleeping bags just seemed to grow legs and walk out on their own. So Mary-Ellis decided to build a chain-link fence in the middle of the first floor of the office and quarantine all the good stuff in a cage, right where everybody could see it. That put an end to disappearing stuff.

Later on, when I was running my own business, those solutions made a lot of sense. Every dollar taken out of circulation in your company is a dollar out of your pocket. And every dollar brought in helps your bottom line. Until then, I had never really thought about how, as an employee at any level in the television business, you could be viewed as an asset, a potential for earning—or the opposite. It became clear that these rules of order that Mary-Ellis created were part of the growth of the company. But on that same note, she ran the enterprise as a family—a family business. No matter how tough she could be—and, yep, I saw her bring grown-ups to tears—she actually cared about us and wanted us to be our best. Her message was—*I expect a lot from you, and I will reward you for the effort.* These were two kinds of motivation, for sure. But the idea that she was training us to be the best spurred us on. Exhibiting the passion and purpose to improve would win the reward of her approval. That balance of setting high expectations coupled with rewards goes on the list as *Motivation Lesson #5.*

Just as the kids on *Road Rules* faced challenges in every episode with surprise rewards at different intervals, we enjoyed elements of adventure and surprise that were stock-in-trade for Mary-Ellis. When we finished logging all of season three, she arranged to take the five of us loggers out to dinner with her at Delmonico's—an upscale restaurant that was in another world to yours truly. Going out to a swanky restaurant with your boss? That was big-time, a Hollywood-here-I-am moment.

The moral of this story is that the time spent gaining expertise at the ground level gives you a foundation upon which to build. Once you've conquered those fundamentals, you can then begin to accelerate—armed with knowledge about where you're headed.

WHAT RESOURCES DO YOU OFFER?

Walk into any office or work setting, and you will pick up on an atmosphere that lets you know everything you need to know about who's in charge. You'll be able to identify a leadership capacity of *motivating resourcefulness*. Leaders know how to bring out distinct resources in each member of the team—call that *Motivation Lesson #6*—and are also able to motivate teamwork, collaboration, and healthy competition, all while fending off problems before they occur. Mary-Ellis Bunim and Jonathan Murray, different as they were from each other, created an atmosphere for resourcefulness and teamwork to flourish. As a result, creativity flourished. And a key to that was diversity.

Bunim-Murray was unique in the 1990s entertainment business for the company's commitment to showing diversity, like the casting of Pedro Zamora, a gay HIV-positive Cuban-American whose rapid decline and subsequent death from AIDS was documented in the third season of *Real World*. BMP pushed so many boundaries in the early years with multicultural and minority casting choices, while tackling taboo yet relevant subject matter, that they have been credited with legitimizing reality as a serious form. They cared about telling untold stories. They offered their own perspectives too. Later on, Mary-Ellis became a single mom, after her divorce, raising her daughter at the same time that she was building and running the company. In casting, she recognized the importance of strong, independent voices. Jon, a gay man in a longtime relationship and soon to be raising a family, was always a champion of diversity and giving voice to those not used to having one in television.

In promoting resourcefulness, BMP inspired creativity from all of us. Perhaps it was because Mary-Ellis and Jon were still in the throes of making up the rules of the reality game and had no choice but to teach all of us who worked for them how it should be done. None of us could have come to them with expertise, after all, as there would have been nowhere else to learn what they were in the process of inventing. I'm talking about every facet: from story development to casting to the technical rules of how to film and edit the raw footage of reality. In turn they assembled an A-list team of gifted producers, directors, and editors—many of whom dominate the field today.

These other players weren't necessarily mentors to me, but I was fortunate enough to watch and learn everything I could from them. At the top of the list was Clayton Newbill, a co-creator of *Road Rules* and its show runner during the time I was at Bunim-Murray—and who today is the executive producer of *Shark Tank* and *Beyond the Tank*—who represented the utmost in production precision. Everything about his approach was detail driven, combined with focus, discipline, and planning. Clay, number one at getting the trains to run on time, did what he does better than anyone—and, later, when he championed me and my desire to get out into the field, taught me the meaning of resourceful.

Resourcefulness can be your golden ticket. It's evidenced through such traits as the ability to *take initiative*, to look for ways to *innovate*, to draw from your own experiences and expertise as a *creative thinker*, and, importantly, to step up as a *problem solver*. Resourcefulness is often on display in how you respond to challenge. Do you become frustrated and blame someone else? Or do you embrace it and look for solutions?

For example, a major technical challenge I encountered with the postproduction process was the lack of protocols for organizing all this footage that was being generated. The problem became apparent as soon as I was promoted to post coordinator and I received a call from an Avis car rental office in Wichita, Kansas. The agent got down to business, saying, "We found your box with this phone number on it."

Seems that the crew from the Wichita shoot had turned in the rental car with the box of videotapes still in it and had flown off to Florida to set up the next shoot. After the Avis people overnighted us the box and we started sorting through the tapes, I realized that there was no system in place for relaying what the time sequence was for the tapes that were being sent. My solution was to create a logging/labeling system for the camera assistants in the field that they were to use to track the order of how the tapes were shot and how many were shot each day. The camera assistants would then type out their log, fax a copy to the postproduction office, and then place a copy as well in each box for shipment. This way, when the tapes arrived, we would know if anything was missing. The system also created a more streamlined way for the production offices to communicate with producers in the field.

So, as I learned, being resourceful—making it happen—had a lot to do with thinking ahead and being proactive. The lesson here is never to be afraid to propose an improvement to the status quo. If you see something that's inefficient or a system that's missing, take the time to understand what's not working, then develop a plan to address the issue and take it to the powers that be. Better yet, if you can bring others on your team to be part of the plan and make it happen together, everyone wins.

Certainly, that was my experience at Bunim-Murray, as I increased my value to the operation as someone who could anticipate problems and avert them before they happened. But there was a hitch. Whenever I asked about transferring out of postproduction and into the field where the action was taking place, there was no incentive to say yes. After all, I had no field experience, or so I was reminded, and was doing such great work building protocols in post. Or maybe they didn't think I was ready. That then became a challenge I had to overcome. Making the best use of my time, I did so by becoming even more proficient in other aspects of production—like reality storytelling.

Interestingly enough, many of the story lines on *Road Rules* were actually about lessons learned in resourcefulness when responding to challenges. Take season four, aka the "Islands" challenge. This season, the first to include other modes of transportation in addition to the Winnebego, had it all: fun, pathos, conflict, heart, and five lovable cast members all with relatable backstories. They had to figure out how to work together in ways large and small—overcoming fears of flying, swarms of bees, camping in the middle of a torrential storm, and other physically challenging missions, along with mental challenges (puzzles, riddles, word jumbles, Morse code, etc.). Solving clues would then send them to the right destination for their next challenge—like helping the Coast Guard with a search-and-rescue mission, competing in an open-mic stand-up comedy show as they attempted to win prize money for survival, and actually surviving a night on a deserted tropical island. This was before *Survivor*, around the same time that the Swedish reality series aired, so our five kids were practically the test case. One of the funniest lines of the season happened as they were being dropped off on the shoreline and one of them predicted it would not go well, saying, "I read *Lord of the Flies*."

Even though I wasn't in the room when many story ideas were

brainstormed, I had a front-row seat to BMP's revolutionary approach to development. Lest we forget, up until this period—1998, 1999—the arena for reality TV was very much on cable, not yet hitting big on network. As rulers of their dominion, Jon and Mary-Ellis needed to tap all their resources to make the most of their position.

How? Well, every now and then, they would bring in free lunch from Panda Express for everyone, put us into working groups, and have us pitch ideas for new shows or for episode challenges on existing shows. Mary-Ellis might say, "We want each group to come up with three ideas for what the next *Real World* should be and what the job they're going to undertake is." They turned the effort into a contest. Jon would say, "OK, guys, we want to develop a show on dating. If we were to develop a show that was a cross between *Real World* and *Road Rules*, what's our dating show about?" Sometimes these development contests became lightning rounds where they'd throw titles at us for upcoming episodes—like "Next episode is called 'Mary Had a Little Lamb.' What's the premise of that show?"

Some of us had strong ideas. Some of us were good at pitching and getting up on our feet in front of everyone. Some of us were good at both. Our groups became teams, like the kids on *Road Rules*, and we competed to see which team could produce the most winners—as determined by a vote from everyone. Then Mary-Ellis and Jon would award the top three individual ideas with first-, second-, and third-place prizes—usually gift certificates for the movies or a bookstore, or for first-prize awards, maybe a really expensive ten-speed mountain bike (as I won at one point). In true reality-TV fashion, Bunim-Murray found a way to make entertainment out of work.

The approach was totally innovative and, in hindsight, smart business. At the time, it didn't occur to us what a great deal they were getting with free show concepts from the peanut gallery. Later on, when I found out how much the Panda Express cost, I'd joke that it would have been better had I just not eaten that lunch and sold them the ideas. Then again, I was being given the equivalent of a Harvard education in a burgeoning genre and learning the show business fundamentals of what made an idea marketable. What's more, this process revealed one of my most valuable resources—all of those years of watching television that had given me this vast creative library to draw from. Another eye-opener. My accumulated record of TV content gave me an advantage in winning these contests. Plus, the ideas, as I came to understand, didn't have to be 100 percent original, as long as there was some new twist or take on the older version. In the back of my mind, I'd always think of home and watching the *Gong Show* with my father's voice asking me and my brother, "What can you do? What can you do?"

After I won that expensive bicycle, ideas for unscripted shows began to proliferate in my imagination. I'd pitch them to my wife, and if she liked an idea, that was validation that I was onto something. In particular, I became pumped about a concept I had for a music-and-dance show that took me back to all those hours of watching *American Bandstand* and *Soul Train*. A more recent precedent had been MTV's *The Grind*, and now there was nothing in that space—an opportunity for me, I thought. My challenge was to fine-tune a premise that lent itself to a documentary format that was also a vehicle for entertainment. The situation had to be ripe for finding stories and characters that were compelling, as in dramatic and/or comedic or just loud enough to warrant viewership. Adding what I already knew from both the news and the game show worlds, I then began to conceptualize a music-and-dance show that followed young Angelenos into the hot, happening nightclub scene that was hopping in the late 1990s. The more I thought about my idea, what I eventually called *The Guest List*, the more I tried to think like a producer in terms of how to envision possible episodes with mood and tone and timing.

Obviously, it was all well and good to have these ideas, but without the knowledge for executing them to be gained from working in the field, there was little I could do to bring the concepts to fruition. For that reason, when I was finally offered the opportunity to go out on location and actually be on the production crew—but again in an entry-level job—I went for it.

Previously, every time I'd asked about filling a spot as a production coordinator, I was told that, unfortunately, I didn't have the experience of working in the field that the job required. My argument was that, hey, I've been here in postproduction, rising up in the ranks, building all these protocols, and that's what I can offer in production too. That held sway with the producers in the field. But, once in the field, like playing Chutes and Ladders, I had to now start on the bottom rung as a camera assistant. Not a cameraman but the assistant who carried and loaded the videotapes. What? Somehow I'd gone from logging tapes to carrying tapes. However, coming from the "we try harder" school of outhustling, outworking the competition, I continued to prove myself, killing it at the job I'd been given and at the same time really getting to learn the jobs up ahead of me that would lead to the one I really wanted—executive producer.

Back in the days of working on *Big Deal*, my dream of becoming an executive producer was wildly ambitious. It was a way of fine-tuning my original dream of just working in television. But now that I'd been at BMP all this time, I knew what an executive producer actually did, and I could legitimately see making that my reality. In fact, at the ripe old age of twenty-seven, I went so far as to give myself a deadline. If I hadn't achieved my goal of becoming an executive producer by the age of thirty, I vowed that I was going to move on and do something else. Now, that may sound extreme. And, in fact, I may not have actually called it quits at that point. But as they say— the difference between a dream and a goal is a deadline. If I wanted to really make it happen, setting that deadline was also a reminder that I was still committed to betting on myself.

For that reason, shortly after paying my dues as a camera assistant, I turned down the promotion to cameraman that was offered to me by Glenn Taylor—who went by the nickname of GT—a well-known and respected director of photography and now a director. I had been his camera assistant and we were headed next to shoot in the countryside of New Zealand, and he told me, "You are going to make a great cameraman one day. Come here, and I will show you everything you need to know about the camera."

When I declined his offer, I had to explain, "I'm going to be an executive producer one day. But thank you."

Anytime I run into GT or people who know him, I am reminded of that story. I knew already that becoming a cameraman or a director wasn't a stepping-stone to my goal of becoming an executive producer. That meant waiting a little longer. I knew this was an opportunity that I had passed up. But was it the right opportunity? Did it move me closer to my goal, or was it a detour that might lead to getting locked into a path that wasn't for me?

Those are always relevant questions to ask yourself when you are given an opportunity that may be appealing in the short run but won't move you toward your long-term goals. And as you assess those goals, you always have the resource of setting a time for when you hope to achieve them.

GROWTH LEADS TO OPPORTUNITY

One of the classic pitfalls for anyone who is a go-getter and goal setter is being so caught up in where you're headed that you don't savor the journey. After all, that's part of what made *Road Rules* fun to watch. Cast members made discoveries about themselves through the ups and downs of their adventures that led to growth. In turn, the cast members would find that growth could be one of the engines of opportunity.

Those were lessons taught to me by working in the field. I was living the dream, doing what I loved, not making much money but learning from the best in the business and adding my own innovations to the mix. Not to mention getting to travel, as I had fantasized about back in high school. My work in production let me follow the cast on adventures hiking the Northern Trail, into the wilderness of the U.S. and Canada, later to the Outback of Australia, and, after that, to major destinations in Latin America. As cast members made the discoveries that led to the rewards they'd receive as a team at the end of each season—European vacations, new cars, state-of-the-art computer equipment—I felt that my reward was being able to learn and grow in television. Awesome!

In the midst of all this growth, I decided, what the heck, I'd approach Jon and Mary-Ellis about my idea for *The Guest List*, among other possibilities I'd been developing mentally. Now that I was mastering the execution end of the equation, I ambitiously thought they'd be thrilled when I said, "By the way, I have some ideas—outside of the free lunches—that I'd love to come pitch you guys and that I'd love to make, that I think would be good shows."

They didn't take the pitch for *The Guest List*, although I do recall that Jon still had something encouraging to say about the effort to think along those lines.

And that was fine. If they weren't going to be a resource for enabling my goals of developing and producing a show, I realized, maybe that was a sign for me to do it on my own. The next thing I knew, I'd taken over most of the garage in the house Adriana and I had bought by this point and I turned it into my office/studio. Where else besides a garage did anyone build a brainchild or a business from scratch?

Becoming an entrepreneur and having my own business were not the initial goals. I just wanted to take my idea for *The Guest List* and shoot the pilot episode and then try to go sell it, knowing almost nothing about that aspect of television. What I did know was how to rally the troops to my cause. For starters, I got Eric Nies, one of the original stars of *Real World* and the host of *The Grind,* to come on board as my show's host and gatekeeper of the club. The show was going to focus on how this group of twentysomethings had to face challenges in getting onto the guest list of the dance club. The cast was made up of friends of Adriana's and others who came on board for the fun of it. We shot the pilot at an actual club in Orange County. For production help I tapped some of my friends from Bunim-Murray, including sound and camera people who brought the equipment and videotapes, more or less at no cost, and helped me access stock footage that I could use for free.

Instead of paying Eric Nies anything up front, I cut him in on the deal. This was all new to me. At the time, Eric's manager was his sister. Just before we shot the pilot, she called to say he was all set to fly out to California for the shoot, and she wanted to get his travel in order. Meaning? She was checking on whether the airfare had been arranged and what car service would be picking him up and at which hotel he would be staying.

Holy shit! I didn't have the money for any of that. Too embarrassed to tell his sister, I said, "Let me get back to you with the details."

After pondering how in the world I was going to come up with money I didn't have, I called her back to confess that there wasn't enough in the budget for travel and that I needed to keep the money on the screen, therefore enhancing our chances of getting the pilot sold. Instead, I could pick him up at the airport and offer him the guest room in my house, and he could have whatever food was in my fridge. Somehow, that ended up being acceptable.

With that covered plus all the volunteer efforts, along with the loaned equipment, I was left with a budget of only twenty-five hundred dollars that I needed to have for getting the pilot shot, edited, mastered and duplicated in order to be sold to television.

Being resourceful, I decided to go sell the most valuable possession I had at that time. Yep, you guessed it, the twenty-five-hundred-dollar mountain bike that I had won as a first prize in an idea contest from Bunim-Murray. Was I sad to see it go? Yep.

But I sold the bike, got the money, and used it to independently produce the pilot for *The Guest List*. It was a thing of beauty, if I did say so myself.

Actually, after I showed it to Jon and Mary-Ellis, they agreed. They went further and decided to take it on, meaning that they would try to sell *The Guest List with Eric Nies* as a Bunim-Murray production.

After two and a half years as their protégé, I could not have felt more validated, even though the show ultimately failed to sell. Granted, I was disappointed, not to mention that I was now out one really cool mountain bike. Of course, years later I would be in a position to buy an even cooler state-of-the-art mountain bike. And, more importantly, I had figured out the road rules that led me to deciding—*Hey, you know what? I can do this on my own. I can make it happen. I don't need anyone else to tell me yea or nay.*

That realization was very much in my mind when I came to one of the most pivotal turning points in my career at Bunim-Murray. At this stage, I'd been at the company for three years, having spent the last year ascending the ranks to production coordinator. For reasons I couldn't explain, I'd gotten stuck. Instead of being promoted to production manager, which was the next step up that was merited by the work that I was doing and a stepping-stone to being made executive producer, my ultimate goal, I was told to wait.

Nothing that I could do or say seemed to alter the situation. Pay raises had been easier to get. But moving beyond production coordinator was off the table.

Everything came to a head with the job selections for the eighth season—*Semester at Sea*. The previous season had taken us to Latin America, mainly Mexico, but this next season was something out of my wildest travel dreams. *Road Rules* would be taking place on a Semester at Sea cruise ship and traveling down to Cuba, through the Caribbean and around to South Africa, and onto the other side of the world. I couldn't imagine anything I'd rather do and had no hesitation in reminding the powers that be of my desire to come on board in the first position as production manager on that boat.

The answer was still: "No." Why? I wasn't ready, they said, and I was still improving as a production coordinator. But I had done that and killed at it, as I quickly asserted. They were unmoved. My pay improved, but as for a promotion with greater responsibility, "Sorry, Cris. That's the best we can do."

The first person I called for advice was my mother. She listened, and even though she had no sense of what the different production titles meant, when I explained that I'd been offered the same role again, she said, "Forget it. You can't do that job."

"Except it's a trip around the world. Semester at Sea. I'll never have this chance again."

"Cris, you want to be executive producer? This is a detour. Don't come off course."

And that was that. My mother had always pointed out that if you set goals for yourself, you should only do the things that moved you in the direction of accomplishing those goals. Everything else, she believed, was a distraction, delay, or detour. Sometimes detours could take you on a route that could be valuable in the long run, if you got back on course. But in her view, this could well be a detour that would lead off in a direction of complacency and comfort. Tina Abrego almost always came down on the side of keeping your eyes on the prize.

Looking back, I imagine that Mary-Ellis and Jon believed that I would be ready one day. At that time, however, they couldn't see past the guy who'd arrived three years earlier as a tape logger—even though I'd never been shy about asking for the promotion. Each time I went in again to say something, I'd remind them how many times I'd already asked, pointing out, "Every time I come in here, it's been a no. I don't see any opportunities when I'm seventh in line behind everyone else. What's it gonna take for you to trust me with a project?"

The two took turns reassuring me with promises of "In due time" and "Be patient, be patient."

"I am patient. I just know what I can do."

As a boss of my own company, later on, I would have much greater empathy for what Mary-Ellis and Jon must have been thinking. Over the years, I'd hear the same from many an ambitious member of my production staff. Many times I would have to say, "No, you're not ready."

The reaction of my employees is often similar to mine back in 1999 after I didn't get the promotion on the Semester at Sea season: "Then I'm leaving."

Bunim-Murray's response to that, as I recall, was not so different from when a parent says, "Hey, if you don't like the rules in my house while you're under my roof, go find your own roof and live on your own." Well, what Mary-Ellis and Jon said, in effect, was: "Hey, if you want to run your business, you should go run your own business. Move across the street, then."

That was what I did. And it was almost across the street—where I set up shop in my own garage.

My peers thought I was crazy for leaving BMP. Still, it was the only move left to me. Being stuck was not going to happen. It was time to figure out how to turn my growth into a new opportunity.

In the short run, I had my regrets, even after resolving that I had to leave. But in the long run, I'm grateful that Bunim-Murray's stance forced my hand. I needed to get beyond the thinking that someone else was going to act like a fairy godmother and wave a magic wand to turn my dreams into reality.

In fact, whenever I'm asked about how I became an entrepreneur in the first place, I give credit to necessity as the mother of invention. It's a lesson from Entrepreneurship 101 that I stress for everyone and raises a question you may want to put to yourself: *Are you waiting for someone else to give you permission to make your goals happen?*

The next question to ask yourself is what resources you need to take your dreams to the next level. Even if you don't have them at your fingertips, being resourceful also includes having the vision to see that there might be another route to your reality. If you doubt that, I'm about to prove that you can pave your own road—even if there may be pitfalls along the way.

six

Everything I Know Now That I Wish I Knew Then: *Timing, Partnerships, and Wild Cards*

All you need in this life is ignorance and confidence, and then success is sure.

—Mark Twain

S o you think you can be an entrepreneur? If so, I'm here to encourage you. If not, I'm still here to let you know that the fundamentals of becoming a successful entrepreneur apply to turning your dreams into reality.

The operative principle that you are still in the *business of creating opportunity for yourself* doesn't really change from how you may have approached opportunity creation while working for others. But you now are responsible for the bottom line. That's why your challenge as an entrepreneur will be not only to create opportunity but also to *avoid the common pitfalls of launching your own company.*

Whether or not you have any plans to one day launch your own business, I've always felt that a key to owning your success comes from thinking like you're the boss. As the boss of you or your team, you don't always get the credit for the success, but you'll always be credited for the fail. That's a fact. But guess what. Learning from failure is how you become the most successful.

Nobody likes to hear anyone else say that you learn more from what you did wrong than from what you did right. Nobody likes to hear that your application or pitch or request has resulted in a response of "No, I'm sorry. We're going to pass" or any of the other standard or even creative forms of rejection. Nobody likes to hear that your most promising chance at hitting it big has just flopped. Trust me, if given the choice, I'd come home with the trophy every time, if that was even possible. But, of course, it isn't. Nor should it be.

Even these days, I have to remind myself how to put failure in its place. For example, five or so years ago, I took the lead in pitching a show to the Food Network. This time, when I made the trip to New York, I came ready with a suit and a team and a killer presentation.

"Killer" was the operative word. The concept we'd developed had come on the heels of the outdoors shows that were thriving on Discovery and the History Channel, along with the huge success of the cooking shows that were booming on the Food Network. Borrowing from both winning formats, our new show idea featured a hunter who was also a chef and it was called *Kill It and Grill It.* On the episodes, the hunter might go out and kill a moose or a buffalo or rabbits, and then he'd turn to the kitchen side of things and transform the game into a sumptuous feast. A similar BBC series had been done with much success, and we had great stats on why that boded well for the Food Network.

So we're up early, hitting the hotel gym, getting our coffee, and feeling pumped. Soon we head on over to a meeting with all the decision makers, including the president of the network. I walk in there, confident as can be, and thinking back over all the years when meeting and pitching the president of a cable channel on a first pitch almost never happened.

We sit down and make small talk, and then I seamlessly weave my way into the pitch and start to describe the concept and why it's like nothing Food Network's ever done and how we couldn't think of a better home for *Kill It and Grill It*.

"Did you say *kill*?" the cable channel head asks with a tone of displeasure.

Not a good sign. But I continue, ignoring that *Twilight Zone* music that's starting to play in my instincts. Something is just off.

Trying not to read anything into that, I cue up the PowerPoint that has photographs of this beautiful wilderness with still shots of how the hunter tracks and hunts and finds the elk or whatever the game is, kills it, and then how he carves it up and gets it ready to be cooked in the great out-of-doors.

I can see from the corner of my eye that the president of the Food Network is not happy. His face is red and angry. His arms are folded. Everyone else on his team is looking at me oddly, which is definitely throwing off my pitch. What can I do, other than good-naturedly proceed?

At about the point I'm discussing viewer stats and hunting-cooking demographics, he interrupts, asking in a tone of disgust, "What does killing animals for sport have to do with the Food Network?" He goes on to deliver a lecture about protecting animals and not exploiting them for recreation or entertainment.

These are usually the moments when you want to joke, "So it's a no?" as you tiptoe backward toward the door. In this case, no need, as the meeting came to a fairly abrupt conclusion.

Thus ended what might have been the worst pitch of my career.

What had gone wrong? Call it a wild card that came up. Or

somehow in all the preparation and research, I did not uncover the well-known fact that this executive was a high-ranking official with PETA—People for the Ethical Treatment of Animals! When I say this was well-known, let me add, obviously, it was not known to me.

The truth is that we never sold that show, for reasons that had more to do with timing than anything. But I'll never forget leaving that meeting and turning to my team. We just stood there and were all like—had that just happened? Had we just pitched a show about killing animals to a board member of PETA? Of course, the world did not come to an end because of that fail, and my future in the entertainment business didn't come to a grinding halt.

The lesson was twofold: 1) Failure is not forever, and 2) Failure affords you the opportunity to get it right the next time. And you can file that under "Everything I Know Now That I Wish I Knew Then."

The irony? If I had known everything ahead of time about all the potential pitfalls of starting my own company, I might have been discouraged from doing it. A little bit of ignorance isn't necessarily a bad thing. For that reason, I really believe that the Just Do It approach is the only way to study Entrepreneurship 101.

FINDING YOUR CALLING CARD

There is no right or wrong way to hang out your shingle and let others know you're open for business. Obviously it helps to keep your overhead low while you spread the word. What really helps is to have a success or a credit to your name that you can use as a calling card to inspire confidence in those who might want to do business with you.

Keeping expenses to a minimum wasn't an issue for me when I was first starting out on my own. Since I'd already produced the pilot episode of *The Guest List* and had gone through the basic steps of setting up shop as a business, the rent-free place to get started was still the garage in my home. My first office had no windows, no air-conditioning, no real furniture other than a folding table and some chairs. What I did have was vision and a plan to re-create the passion and purpose that I'd found heading up a team that I'd assembled for that project. After all, I'd already experienced the reality that if I could see an idea in my mind and translate it to paper and then put that to tape, I could actually make it happen. That being the case, I resolved that this was what I should do and not be afraid to go for it.

But as I sat alone in my garage, I faced up to the latest catch-22. Though I was now in the business of creating shows that I could make and sell as an executive producer, I didn't yet have a track rec-ord as an EP that could also serve as a calling card so buyers or networks could confidently invest in my projects. The solution was to go out and get the credit by getting myself hired as a freelancer. This led to a stint working as an associate producer for Paul Stojanovich of *COPS* fame on a pilot for a new show called *Young COPS*.

Before I'd wrapped on that job and had to then wait to see if the pilot was picked up (it wasn't), I received a call from Clay Newbill at Bunim-Murray.

A new show called *Making the Band* had just been given a green light, he said, and there was a job for me on it. "It's the promotion you want," Clay went on, "and it's yours unless you say no." The title was coordinating producer, a step or two up from where I'd gotten stuck before, and much closer to executive producer.

When I heard that it was going to be BMP's first unscripted show for network television (ABC), I was all ears. At that point in 1999, Mark Burnett had only gotten his toes wet with reality TV on a cable show called *Eco-Challenge*. *Survivor*, the series that was about to break reality wide-open on network TV, was a year off in the making. *Amazing Race* was two years away.

Making the Band, a forerunner for many a music-competition-format show to come, followed the nationwide search for talent by music manager Lou Pearlman—who discovered Backstreet Boys and *NSYNC. The episodes centered on the process of paring back a group of twenty-five young guys down to five finalists, who were then groomed into the ultimate boy band. It was an amazing experience for me although absolutely grueling. Shooting on location in Florida for nine months, I worked alongside Clay Newbill and learned from his mastery as we also became great friends. As usual, I commanded my area of responsibility as well as taking charge of handling everything that wasn't being done by the producer next up in the line of command. Before long, she was moved to a story-producer role—and I was made a producer.

Boom, that's it, I thought. I'm so close to executive producer now—that's next!

Not so fast. When I asked, the response was "Sure you can take over the responsibilities," and I got a bump in pay, but again, there was no negotiating for the executive title that would let me captain the ship of production, a role I'd promised myself I'd have by the time I turned thirty—two years away.

After finishing the entire run of *Making the Band*, my plan was to forge ahead with ideas of my own that I hoped to sell. But before I left BMP again, I got thrown a wild card when I was contacted by an executive at MTV, a great guy by the name of Temple Williams; I'd never met him, but he would later become a most valuable member of my team, as he is today. Temple wanted to know if I was interested in working on a new series called *Fear*. The show was similar to the recent blockbuster movie *Blair Witch Project*, and combined elements of *Road Rules* with challenges to a group of kids to go into haunted places and document supernatural phenomena. After meeting with one of the companies involved in the project, I was offered a producer position—that is, once the show was green-lit. Before I could say yes, however, I had to officially give notice at BMP so that I could be replaced.

To complicate the timing, the start for *Fear* was delayed for another six months. The message was just to sit tight and wait. Welcome to the real world of self-employment. In one half hour, you can go from having too many jobs to being out of work. How could I be unemployed for six months? The answer that every entrepreneur learns has to do with good old-fashioned multitasking and saying yes to all opportunities. So as I began to rustle up my own projects, I got another call from Temple about these guys who were making funny videos with physical comedy and that MTV was trying to figure out how to create a show for them. This was a chance to help shape a series from the ground up for a crew that turned out to be the original *Jackass* guys. In addition to the pilot that I helped develop—by teaching these crazy skateboarders and cutups how to do reality TV—I went on to work for hire on nearly ten more episodes.

When Bunim-Murray got wind of my new job, Mary-Ellis accused MTV of "poaching" me as the result of contact made on BMP productions with another MTV executive; she even threatened legal action. That didn't seem fair. So I made my case to Mary-Ellis and Jon, explaining in person and in writing that I had never met with the executive they thought had poached me; that, in fact, Temple Williams had been my contact all along. The situation resolved itself. From this experience, I concluded that business disagreements could be cleared up with direct communication, person to person, and without legal battles. Boy, would I later be proven wrong about that.

At last, *Fear* was given the official green light, and I dropped everything to go interview with Beau Flynn—now known as a huge blockbuster movie producer. Beau's partner at the time was Dawn Parouse Olmstead—now the head of Universal Cable Network and a major force in television—and the two were about to lend something new and different to reality TV. In another stroke of great timing, I'd be there to learn from Beau and Dawn as they shepherded MTV's *Fear* into being.

Neither Beau nor Dawn had ever produced an unscripted TV show. Beau had produced scripted features while Dawn had made mostly TV movies, also scripted. My expertise in reality was obviously what had made me MTV's choice for the job. But I still had to get a thumbs-up from Beau.

To do so, I go for the interview at his office and am asked to take a seat in the small lobby adjacent to his inner sanctum. From where I'm sitting, I can hear him reading the riot act to his poor assistant. He's on a rant, yelling about why he's tired of telling her what has to be done, how she needs to learn to think one step ahead of him and to be more proactive if she has any hope of lasting in her job.

I have a choice: Stress out or create an opportunity. So I decide to go into the interview—proactively—and be very explicit about what I can and will do for him. As he finishes up with his assistant, he calls me in, shakes my hand, and says, "Well, tell me about yourself."

Not wasting a moment, I tell him about all the stuff I've done and then say, "Look, I'm most interested in an opportunity to be the executive producer. You might be wondering why I think that I'm ready, and I'll tell you. The truth is, I'm a person who thinks ahead. Ask anyone I've worked for. I'm always one step ahead of my bosses, because I think that's my responsibility." I have just regurgitated to him everything I'd overheard.

He was amazed because, as he said, he was just talking about that to his assistant.

And I was in. Not as executive producer but as supervising producer, one step down from EP, and both Beau and Dawn rolled out the red carpet, giving me full confidence that I could and would deliver on their expectations. *Fear* was one of the most creative and technologically challenging opportunities that I could have been handed, and to this day, it was one of my most memorable producing experiences.

In addition to giving me leeway for developing new technology for shooting our young paranormal investigators, Beau and Dawn encouraged me to borrow from their arenas of expertise in scripted storytelling, like art direction and set design. The environment would still be real, just enhanced to better evoke the terrifying elements of the scariest of films. The reactions of the cast after being dropped into a horror-movie setting—albeit a slightly touched-up one—were still totally authentic. This was a first for me: the merger of the two worlds of scripted and reality. The magic was being able to keep the integrity of an unscripted show and combine it with the production value of a scripted project.

At one point, as an example, Beau and I were scouting locations with haunted histories, and he looked at the structure and said, "Well, that's an interesting white house but I envisioned more of a creepy old farmhouse."

"Right. But it is a white farmhouse. Just that it's kind of new."

"So what?" He shrugged and then suggested, "Let's build a flat." He went on to explain that it would just be a fake facade in the front, and it would be old and creepy with peeling paint and a gothic ghost-story look.

When I first learned that I could create the environment to enhance the visuals without compromising story, I was like—holy shit! My background from BMP was deeply documentarian. But now Beau and Dawn baptized me in the gospel of showmanship and entertainment. There was something liberating to know that you could be creative in capturing reality.

The other way in which I grew by miles was in working with the talent. The structure of *Fear* involved a competition in which the five kids would document suspicious phenomena and get past their fears. They knew up front that they were going to be scared, so my job was to coach them through the reality of being terrified but not to the point of flipping out and quitting the show. Once they had flown in to the city where the location and the lodging were, I would bring them into a stripped-down hotel room. No television. No telephones. No clock radio. I would literally black out their hotel windows with tinfoil and duct tape so they had no sense of time. The only reading materials were books on spirits, ghosts, and other paranormal phenomena associated with haunted places.

They weren't required to read the books, but I'd have them placed strategically on tables and in obvious spots and they would be told that they could read up on the kinds of things they would be investigating. Before being taken to the location, all five of them went through a forty-eight-hour series of exams—medical and background checks as well as psychological examinations. A team of professionals who were the real deal would come in and conduct these tests and would not hold back if there were concerns.

Once each of the cast members had been approved, I would come in and let them know how the show would proceed. I'd explain, "Listen, when this thing gets started you are going to be taken to a location that—whether you believe in ghosts or not—we're here to investigate because people have seen ghosts there." All of that was true and logical. But to get them in the frame of mind of a horror movie, I'd warn them to be mindful of their physical safety and to know that whatever happened, it was real.

After that, we'd get them hooded up and drive them to the location—but they'd have no clue where they were—and I'd tell them to count to one hundred very slowly as we all left. And then, alone, they'd pull their hoods off, and cameras would be turned on and taping.

Every kid on the show was a standout. A few times we'd have to go pop in when someone seriously freaked out. But overall they were fantastic, and the show was a big deal, a huge hit for MTV.

Fear was the calling card my career needed. From then on, my reputation was as a producer who could take on the most problematic shows, because of the talented production staff I brought on board and for how I coordinated the energies of the sixty-member team. Truly, the make-or-break part of every hit show comes down to that team—the kind of team that goes to war together, that solves the biggest challenges together, and that excels in every way together.

After I did the first six episodes of *Fear,* MTV came back quickly and ordered two more seasons. But my executive producer credit was still off the table—for reasons that I came to understand as having more to do with not wanting to give up creative ownership and future royalties as opposed to shelling out the money in the short term. I played ball through the third season, just as my twenty-ninth birthday was suddenly upon me. The deadline I had set for myself still held, as far as I was concerned. Somehow, someway, I had to make it happen.

This was in the same period when *Survivor* culminated with a viewership of 50 million watching its first season's finale. The second behemoth, *Amazing Race,* was now on the air. And *Fear*—with its riveting must-watch scenes of abandoned buildings and haunted locations and kids running around inside in the dark, screaming for their lives—was continuing to grow its audience.

And then 9/11 happened. Timing changed everything. The truly horrifying images coming out of the towers were all the fear and all the reality that could even be contemplated, let alone watched. *Fear* was unceremoniously canceled and, in fact, the third season never aired. Rightly so too. The mood of the country altered overnight. The nation, now gripped with real fear and real sadness, needed comfort and hope, in turn making reality TV somehow obsolete or just inappropriate.

The fact that I was suddenly unemployed was not the worst thing that could have happened in that terrible time.

GRAB FOR THE BRASS RING

If launching my own company taught me anything, it was just how tough it really is to put yourself on the map as a new business while also marshaling your resources of money and time—especially when you are the last to get paid. As I would later find out, the majority of entrepreneurs fail in their initial attempts at going into business for themselves. Even the most visionary, economic-savvy leaders in industry have been known to stumble and fall in the early stages of building their own companies. Knowing that should not be a disincentive: It should be a reminder to embrace the desire for independence that makes your efforts valiant.

More than anything, I loved the freedom of holding my own cards, win or lose. This period, one of the most productive and creative stretches of my life, also validated the advice given to me by my mother. If you don't love what you're seeking to accomplish, no amount of success—in terms of money or status—is going to lighten the load required to attain your goals. If you don't love the path you've chosen, the struggle to overcome the odds is going to be filled with pain, frustration, resentment, and failure without lessons. If you can fall in love with the growth that comes from struggle, and if you choose to feel that you're richer for what you've learned and discovered, you will find the means for experiencing daily success. Learning to value the growth that comes from daily struggle can go on the list as *Motivation Lesson #7.*

The fact that the executive-producer title continued to elude my grasp was only a reminder that I was going to have to give myself that title—by selling a project of my own. And in Brass Ring, the production company that I founded with partner Rick Telles, the possibilities for doing that were coming closer and closer to our reach.

Rick and I had met while working at Bunim-Murray. Rick, a handsome, friendly dude, was ten years older than me and had begun his career as a soap actor—where he first met Mary-Ellis—who brought him over to BMP. What Rick really wanted to do (as I later understood) was to direct scripted film and television; for him, reality was more of a stepping-stone and not what he was most passionate about. Still, Rick was right there, nodding in agreement whenever I'd say, "You know what? We could do this on our own. We should start our own company."

As time went on, especially once I'd left Bunim-Murray after *Making the Band*, what was once only talk began to take shape as the real deal. Theoretically, I was going to take the lead in developing, selling, and producing shows while Rick would be able to direct when we went into production. When we started throwing around possibilities for what to call the company, Rick's girlfriend suggested using Brass Ring as the name. I'd never heard that term before, but once the meaning and derivation were explained, I loved it.

Thinking big, we became Brass Ring Entertainment. Nothing could have felt more right to describe what I saw as our mission— reaching for the brass ring or the highest prize, ready to go for it, bringing some swagger to the game, as not only a production company but a full-on entertainment entity.

For anyone with a dream or anyone ready to think like an entrepreneur or reinvent yourself in your quest for reality, there is something powerful about taking on an ambitious name or title for your endeavor. It's about seeing your mission as something larger than just you.

Not much groundwork was actually laid for Brass Ring in the time span leading up to the cancellation of *Fear*. I had been able to bring Rick Telles on board for work on that, and then also made a deal for Brass Ring on a TV reality miniseries for the USA Network called *Cannonball Run 2001*, another production for Beau Flynn and Dawn Parouse Olmstead. The miniseries was based on an actual race (from which the Burt Reynolds movie took its name) but in custom-built and souped-up antique cars. Six teams of three drivers each (one of whom was considered to be a mismatch to the other two) were to compete for the $100,000 prize, all while figuring out clues and shortcut routes along the way.

Once again, I loved building the team—which included being able to bring my brother, Steve, in on the production. His expertise led to rebuilding one of the cars overnight after it had broken down. I was also able to make a recommendation to pair Beau and Dawn with Gary Benz and his GRB Entertainment production company. Gary was a hero of mine, starting with his pioneering work on *That's Incredible*. He also happens to be one of the most upstanding and endearing guys in the business. The other highlight was having Ben Samek on my team as one of the producers. We had first worked together on *Fanatic*, a freelance reality series I'd done before bringing Ben to BMP, where he worked with me on *Road Rules* and *Making the Band*. On *Cannonball Run 2001*, Ben and I not only had great rapport but I saw firsthand that his business brain could compute and resolve the most tangled set of variables in no time. Even though Brass Ring wasn't in the position to hire him, I promised myself he would be the first guy I'd hire once we were. Later, after a brief stint working for the competition (*Amazing Race*), Ben accepted work on a Brass Ring project. From then on, he would become such an important part of my career that today there is no major move I make without his input.

The series we finally sold, some months before my thirtieth birthday, was a project called *Hitchhiker Chronicles* to FX. At long last, I was able to award myself my first executive-producer credit on an unscripted series that I created and got to produce. Hallelujah. The monkey was off my back, and I was ready to take on the world. Setting the next goal for myself, I have to admit that my dream had always been to be written about in *Variety,* the Hollywood trade paper that I'd read cover to cover whenever I could sneak a copy out of someone's office. All I needed, I figured, was to score a big hit.

Hitchhiker Chronicles was our take on *Taxicab Confessions.* Our hosts had hidden cameras in their various vehicles and would pick up hitchhikers, interview them, and document their stories. The confessions were touching, uplifting, funny, and bizarre but rarely too heavy. As we were still in the wake of 9/11, that was where the tone needed to be during this deeply somber time in the country.

No *Variety* piece yet as other wild cards showed up—like figuring out how to get paid on work delivered and then creating some cash flow while we shopped other projects, hoping to close those deals. In early 2002, during a lull in my work, around the time that I was trying to get something going with the idea inspired by the Lipton Sizzle & Stir commercial, Adriana learned that she had been let go from the accounting firm that had employed her all this time. Not only that, the very same day she confirmed we were expecting our first child.

Not that I needed more motivation to close some of our pending deals, but I certainly pushed harder than ever. Even though offers of work-for-hire projects were starting to trickle in, I focused every-thing on building Brass Ring. The timing was right for that. After coming to a standstill for months, unscripted television suddenly roared back to life. Inspiring true stories mattered now. Competition formats again struck chords with viewers who responded to stories of people down on their luck being given second chances.

In this groundswell, producing peers were being handed fat five- and six-figure salaries on freelance jobs. Colleagues at the top of this trend reported offers of two to three hundred thousand a year—and with no risk.

The best reality pedigree in town, many would agree, belonged to anyone who had worked at Bunim-Murray. I started hearing reg-ularly about who got poached from BMP for jobs that used to pay fifty to seventy-five thousand but now were three and four times that. One of my former colleagues was lured to NBC for an overall deal rumored to be upward of a million dollars.

We all had the same reaction: *Holy shit!*

Everybody I knew in my arena wanted to ride the new gravy train. But any suggestion that I should follow suit, I resisted, and insisted that I didn't want to ride anyone else's train. No more free-lance or working for somebody else. I kept saying, "I'm a company now. I'm a company now." The concept of quitting or failing at mak-ing my own business a reality was unacceptable.

I believed that with great ideas and a track record in execution, we'd prevail. News alert: There is more to running a TV production company. Yes, you own the ideas, and when a show really hits, you've struck gold. But on the road to the gold, you can go broke. Turns out that even after you've sold a show to the buyer (the broadcast network or a cable company), the money you get from them is required to make the show. In theory you are supposed to keep ten percent of that payment for your part in producing that show. However, as many entrepreneurs can attest about work-for-hire, if your priority is to make the best product possible, you often end up putting a lot of the money you're supposed to keep back into production, materials, labor, and all the other costs you incur—keeping only what's left over for yourself. You might make less than the ten percent or only break even. Sometimes the overages in expenses cause you to come out of pocket and you can actually lose money on the job. But if you charge more, you can bid yourself out of business or lose an opportunity to your competition.

This is a familiar predicament to many freelancers. Whenever you're hired to provide a service or product on order, there are expectations to be met. Your customer may ask for changes and improvements that you haven't budgeted; and because you want them to be repeat customers, you say yes to those changes to make them happy, even when you're eating into your own profits. In the short run, that doesn't always make great business sense. But if you're playing the long game, it can be worth it to invest in your repeat customer and develop relationships that lead to repeat business.

The challenge for us as a fledgling company wasn't just that we were putting everything into the production and being the last to get paid. It was also being liable for everything that went awry.

We made every mistake conceivable. For example, we didn't know that we needed to get insurance. Everybody knows that. Not us. We found out after we flew some cast and crew to London without a policy in place. Fortunately, nothing bad happened, and we were able to get the insurance after that. But still, all of this was outside of what I loved and why I was in the business: making television. Obviously, I had much to learn.

Early on, Rick and I were advised to hire an attorney to go over those kinds of concerns with us and to make sure we were legally protected, given all of this liability. The advice that I deeply, sincerely wish that I had been given then was not to rely on a sole lawyer for both of us. I thought, stupidly, that it would cost each of us more money and more headaches to have separate lawyers, as opposed to one lawyer who would be looking to protect Brass Ring as a whole. The last thing that I thought about was what would happen if for some reason we chose to end the partnership. We were cool, right?

In the months leading up to Adriana's due date, I did spot some signs of concern—to me. Rick didn't seem to be as frustrated as I was about selling another show. Instead of ramping up to play in the big time, what we'd been working toward, Rick's focus wasn't there as much, in my view. Somehow we weren't on the same page, as I recall from one pitch meeting with an executive at UPN.

Rick and I usually pitched well together. His background was as an actor, and we would trade off, normally, taking turns telling the story and making the case for the show we were pitching. But that day, as I was in the middle of building to the moment where Rick could take over, he looked distracted. So I went on by myself and tried to turn it over to him again, but once more he didn't join in. I finally stopped and said, "Rick?"

At that point, he apologized and asked, basically, what he had missed.

That's when I knew that things were about to go south. And fast. Of course, I didn't want to see it. Rick was a good person who'd been in the trenches with me in starting this company. But could I count on him as the stakes got higher? Much as I wanted us to make it, I had this gut feeling we could easily implode.

And yet, I chose to ignore that instinct. Spoiler alert: When and if you have a strong gut feeling about something, pay attention. I did not, opting instead to focus on the good and all the opportunity that soon came our way.

Everything happened all at once. Finally, we sold our next show, one I had created that was called *Surf Girls*. It was inspired after I'd read a novel by Joy Nicholson called *Tribes of Palos Verdes*, a female-driven story of a surf cult in a privileged beach community in the LA area. Nothing like that had been tried in unscripted TV, and I thought it was a phenomenal story that would make a great series. Although I'd been pitching it as a docuseries that would follow girl surfers everywhere in pursuit of the ultimate wave and everyone loved the pitch, somehow I couldn't sell it to save my life. Then, all of a sudden, the feature film *Blue Crush* was about to open, and the advance press was sizzling.

My phone began to ring right away. Among the calls was one from the folks at MTV who knew about my project. We were family at this stage of the game, and I went back in there, was approved to head up the production, own it and produce it, and sold the show. I then sweetened the deal by bringing in the surf gear companies Roxy and Quicksilver.

On a roll, *Surf Girls* was set to be shot in Tahiti, Australia, Fiji, and Hawaii. My dream job, it was a show that I created and sold, and now I was going to make it while traveling to outrageous destinations. Not skipping a beat, as that was coming together, I then teamed up with Gary Benz and GRB to help develop and sell a show that I didn't create called *Next Action Star*—a competition format for finding the next American heartthrob or sweetheart action star, male and female. The pitch I developed and brought to NBC (where they loved it) hinged on us being able to partner with the biggest name in Hollywood action movies: Joel Silver. He had done everything from *Predator* to *Lethal Weapon* and *Die Hard* to *The Matrix*—and all their sequels.

Along with Gary Benz and Rick Telles, I developed an irresistible presentation and went to meet with Joel Silver at his offices on the Warner Brothers studio lot in Burbank. We arrived early and were led by not one but two assistants to sit in the outer lobby of this imposing yet hip office. This was definitely Hollywood. Without hearing a word as to the reason for the delay, we sat there for about an hour.

By this point, I'm starting to feel annoyed but am cool as I check in with an assistant who goes to see if the Silver team is ready, just disappears, returning thirty minutes later to say, "Come this way."

We follow the assistant into the waiting area outside Joel Silver's office, and we proceed to sit there for another forty-five minutes. Now I'm pissed. We're all pissed.

To make this more painful, there are three members of his team, producers and development execs, who are at desks nearby, and Joel has an automatic door that he opens and closes constantly so he can scream at them.

"This is bullshit," I say to Gary and Rick. I might have been even more colorful with my language. This was some *serious* bullshit.

Finally, the door opens and Joel yells, "Bring them in!"

We get up and walk into Joel Silver's office that is dominated by the lifelike statue of the Predator from the movie. And without greeting us, Joel—a bear of a man himself—walks from his seat where he would normally sit all the way around to the front of his desk, stands there as we three walk tentatively toward him, and he sits back on the edge of his desk and he looks right at me and roars, "Tell me who the fuck you are so I know who I'm dealing with!"

And as I take a split second to register his question, I flash to an image of a headline about me in *Variety*—not for any show business success but for punching Joel Silver in the face! Great, I finally make it into the trades just in time for the end of my career. I'm usually the guy who can handle the yellers and the screamers, but where I come from, when men raise their voices and confront other men like that, there's going to be a physical altercation. And all I can think is if he put his hand anywhere near me, it's going down

Instead, as soon as he said this to me, leaning back on his desk and glaring, I walk up to Joel Silver, look right at him, and say, "I'll tell you who the fuck I am! I'm the guy who developed this show and the guy who is gonna make this show a hit!" Then, talking fast and loud, I reel off a few credits and end up telling him about being from El Monte, and, if I recall, that I was a high school wrestling champion. Just in case.

No sooner have I finished this response than Joel smiles big and says, "Great. Have a seat."

After that, the three of us took seats and had one of the best pitch/deal closings ever. I found out that a lot of that bluster was Joel's mechanism for getting rid of people on whom he didn't want to waste his time. I also found out that as abrasive as he was with his own people, they all seemed to love him, as if that screaming was just how he would say, "Pass the !#(%^) ketchup!"

I will admit that as we walked out of that meeting, Gary Benz turned to me and said under his breath, "Cris, you know you're crazy. I can't believe you did that."

The production should have been a hit, and I certainly did everything in my power for it to live up to its great potential. NBC poured millions of dollars into a budget that grew exponentially every day. It was bananas. There were lots of lessons to be learned about why the Hollywood-movie-blockbuster mentality needed to have some of the budgeting constraints that we reality TV producers knew well. On the other hand, as the summer of 2002's breakout hit *American Idol* had just proven to everyone in its debut year, in revisiting formats like talent competitions you've got to have high stakes and high production values. The saying "Go big or go home" was absolutely applicable to *Next Action Star* and to Joel Silver—who taught me lessons about the power of boldness and loudness in media. We got along well, even to where he wanted to deal only with me on the production; whenever he was on set, I had to be there.

That vote of confidence translated into later projects that I would do for Joel Silver, as well as a healthy ongoing business relationship. When it finally went to air, *Next Action Star* didn't do as well as it should have, but, as I was going to learn over and over, timing is everything. Even the most powerful players in Hollywood—or in any industry for that matter—can't control every variable that can impact business success.

All you can control as one person or one company is how honorably you live up to your commitments, how hard you're willing to work, and, as I had yet to fully grasp, how smart you're willing to work.

What does it mean to work smart? Well, the next several months would reveal to me how stupidity can put you out of business.

TIME WILL TELL

If you are a parent or plan to be one anytime in the near future, you probably can understand how your priorities and goals can shift in that moment when your child is first placed in your arms. The arrival of my son, just in time for Thanksgiving, was a cause for great celebration for me and Adriana, as well as for our parents and all of our extended family. What changed for me was now I had a goal that was new—the deep desire to be a great parent.

That quest is much more difficult than a slew of other worthy endeavors and, no doubt about it, the most personally rewarding job there is. And as my wife will be the first to remind me, it's a job that requires time, not just guest appearances by the parent who is otherwise out of his mind with work, not just well-intended time to be there long enough to briefly come home and help diaper, feed, and entertain a growing baby boy—and cut Mommy some slack.

In this equation, as most young couples and first-time parents know, nobody wins the "Who's got it tougher?" competition. There wasn't much I could do to help at home, unfortunately, as it was now undeniable that the Brass Ring partnership was in peril.

One of the biggest lessons that I was about to learn is that sometimes just because someone is your friend that doesn't mean you two are suited to be business partners. In my own team-building approach—with my "the more the merrier" or "share the wealth" mentality—I assumed that it would be fine to develop my production company as a partnership. That in and of itself is a worthy approach. But a partnership in business is a lot like a marriage. Once you get hitched in a business partnership, you are legally entangled. That means that before you tie the knot with something as important as your dream at stake, you had better do your due diligence to make sure that the two of you are suited as partners.

Partnerships shouldn't be about convenience or compatibility or friendship. This isn't to say that friends never should be business partners. But it's not a proven recipe for business success. Also, Rick and I never had conversations about shared vision and shared goals; we never talked about how or if our respective skill sets would balance and complement each other's. The failure to have such discussions came from my own lack of experience.

As things started to go south, I made the further mistake of thinking that I could manage both *Surf Girls* and *Next Action Star*. In fact, MTV had made the deal based on me being first position—meaning that any other work would come second. But then NBC and GRB asked for the same deal, that I be first position on *Next Action Star*. Well, I couldn't, as I had already committed to MTV. What were the options? We're talking about MTV's $3 million budget and NBC's $25 million budget. If anyone was going to budge and let me put Rick on one of the shows, it was going to be MTV. And so after much conversation and the help of agents, MTV OK'd him to take the first position and travel with the show to all the major surf locations. While he flew off to do that—unfortunately with a flare-up of his back problems—I was immersed in *Next Action Star*, a colossal production of epic proportion. No hype. Not only was it NBC and Joel Silver, but a lot of it was scripted and had to look like a movie, not a TV show.

Surf Girls had been fine when it was in preproduction and had been shooting locally—and I was checking in regularly—but the minute they left the country, it was a debacle. Rick's back was an issue, people were quitting, and MTV wasn't happy with the content they were getting. All I could do was reassure everyone that we would fix everything in postproduction. Sure enough, once everyone returned and we started the edit, *Surf Girls* appeared to be back on track.

Next Action Star continued to be all-consuming. I'd leave the house every day at five forty-five in the morning and return at midnight or one a.m. That was until the next crisis that lit up on *Surf Girls* when MTV decided they were unhappy with the edit. Now our agents put us on notice, saying, "They don't think that you have control over the show, and they're gonna pull the show from you."

Now I go straight to MTV and beg them not to pull it. They relent. Instead of killing it, they choose to send in one of their own editors and I agree, promising, "I'll get involved."

So now I leave my house at five forty-five in the morning, leave *Next Action Star* around midnight, and go to *Surf Girls*, staying until two or three in the morning, and then go home for whatever sleep I can get and a shower. Of course, I feel terrible that the only time I go home is for an hour or two here or there. And nobody at home is too thrilled about me either. Whenever I just put my head down for a bit, first thing I hear is Lexi—my Rottweiler, who has to be outside because of the baby just being born—crying to come inside, scratching at the door. Next the baby starts crying.

Every night it's the same thing, the whimpering and crying, the no sleep. With Lexi and a newborn baby, I can't explain that it won't always be this way.

And then, after everything, we can't save *Surf Girls*. MTV says, "Guys, you're out. We're bringing a producer in, an outside producer to take over and run everything from here on out."

A crushing defeat. *Hitchhiker Chronicles* was a show we created and sold but we didn't own. *Next Action Hero* was not our idea, and we didn't own it. But *Surf Girls* was ours. We were owners of it, and I went to the mat to sell it as a show we could do on our home turf of MTV and own the whole show and be responsible for it.

So Rick and I are sitting at a rented edit bay we had in North Hollywood, and I'm beside myself at how badly we've blown it. It's one thirty, almost two in the morning, and I say, "I can't believe it. After everything we worked for, after we finally get our own show that we created and get to own. And they let us produce it. We held our ground. We laid our necks on the line, our friendships. We pushed them into giving us the chance, and we blew it. You know what I'm saying? We blew it. We blew everything that I've ever wanted to do."

Rick does not say a word. Instead, as best I can recall in that moment, he breaks down.

And I say, "What? Why are you crying?" Probably the f-word was in the mix somewhere. Was he kidding me? I'm out of my mind from the crying at my house and now this? So I repeat, "Why are you crying?"

Rick goes on to say, in effect, that he can't take it anymore. The hours. The stress. And then he tells me that the truth is he doesn't even want to be in reality TV. He had wanted to direct scripted television, and working in unscripted wasn't what he wanted to be doing with his life. "It's too much. Not sleeping, being in pain, being yelled at."

I stare at him in stone-cold silence.

And that was when Rick Telles said emphatically, "I want out."

From the instant that he said that he wanted out, that was the end of our partnership and the full implosion of Brass Ring. We began the messy task of working our way out of whatever obligations, commitments, and revenues owed to us still existed under the umbrella of everything that had been generated. In deciding to go our separate ways and divvy up the properties, he was going to take any of the scripted ideas we had been developing and I was going to take the reality ideas. And we would split anything that came from existing projects already in development, in particular one show that was now moving along—the one inspired by the Lipton Sizzle & Stir commercial.

The way I see it today, as I look back at the mistakes I made not just with my first partnership but in other deals and inexperienced decisions made down the road too, I probably spent about $15 million in earning the wisdom that these mistakes cost me. I actually consider all of these years to be my graduate degree—master's and a doctorate and postdoc too—in reality. Pricey but worth it.

One of the best pieces of wisdom that I can share was how wrong I was when I decided that everything was over for me and my career after Brass Ring came to an end. I really thought that once you failed, nobody would give you the time of day ever again. No two ways about it. I was a failure. I'd been stupid, and now I was embarrassed.

What I was going to discover is what I hope you'll take to heart—that the lessons of failure were both important and necessary. Besides the lesson that 1) failure is not forever and the fact that 2) what you learn from your mistakes can be used to inform better choices on your way to true success, I should add that 3) failure teaches you to stay grounded, to keep your ego in check, and above all, 4) failure teaches you the true value of time.

In the grand scheme of things, most of our successes and failures aren't as earth-shattering as we think they are in the moment. Time gives us the ability to gain distance, perspective, and, again, a chance to process the lessons. Time teaches us not to be thrown by the rise and fall of good and bad days but to find our even keel. How we move forward or fall apart is up to this lesson—that only time will tell.

What I didn't know in the immediate aftermath of the Brass Ring disaster, that I do now, is that this was a rite of passage that the majority of entrepreneurs go through. An overwhelming number of first businesses crash and burn.

As a test of whether or not I felt like my days as an entrepreneur were over, at my lowest point after Brass Ring's breakup, I received a call from my friend and colleague Gary Benz. He offered me a salaried job that came with two shows that I'd be running, right away. The money was more than I'd ever been offered in one salary. I was tempted, just as I'd been tempted by a similar offer from Clay Newbill to come with him to work at ABC.

"Let me take a day to mull it over," I told Gary.

The moment of truth came for me on the drive home. No matter how I sliced and diced what I'd just been through with Brass Ring, I couldn't see myself ever getting the same chances again. But was I ready to give up and forget the possibility of creating, selling, and making shows of my own? No, I wasn't. I had touched my dream. I had tasted that reality. That taste was all I needed to see that the money was not the dream.

I thought of what my mother had told me over the years—not to go off course, not to take the easy way because too many people got stuck on those detours, settling for less than their dreams.

That message came through, and I knew what choice I had to make. But I will still never forget explaining it to my wife. At first, when I walked into the living room and said, "Gary Benz offered me two hundred thousand dollars to come work for him," she just exhaled, as if to say—*Thank God, we don't have to worry.*

That was before I added, "But I can't take the job." If I went to work for someone else, running two shows, I'd never have time for my own projects. As always, I had to bet on myself.

After all, I still believed in playing the long game. Could I make my dream a reality this next time? Only time would tell. That's the truth of the long game—what I contend is the only game there is.

seven

Surreal Life: *Reality Is a Contact Sport*

You will not get my vote. It goes to Richard. I hope that is the one vote that makes you lose the money. If it's not, so be it. I'll shake your hand, and I'll go on from here. But if I were to ever pass you along in life again and you were lying there, dying of thirst, I would not give you a drink of water. I would let the vultures take you and do whatever they want with you, with no ill regrets.

—Susan to Kelly,
Survivor: Borneo (Season 1)

"Fake it till you make it" is a saying that you hear a lot in my industry. For those who find themselves on unfamiliar turf or attempting to navigate higher, more competitive levels of the game, there's nothing wrong with looking for ways to fake it until you make it. Yet again, that's the irony about the entertainment industry, where there are no set rules, and as part of the hustle, everyone is more or less faking it until they seriously make it. But that skill set is only helpful up to a certain point. After that, you have to be able to deliver. How you go about delivering all depends on the business principle of *daring to change the game—and even write your own rules.*

That was a lesson that I took away from the fall of Brass Ring. I had to be able to win on my own terms, not just by playing the same game as most people but by actually delivering value to the marketplace. Sure, you can fake it till you make it on the way to getting the opportunity, whether it's getting hired for a job you've never done before or landing a meeting with that power broker who can say yes to your proposal. You can fake it till you make it as you figure out the lay of the land to help you gain a foothold in your new arena. In show business and in other marketing avenues, you can even fake it till you make it in getting the sale. But in the end, you can't fake it if you want to truly make it. In the end, to be successful, you have to deliver.

There are numerous ways to interpret what it means to deliver in your arena and on your terms. In the business of selling and making television, my journey with Brass Ring led me to the hard-hitting conclusion that the time had come to deliver not just a show that had been green-lit but one that was a real hit. In fact, even as I pulled myself up off the mat after the breakup of my company, the show that would lead to delivering that success was already in the works. Only, I didn't know it yet.

Why not? Because, for a betting man, it was about the most unlikely of successes that could have been delivered in a big way. The lessons ahead all come under the heading of *Advanced Entrepreneurship*, where changing the game with *gut*, *grit*, and, especially *risk*, all can lead to success.

RISK BEING ORIGINAL

The question that comes up time and again for start-ups of every kind is how they can compete against the big guys. There are a zillion ways that anyone with an Internet connection these days can launch his or her own online business and turn dreams of success into rapid reality. But, in truth, the businesses that really make it are not in the zillions. The ones that succeed all offer something different, something that the more established offerings don't. Those that really make it usually start with the risk of being original. Being so crazy, over-the-top original can backfire. That's why the saying "Jump the Shark" came to be. It's a reference to the scene on *Happy Days*, when Fonzie went waterskiing and did a stunt to avoid getting eaten by the shark. Original? Maybe. But not believable. Not for that show or that character. A massive fail.

Most businesses, by the way, are risk averse. Why invest in something that's different and has no track record? What happens if the super-original idea or product has just jumped the shark and can't gain traction? Most industries, including Hollywood, play it safe. That's why it was always going to be a really tough sell to convince executives to buy a show based on the idea of putting less-than-prime-time celebrities on a reality TV series.

At the start, all I had to go on was my instinct that it would be fun to watch a show with celebrities who don't belong together— Mr. T., George Hamilton, Sally Jessy Raphael, Little Richard, and so on—if they could live in the same house as a reality TV family. The first log line? *"Real World* with celebrities." But that's all I had.

So I discussed what to do next with my then agent at UTA, the agency that had signed Brass Ring in the midst of beefing up their reality TV division. I'll never forget the article in *Variety* that cited the reasons UTA had signed those of us who were in the up-and-coming category, noting, "We want to find as many original voices as possible. We want trailblazers. We don't want people who are copycats." How cool was that? Even more cool was getting my name in *Variety*! Another goal checked off the list.

My agent agreed that there was something original to the concept of *Real World*–meets-comedy so far. But to do what I was talking about, she said, "You've got to know the Mr. Ts of the world." As it so happened, UTA had another client, Mark Cronin, who was responsible for the FX series *The X Show* (a nightly talk show with comedy) and was already working in various capacities with celebrities like Gary Coleman and Erik Estrada. The agent recommended that Mark Cronin and I should meet so we could talk about a possible collaboration.

When I first met Mark at a restaurant in the Valley, I'd barely sat down before he had me laughing. One of those guys who is naturally hilarious, Mark was tall and thin, probably about ten years older than me, and a good-looking fellow with a slightly receding hairline, which made his facial expressions seem that much more animated. His timing was impeccable, as good as any stand-up comic's. I began to sense that we had very different yet also complementary personalities. Whereas I can be outgoing, Mark was more aloof, almost in a goofy way that reminded me of a kid—jovial, imaginative, and entertained by his own creative antics. He was not only smart but, sure enough, he had graduated from Penn with an engineering degree.

How does an Ivy League grad with a major in chemical engineering end up in television? As Mark explained, he had done comedy at Penn but after graduation went for the big high-paying serious job working for the company that made Teflon pans. Missing his creative outlet, he started submitting funny sketches to a local comedy access TV show at channel 9 that Howard Stern was producing with the team from his radio show.

So one night he was settling in to watch the show and was shocked to see that they were doing one of his sketches. Instead of suing them, Mark convinced the producers to hire him instead. He quit his engineering/marketing job and went to work for Howard Stern and eventually to being part of Stern's megahit television specials. That was his stepping-stone for moving to Hollywood.

Besides the fact that I was a huge fan of Howard Stern and his comedy—so outrageous and inappropriate, often just exactly what you're thinking but were afraid to admit—I was impressed that Mark had worked with other pop culture personalities on a range of mostly comedic projects. Weirdly, he had actually been the executive producer of *Big Deal* when I was starting out, even though we didn't interact at the time.

Mark Cronin embodied originality. As we started to talk about what the format might be of a show conceived as "*The Real World* with celebrities"—what we intended to call *The Surreal World*—Mark immediately began to push the comedy envelope. He was a visionary, not just with humor but also with strong writing. In short, we clicked. We went on from there as we focused on how to develop the concept, the show's structure, and the pitch. That old expression about how innovators think outside the box would not have applied to Mark Cronin. For him there was no box.

We balanced each other well. While I also was creative and had vision, I had the practical logistics training in unscripted formats that allowed me to know what could actually be done. To a certain extent, I was an oddity in the business in that I could develop ideas creatively, execute in production, and also oversee postproduction. Being multifaceted in those respects was helpful for harnessing Mark's originality.

Early on, I could see how we brought out the best in each other. He helped me sharpen my comedy chops that, as much as I loved humor of all kinds, had never had much of an opportunity to develop in reality TV. I helped him focus his skills in more narrative or dramatic storytelling, which he had not explored much in his work.

Development was always fun with Mark. In one creative session, for example, we had to come up with episode concepts **for our family** of celebrities once they'd exhausted the more practical steps of moving into their Hollywood house, going out shopping for groceries, and fixing meals together. We listed all the more exotic outings and adventures like *Survivor*-type camping trips, jaunts to Las Vegas, visits to a nudist colony, producing their own talk show, and even having a wedding take place during production. We wanted to up the ante and do something way out there, so Mark suddenly announced, "In the episode, they go to outer space!" He just went for it, describing how we would let them get on a rocket ship, blast off, and get all the way into outer space. He was all in, saying, "C'mon! Think of it! Tammy Faye Bakker and Ron Jeremy floating around in zero gravity!"

I let him go on for a bit and then reeled him in, laughing and then saying, "Nah, we're not gonna go to outer space. But what if we set up time at Space Camp, where they train the astronauts?"

Mark thought it over and then got all excited about astronaut training.

We balanced each other like that all the time. Though Mark had worked with some of the celebrities we envisioned as part of our cast, we couldn't exactly attach any of them until we sold the project. As a no-brainer, I suggested for our first pitch that we go to Bunim-Murray, assuring Mark, "Hey, I know Mary-Ellis and Jon, after all. And this is basically celebrity *Real World* with comedy. Why wouldn't they snap it up before we pitch it around town?"

Why wouldn't they? Well, Mary-Ellis had a lot to say about why not. Not holding back, she delivered a lecture and a complete dressing-down that was along the lines of "Who do you think you are?" Jon said little as she continued. "We created this genre. We created *Real World*. Why would I do this with you? Why would we partner with anyone else on something we created?"

In hindsight, I understood that she had her points. Maybe I was naive, but I thought as my mentors they would welcome the fact that I'd taken what they taught me and done well. But, sure, the moment can be unsettling when the student may be ready to be on the same stage as the master. For his part, Jon Murray waited many years to tell me how much he regretted not partnering with us on a show he believed at that time would do very well. He said this to me recently at an annual convention for television and broadcast professionals. For Jon's numerous accomplishments as a television pioneer, at that conference he received the well-deserved Brandon Tartikoff Legendary Award. Sadly, Mary-Ellis had passed away only two years after I went to pitch to them that day, and I wasn't able to acknowledge her contribution to my success. However, when I met up with Jon at the convention, I certainly expressed my ongoing gratitude to him as well as to his late partner. That was when he told me how he had really felt about the show that I'd last pitched to BMP, saying that it was a form of homage to *Real World* but really its own creative entity. He told me that in private before we were to be interviewed in a Web broadcast together. Then, with cameras rolling, he repeated that story in public, again describing how much he regretted missing out on the success he knew the show would attain. Jonathan Murray was the one receiving the award at that convention but those words to me were my own prize.

If anyone could see a diamond in the rough, Jon was someone who could. That being said, what we had first called *The Surreal World* was still an unlikely contender.

Whenever you choose to risk being original, just know ahead of time that you are now changing the game. Not everyone is going to get it or get you. But if I might give you a suggestion about that—and we can add this to the list as *Motivation Lesson #8*—it doesn't matter if *everyone* doesn't get it. If you really believe, chances are that somebody else will too.

IT ONLY TAKES ONE PERSON TO SAY YES

The fantasy scenario for anyone in the business of selling yourself, a project, or a product is that you manage to spark a bidding war that increases the market value of your work. That's the best-case scenario. But in high-risk situations, when you're changing the game and going against the grain, be prepared for another kind of reality. This goes back to Networking 101—it just takes one person to say yes. Your challenge is not giving up along the way.

In hindsight, I know now that being rejected by BMP and having to come up with a new name for the show was a blessing in disguise. Since we couldn't use *The Surreal World,* we changed one word and made it *The Surreal Life.* An easy fix. By differentiating ourselves from all comparisons, Mark Cronin and I went further in developing our creative stamp as collaborators. We quickly got away from the Lipton-commercial description and only used *Real World* as the departure point in our pitch. Instead, we honed and built *Surreal Life* together by drawing from story lines and characters in classic scripted sitcoms. We printed out titles of episodes from the likes of *I Love Lucy* and *All in the Family* and then put our heads together to invent ways of translating scripted timeless comedy situations into reality TV.

The pitch was phenomenal. To this day, the pitch for *Surreal Life* is still one of the best I've ever taken out. It was so fresh, so different, so damn fun. We dispensed with the usual sizzle reel—the video presentation that gives a hint of the tone and format of the show. At a minimum, you should always go in with something to show, a PowerPoint at the very least. But this was such a forward and new idea that there was no way to present a sizzle reel without casting, which we couldn't do without a deal. We had to figure out how to pitch what no one had ever seen or conceived of before—iconic celebrities living in a Hollywood mansion somewhere and fixing their own breakfast, brushing their teeth, even making their own beds—without showing the famous individuals themselves.

The solution? We went into meetings and put on a live comedy show, acting out all the different possible scenarios we could imagine. Mark was a spot-on mimic, and I could hold my own, so we'd set up a hypothetical cast and then play the different parts. We hadn't even called any of these celebrities about the show, but we portrayed them in our live sketches, posing questions like, say, what would happen if you had an early-morning conversation between rocker Bret Michaels (from metal band Poison) and Gary Coleman (from *Diff'rent Strokes*)?

"Just imagine," I'd begin, "what would happen if Gary accidentally uses Bret's toothbrush." Then I'd be Bret Michaels getting metal mad and accusing Gary Goleman—as played by Mark Cronin—who would then use the famous line "Whatchoo talkin' bout, Willis?" Or, in that case, "Whatchoo talkin' bout, Bret?" Or just imagine, what if it was Charo as the "mom" of the house, and she arrived and there was a puppy that she loved and named "Coochi"? And then, what if a rapper from a hard-core rap group like Public Enemy arrived next—say, Flavor Flav—and he wanted to name the dog something else? Say "Boogie." Of course, that was the running bit and we'd throw everyone into the mix, like pop star Britney Spears getting upset when Coochi/Boogie peed on the carpet and she was like "Oops you did it again."

We'd have executives literally falling out of their chairs. We went to VH1, where we knew they needed programming, and we brought the room of execs to tears. They were absolutely crying from how funny our pitch was. But as soon as they wiped their eyes and caught their breath after all that laughter, they looked at one another and at us and said, "We can't buy this. It's a skit." Someone else in the room said, "How would you even book it? Who would actually do it?"

Not surprisingly, our agents followed up to say, "They passed."

Undaunted, we went out to all the networks, trying to work our magic in the room. We went to MTV (under the same Viacom ownership as VH1), where I knew lots of the executives. We owned the room. The agents' report? "They loved you guys. But they don't see how it's a show. Pass."

Instead of going back to the drawing board on how we were selling the show, we went bigger and bolder, pitching it not just as a soft-format docuseries, but, really, as the first reality sitcom. We went to CBS, NBC, ABC. The pitch killed. They applauded. They stood up and cheered. But the verdict was the same. They loved us, but they would never do it. They would either say that there was no such thing as a reality sitcom or that it wasn't their area. Everyone wanted big-competition format à la *Survivor*, *Amazing Race*, and what was then the newest contender, *American Idol*, which was getting ready to air in the summer of 2002, around this same time period.

One by one we exhausted all of our options. Everyone came to the same decision: "Pass." The irony of ironies was that this was one of the best pitches that anyone had ever witnessed, yet it just couldn't sell.

Finally, we go to the WB Network for our last pitch. We meet with this executive named Keith Cox, who's in scripted television. He's not even in reality TV. But, knowing this is our last shot, we go in like tour-de-force performers on their last night of the show and bring the house down. By that, I mean Keith Cox loves us! He can barely stop laughing, and when he does, he gets it. He sees it. He wants it!

But wait. Nothing is ever that easy. The next day, our agents put us on the phone with Keith Cox, and he reiterates, "I love the idea. I absolutely see it."

We can hear the "but" before it's out of Keith's mouth. And indeed it follows next, as he explains that the problem is that Jordan Levin, his boss, doesn't get it. Normally, this is where you hear the apology and the wishing you the best of luck with your show anyway. Instead, Keith tells us that he has gotten his boss to agree to a compromise option. He goes, "Look, I'm putting myself on the line to do this show. The deal is, if you guys can confirm that you have a cast of actual names booked for the show, then I can order it."

In that one moment, I knew that *Surreal Life* was going to become a reality. That is, as long as we could deliver. We would have a show on the air as long as we could convince seven pop culture icons—in one form or fashion or another—to join the first cast ever of a new genre of reality TV.

Once again this was a reminder that no matter how many times you hear no, it only takes that one person to say yes. How do you find that one person who will buy into your dream? First, by *not giving up*, and second, by *believing and having faith that it will happen*, and, third, by *letting go of preconceived ideas about who you think the person who can say yes to you might be.*

Keith Cox, who today is an executive at TVLand and who has been at the helm of many successful scripted and unscripted series, was not the most likely candidate to even give us a provisional yes. But now that he had, we were going to have to overcome even tougher odds in going after the members of our first cast—wherever, whoever, whenever we could.

But we couldn't stop and rest after finally getting a yes. The yes takes you to another lesson—that just because you're in and have gotten hired or have sold a project or have been given an investment, that doesn't mean your work is over. On the contrary, the work has just begun. File that under Advanced Entrepreneurship.

Not just work but, as we experienced, even humiliation, mockery, and loathing. Nobody was laughing hysterically when we went out to the managers and agents of all these various celebrities who were known from TV, film, music, or sports or who had become famous for being in the news or making headlines in pop culture. This was about four years away from the launch of *Dancing with the Stars*, when it would be more acceptable for celebrities to enter a competition format and enjoy an injection of newfound or multiplied popularity. The only example of celebrities on reality TV at the time was *The Osbournes* on MTV. Since Ozzy was the only celebrity member of his family, at that time, the show was more in keeping with other series that documented behind the scenes of major music personalities. In fact, it would have been the opposite of a selling point as far as legitimizing our show for the celebrities we were trying to book.

Let's not forget that reality was still the bottom of the barrel, the scourge of the industry, especially in the view of traditional actors. This was not going to change in the next few years either, as we would see with the impending Writers Guild strike that would serve to fuel the reality boom. At that juncture, every network and every studio in town purged everything they had in development, every deal with writers and show runners in every scripted format. Their reasoning? As they might have said—*What do we need writers for? We have reality television.*

Today it's *all* changed. With the coming success of unscripted—everybody who is anybody wants some kind of reality deal as part of their brand portfolio. We are talking about another dimension in the entertainment universe, something I couldn't have imagined in my wildest dreams.

But a dozen years ago the disdain for reality was everywhere. In that atmosphere, pretty much anyone in the unscripted genre was hated—no, let's say despised—as a group. We could feel it even before the strike, when Mark and I first started reaching out to agents, managers, and publicists of various performers whom we wanted for our show. I'd make a phone call, for example, to Britney Spears's representative and be in the middle of saying, "Listen, we love Britney and would love to have her on our show, a celebrity-driven reality series that . . ." and before finishing the sentence, I'd hear, "Don't you ever fucking call me again!" before I'd hear the sound of the dial tone.

We heard it all: "Forget it!" "Fuck off!" "How'd you get this number?" It was impossible. No celebrity, even a nonworking celebrity who was still waiting for a feature part or a scripted TV part, would be seen anywhere near reality television.

We enlisted the help of a terrific casting director to facilitate some conversations. In many cases, however, to get celebrities to sign letters of intent we had to go to public places like hairdressers and barbershops or post offices and kind of happen to run into them without being too weird. One of the first guys I was able to meet in person was Erik Estrada, famous for his role on the TV hit *CHiPs*. We bonded as fellow Latinos, and he agreed to work on the show, except . . . he wasn't available for the first season's timetable. Then Mark Cronin managed to get Corey Feldman (former child star of both film and TV/turned music artist and recovering bad boy), who gave us our first yes for our debut season. Phew.

That first season, as I recall, there was no method to our madness, other than to take all comers and attempt to assemble a cast that had a modicum of diversity. After Corey Feldman, we started to get more yeses. Gabrielle Carteris (from *Beverly Hills 90210*) was in. Emmanuel Lewis (best known for his role on *Webster*) was a big yes. Then rocker Vince Neil of Mötley Crüe agreed to join the cast.

But the big yes we needed was still out there—the pop culture icon who would also be what Mark Cronin and I called the cornerstone. For our casting concept, the cornerstone was the cast member who was the big marquee name and who could inform the overall tone of the show, hopefully make things happen when they were dull or keep the peace when unscripted crazy moments got out of hand. We took as much from sitcom storytelling and comedy character archetypes as we did from familiar-cast dynamics in reality docuseries. The ideal cornerstone for our first season, we thought, would be MC Hammer, but phone calls to him had not been returned, and it appeared he wasn't interested.

Just to make sure, I arranged to fly up to the Bay Area to meet with MC Hammer in person. No one really knew what was going on with Hammer in those days. After he had sold millions of albums/CDs with late eighties and early nineties hip-hop hits like "U Can't Touch This" and "2 Legit 2 Quit," the word was that he had blown through all that money by living too large with his mega entourage and/or from possible mismanagement. Certainly, that cycle can be an issue for any celebrity whose income skyrockets almost overnight. You get used to the glamorous lifestyle and to being generous to everyone in your circle, only to see all that money go away once you've passed your prime in pop culture.

Again, where I come from, we don't judge. On the contrary, I was impressed that Hammer was now an ordained minister and was apparently involved in new business projects. But whatever was going on, I knew he'd bring a great energy and presence to *The Surreal Life*—just as I told him when we met in his really fancy downtown San Francisco office with a view of the bay.

So I'm making my case to MC Hammer, pointing out how he'll benefit from new fans, the new exposure, the new revenue, and the other advantages that being on a reality TV series can offer, and he comes back to me, saying, "I don't need new fans. I don't need more exposure."

We shake hands nonetheless, and I thank him for his time. Afterward, I'm back at my hotel, and I call Mark and the rest of the team to say, "Damn. I don't think we'll get Hammer."

"He doesn't need to work?" Mark asks.

"Nope, he's doing well."

I've barely hung up from that call when my cell phone rings. It's MC Hammer, who says, without preamble, "Let's talk money. How much money are we talking about?"

"What would you take?"

"Fifty thousand." He is asking for fifty thousand dollars an episode. For a scripted TV series that would have been reasonable for a top name. But for an unscripted series, that kind of money was almost unheard-of—on a new show and for someone who hadn't been in the public eye for a while.

"Twenty-five," I say, as a counter.

"Can you give me twenty-five thousand dollars an episode?"

My comeback is not to hold me to it, but that I will fight to get that for him. He then asks if I can extend my stay for the night and come meet him the next morning. But the address he gives me this time is out in Oakland. When I get there, it's a small house in a less-than-flashy East Bay neighborhood. In that moment, I am reminded that there can be a wide gap between perception and reality.

Hammer met me and showed me around where he really lived. The office suite in the San Francisco building where we'd met the day before? Not his. It belonged to a friend of a friend. In fact, he wasn't working on new business yet. He just didn't want to look desperate. But now that we had gotten past that, he was on board and genuinely upbeat about sharing his spirit and wisdom as a cast member. I was excited that he actually was going to get new fans, new exposure, and new revenue. *Surreal Life* was going to be good for him, and he was going to be good for the show. We shook hands, and I headed back to Los Angeles so we could finish up our casting.

We had built the show so far with a core of five—four men and one woman—a mix of three actors and two music celebrities. To create some balance, we added two more cast members, both women. One was *Baywatch*'s Brande Roderick (also a pinup *Playboy* model who had just been named Playmate of the Year), and, in a move I still say was unplanned genius, we cast Jerri Manthey, whose claim to fame was as a reality TV star from *Survivor*.

We delivered. Keith Cox ordered the first season. A new chapter had begun.

This was a case of breaking a few rules to get that first yes, which led to the next yes and the one after that. Success really does breed success, what you can call *Motivation Lesson #9*. It's a lesson that reminds you how you not only create opportunity but how you can parlay it into more opportunities. Some might call that leveraging. I call it smart.

FOLLOW YOUR INSTINCTS, DEFINE YOUR BRAND

Forgive me for stating the obvious but risk is risky. When you're playing the game your way as an entrepreneur and you're asking other people to buy into your vision, the final product is going to impact not just you, but everyone who signed on. So how do you handle that added pressure? First, by *bringing the best of yourself and others to the task of delivering on your promise.* Second, as I had to learn through trial and error, by *choosing to listen to your instincts and not your fears.*

When the first season of *Surreal Life* aired in early 2003, it was hard to pinpoint what my instincts were telling me. We weren't doing *Amazing Race* numbers although the word of mouth kept bubbling up about how fresh and funny *Surreal Life* was. Obviously, we had hit a nerve. But was it going to be the big breakout smash that was going to redefine what was possible on reality TV? Had we really delivered? Was this "it"? Hard to know. Not yet.

Part of my inability to get a sense of where the show could go was that all of this was happening in that same crazy time period when Brass Ring was imploding and then being legally dissolved. Going forward I would soon create a new production company for myself, 51 Pictures, named in honor of my football jersey number. As a creative and producing partner, Mark Cronin would continue to produce under his company name, Mindless Entertainment. Eventually, he and I would form a company as an umbrella for all of the productions we would do together and, as a combination of our two company names, call it 51 Minds.

That future was not yet foreseen when we were waiting to hear about whether we were going to get picked up by the WB for a second season. This was also a time for a reality check about whether the business side of our venture had been successful. We still had to pay the costs of overhead, rentals, insurance, all the overages like extra meals for cast and crew, extra flights, and cancellations. Every dollar that went out was a dollar less in our pockets as executive producers. If the network gives you a million dollars to make ten episodes, whatever you have at the end is your profit. For us, there was no weekly paycheck or bonus for extra hours worked.

Even though my gut told me that *Surreal Life* had amazing potential, because there were still no guarantees, I realized that it was time to generate more work on my own. Before I did that, however, my new agent at the time, Mike Camacho, then at CAA, had another idea.

Camacho had become my agent during the period when I was starting to clean house after the Brass Ring implosion—at the same time that I switched to a new lawyer who changed my life in this business. Camacho was a colorful deal maker of the highest order who then represented Mike Fleiss, the creator of *The Bachelor*, which was then garnering massive attention on ABC. Instead of doing speculative work while waiting for the WB to say yea or nay to another season of *Surreal Life*, Camacho suggested I do some work for Mike Fleiss for a hefty sum. It would not be a labor of love; it would not be a way to bet on myself as I had always done. It would not be forever. As a break from everything I had done, it would be a chance not to carry the producing burden.

I didn't want to take the job. My instincts told me no. But it wasn't bad timing. Not to mention that Camacho and my new lawyer carved out a deal that if *Surreal Life* did go forward, I would be released from any commitments to Mike Fleiss. There was no real downside, so I said yes.

The main assignment, among others, was to help create and shape a reality show for TBS that was based on *Gilligan's Island* as a competition-combination format. Once we got into production and I realized that other players were running the show, leaving me with no authority, I knew this was not going to work. After my experience on *Next Action Star*, I had made a solemn vow to myself that I would go down on any ship of which I was the captain. If my gut told me that an approach to shooting the show or telling the story was the right way to get the show done, then I would take it to the end. But with maximum responsibility and no authority, that couldn't happen.

Just as I was starting to butt heads with the other powers that be, we got the word that the WB had ordered a second season of *Surreal Life*. The option was left open for me to do my own show and continue on *Gilligan*. But this time I listened to my instincts and said no to continuing with a series that I didn't control.

Even though this was the kind of detour I preferred to avoid, it had been a valuable refresher course in trusting the instincts that we all have at our disposal and are there, if we use them, to help keep us on track. Trusting your instincts is also about observing, strengthening, and honing them—which is increasingly necessary the more ambitious and the higher the level of the game.

This was certainly becoming evident in reality TV. Like reality itself and many competitive industries, it's a contact sport, not for the faint of heart. With no guarantees of how your entrepreneurial efforts will turn out, you have a choice between listening to your fears or following your vision. In choosing the latter, you can then opt to up your game, enjoy the battle, change the rules, and own your success. *Motivation Lesson #10*: Get past your fear and write the rules of your own game You can't own what you didn't create.

And that begs the question: What does it mean to really create and own your success? Strange as it sounds, I saw the answer to that question in the examples of many of the celebrities who had penetrated pop culture in one aspect or another and were now the very individuals Mark Cronin and I were most passionate to meet and cast in *Surreal Life*. All iconic, each of them managed to create and own their success by being authentic and by carving out their distinct lanes, their own brands—if you will. Just look at the second season cast: Erik Estrada (everyone's favorite TV motorcycle cop); Ron Jeremy (actor, porn star, and filmmaker); Vanilla Ice (the white pop rapper/hip-hop entertainer); Tammy Faye Bakker Messner (the televangelist, singer, and author); Traci Bingham (of *Baywatch*); and

Trishelle Cannatella (a reality star and alum of *Real World* as well as a *Playboy* model).

At that point in 2004, as we went into production, with the Writers Guild strike killing every scripted show that wasn't already in the can—or already shot—and unscripted shows coming under major critical scrutiny, we were caught in the crosshairs. From one side, we had to defend the genre of reality altogether. From the other side, we had to defend *Surreal Life* from attacks made by peers in the reality field for not playing by the rules of casting "real" people. Like we were cheating or something. Worse, we were accused of using has-beens, and C-list and even D-list celebrities. The lesson to note was that you know you've created something meaningful and unique when criticism comes at you from all sides. Some of it really was jealousy, reflecting the fact that *Surreal Life* was a critical hit—that a core audience loved watching it and laughing their heads off. I mean, Ron Jeremy and Tammy Faye living in the same house, going on a visit to a nudist colony . . . Need I say more?

The more we were criticized, the more we listened to our instincts and honed our casting brand. Why did everyone harp on "D list" to describe our cast members? I found it offensive. Why demean individuals who at one time occupied prime real estate in pop culture awareness? Mark Cronin and I refused to fall into the trap of grading levels of stardom because the truth is we were redefining what it meant to be a celebrity. We went for iconic individuals, pop culture names who had followings and whose names endured even if they weren't currently on the air or doing any real business anywhere. And while, yes, maybe they had fallen from grace, that didn't change the fact that at one point they were pop culture icons. We felt honored to have them on board, and we always treated them with the utmost respect.

As we developed our own casting template for *Surreal Life*—beyond just whomever we could get—we touted our ensemble as a medley of iconic celebrities. They were not only authentic, true to exactly who they were; they were the most professional of any cast in unscripted television because, naturally, they knew how to move and talk and interact in front of cameras. We also looked for the pop culture icons who would work well in a sitcom-family format. We never forgot that we were in that post-9/11 period when audiences just wanted to come home and laugh at the foibles of others.

By the second season, I realized why producing *Surreal Life* was so rewarding for me—because it was like doing live theater. Not that I'd ever done theater, but that's how it felt. We had a house: a Hollywood mansion that was slightly faded in glory but decorated brightly, like a set of a movie, and the mansion was full of action, interaction, and reaction, all happening at the same time. Producing comedy was much harder than straightforward docuseries. We had to stay constantly on the ball, making sure we'd set up a comedic premise or situation, providing the tools for the cast members to discover the real humor, including assignments and props. We even had to retrain some of our camera operators because, in comedy, the key to the laughter is in the cutaway to the reaction. On *Surreal Life* if someone said or did something funny, the reaction from castmates was usually even more hilarious. So we developed a tempo for shooting and editing that was all in the reaction.

Amazingly, even though I'd done all those other unscripted shows with casts of real people who were chosen because of their big personalities, they paled in comparison to true, seasoned on-air talent. Our celebrities were veterans with not just big personalities but charisma and timing. Once you turned the cameras on, they went to work. They knew what to do. And they would deliver.

A lot of casting folks used to assume that any celeb would be promotable and marketable and would make sense for an unscripted show. But wait. Not all pop culture figures are at ease and entertaining as themselves. Some stars are terrified of being without a script. Some icons are just shy. Others are always performing and never just real. In casting for an unscripted show, I found that until you've met a celebrity in person and had a conversation as if they were on *The Real World* or *Survivor* and studied their behavior as people, you can't really assess how they'll be with cameras on them 24/7. I'd have to assess if they were good storytellers. Were they emotional? Were they extroverts? Were they type A personalities or type B? Were they good people who would not be scary to be around in close quarters for two weeks?

It wasn't enough to say we wanted to book a former star of *Melrose Place* or *The Brady Bunch*. We wanted to be able to create an ensemble whose members would dynamically interact with one another. One of us would say, "Oh, wow, I've got this actor, always has an edge, like he's mad at the world, and I have this other actress who has found peace and who can bring balance and maybe interact with this angry guy." And the other might say, "I have this actress who has a sarcastic attitude and a musician who just got divorced again for having affairs." That's a medley of personalities that would be interesting to watch interact. All of the casting lessons I learned at Bunim-Murray still applied.

As time went on, Mark Cronin and I came up with a blueprint for booking celebrities that was borrowed from sitcoms. This wasn't the standard in reality. We were casting a sitcom family—the Dad, the Mom, the Son who was the comedian, the Son who was brooding and sometimes trouble, the Crazy Uncle, the Annoying Neighbor, the Airheady Daughter, the Rebellious Daughter. We weren't stuck on any of those types, but they would be guidelines for finding those real-life personalities in these celebrities. In that mix we'd always look for the teenager or the young up-and-coming person who doesn't know anything about the business but thinks they're a huge celebrity because they're sexy—which was often the cast member who was the least known.

The idea to cast a reality-TV star as a member of our sitcom all-celebrity household happened by accident. Whenever we talked about the ensemble for the first season, Mark would always remind me that we needed to find our young ingenue.

I'd be thinking—*I don't even know what that French word means.* Mark eventually explained, "You know, the young hot person."

But we couldn't find any ingenue pop culture icons because young celebrities were still in their prime and usually hot careerwise, so they were unlikely to do the show. However, the one place where we could find ingenues who were available and reality show friendly was among the alumni of reality TV. Not only did this have a ripple effect into the entertainment world, sending the message that reality TV can give you a lasting celebrity platform, but it also ended up creating story lines for *The Surreal Life*. Adding that one reality star to the family was crazy—as we saw the first season when the other "real" celebrities sat around waiting for the seventh member to join them and couldn't believe that a contestant from a reality show was on the way. This happened every season. The others in the house would openly look down on the reality star, even saying, "What have you done? You're nobody." Sometimes that reality star would school the others—because, hey, they were now going to be reality stars too!

The high jinks and hilarity continued through the second season, as word of mouth also grew. We did have to compete with the Godzilla-sized reality shows like *Survivor*, *Amazing Race*, and now *American Idol* and *The Bachelor*. We had good numbers but not like the tens of millions that those huge-format shows would have tuning in to their megaproduced finales. Like a sitcom, we would premiere high, level off, and then ride out fairly steady. We had loyal viewers and we stirred up lots of publicity. A promising start, as far as we were concerned.

Not so promising according to Jordan Levin, then president of the WB, the same executive who didn't want to buy *Surreal Life* but was convinced to do so by Keith Cox.

Levin comes back to us and says, "Guys, we're doing great but *Surreal Life* is a sitcom. We have no competition, no elimination, no host."

We try to say, yeah, that's what makes *Surreal Life* different. After all, part of booking celebrities on the show is based on them not having to compete or be humiliated by eliminations. Why have a host who would get overshadowed by the celebs' personalities?

"Well," he says, "I want a competition. And eliminations. And a host."

Mark and I have no idea how to do that. We go back to Levin and argue. We fight. We plead. But finally we give in and develop a bunch of ideas, assuring Jordan Levin and the WB that we're trying to figure out how to do it. But nothing works. So we've got the head of the network getting more and more upset until he announces that he's going to cancel us if we can't figure it out. We go back and forth, and the window for the pickup by the network has now passed. According to the timeline of our deal, since he doesn't pick us up, that means we're free agents.

It meant we were free to go elsewhere with *Surreal Life*. Right at that opportune moment, the stars aligned. Not missing a beat, Mark—who had a relationship with Brian Graden, then the visionary president of MTV Group—pitched the show (unofficially) as it was, as a celebrity-driven sitcom. The answer was swift and certain. Brian Graden told Mark that he'd love to do *Surreal Life* on VH1. Other than its *Behind the Music*, VH1—part of the Viacom group of cable channels, overseen by MTV executives—had yet to find content that connected to a loyal audience.

After Mark reported back to me, I said, "Damn. Let's do it."

But when we told the agent at UTA who had made the deal for us at the WB, he warned us in no uncertain terms, "You will destroy your careers in this town. You guys have got to wait until you're canceled. You're not canceled."

Mark and I were stuck. We weren't canceled, but we weren't picked up. So what were we doing? Stuck in limbo?

To Mark's credit, he went back to the agent and said we definitely wanted to go to Brian Graden and take the show to VH1. We also told the WB that we were going to leave. At that point, our champion, Keith Cox, made a plea for us to stay, saying, "Don't leave. Just give me time. I'm going to get you guys picked up."

The UTA agent repeated his last warning: "Do not do this. If you guys do this, it's career suicide. You can't walk out on the president of the WB when you haven't been canceled."

But, again, we hadn't been picked up either. My position, strengthened by my instinct, was that despite Keith Cox's sincere intent to get us picked up, Jordan Levin was never going to let him and would hold us hostage, and we would be dead in the water. The time had come to bet on myself, as always, and not operate out of fear. "Let's go to VH1 now," I said to Mark. As for all the voices who told us we'd never work again in this town, I just said, "Time will tell. I'm willing to take the risk." Mark was with me 100 percent.

The decision-making process was a key moment for me in owning my own success. There was no way to predict what would happen after we made the move. But I knew that this way, I would have no regrets.

It was insanely risky. But it paid off a thousand times over.

Brian Graden was indeed the ideal executive for the *Surreal Life* and for me and Mark. Everything about our new home was ideal. The timing was perfect, given the fact that VH1 needed attention-worthy content. VH1 was a cable network that was a virtual clean slate, with nothing on it yet to offer a brand recognition. Ours was just the right type of show to give the network what it didn't have. Plus VH1 had endless hours of real estate for scheduling. Without an already predetermined audience, we had the creative opportunity to build an audience of our own.

Sure enough, *Surreal Life*'s next season on VH1 was our magical breakout year, bringing together the most unlikely celebrity family yet: Brigitte Nielsen, Flavor Flav, Charo, Dave Coulier, Jordan Knight (from New Kids on the Block), and our ingenue, Ryan Starr, a reality contestant from *American Idol*. Mark and I could have written an entire hilarious book together on this cast alone.

We went on to do several more seasons of *Surreal Life* over the next three years, along with spin-offs and specials and the development of our brand that led to a whole host of other original unscripted series and that all told would amount to more than five hundred episodes of hit television. At one point, in just a span of one season, we were producing 130 hours of TV per week, just for VH1, one buyer. Unprecedented, unheard-of.

Some could say we put VH1 on the map. You could say they put us on the map too. It was the reality that dreams are made of. We had delivered. And there was so much more to come.

Along with the lessons pointed out already, I'll add that you don't have to reinvent the game to create opportunity and own the success that results. Just don't play it safe. Be bold, be original. Trust your instincts on developing your own brand. You can break the rules if what you have to offer is something you believe worth fighting for. Don't try to fake it until you make it. Own your success by making the commitment to deliver on the promise to yourself to make your dream a reality.

eight

Celebreality

*"Celebreality" is a portmanteau combining the words "celebrity"
and "reality" and is generally used to describe reality TV shows
in which celebrities participate as subjects. The term appears
to have been coined by Michael Gross, writing for The Toronto
Star on May 12, 1991. . . . "It is Kathy Bates and Whoopi Goldberg,
not Kim Basinger and Michelle Pfeiffer. It is Jeremy Irons in black
tie and the sneakers he says keep his feet on the ground. . . .
The new celebrities are human first, famous second."*

—Background for VH1's 2005 popularizing
the term "Celebreality," Wikipedia

We've already begun to look at the business principle that
*challenges you to create opportunities by changing and adapting
the game,* a point we're going to continue to explore here. In tech and
business circles, we hear so often about the need to encourage dis-
rupters who are willing to change and adapt the game. And while I
do agree, it's also important to discriminate between disruption for
disruption's sake and disruption that leads to problem solving and
empowering everyone on the team.

You may not have a literal team. But maybe you have stakeholders
who are invested in your success—your clients, your employers or
employees, your partners, your family, your friends, your community.

Your social media communities count as long as they cheer for *your* dreams. Building that team support, whether it's personal or professional, whether it's gaining followers, getting your content shared, or becoming a celebrity at something, can be an essential part of creating opportunities and of being an effective game changer.

In communicating with your team and your other stakeholders, it's also important to identify what it is that you're offering to the marketplace, what makes it different, and what makes it relevant. Those are lessons I learned quickly as the third season of *Surreal Life* took off, and we began to seriously change the game of the unscripted field.

AUTHENTICITY RULES

Authenticity is an overlooked commodity in the marketplace these days. Maybe it's because we spend so much time in a virtual world that when an experience is real and true, we're drawn to it even more. As entertainment mogul and founder of Motown Berry Gordy used to say, "The truth is a hit"—aka *Motivation Lesson #11.*

That's how I explain what happened after we arrived at VH1, and the chemistry of the cast that very next season struck such a chord with the audience, before we could say "Yeaaaaah, boyeeee" we had two more series spin-offs ready to roll. The monumental success of the third season was unexpected, fast, and amazing. Everything began to move at warp speed. Even with crews of almost a hundred production people soon to be working on these various shows for us, the next five years would make my previous workload look like child's play.

Everyone wanted to know what the secret was. My answer would go back to authenticity in ideas and execution and the development of compelling story lines. Not all the ideas worked. What did work, consistently and powerfully, was the draw of casting a pool of people on television that had not been on TV before as we presented them. Conventional marketing wisdom is to develop content for a specific audience demographic. My approach is somewhat different. I develop content that taps into the chemistry and unique appeal of a casting pool first and in turn galvanizes that corresponding audience. Celebreality flourished, thanks to an untapped casting pool begging to be used and thanks to an audience we attracted that was as diverse as our cast, as well as multicultural, also younger and more urban (as VH1 would say), culturally connected, and, above all, authentic.

Between my 51 Pictures and Mark Cronin's Mindless Entertainment—aka 51 Minds—we produced content that covered those bases well and built that authentic element as part of the comedy. The humor worked because it was real. If you watched a show like *The Bachelor*, for example, the set of a date would be dreamlike, with a sparkle filter and candles flickering and the girl dressed in a flowing gown descending the spiral staircase to the sound of classical music. I would always say, "Who really goes on dates like that?"

In my community and within the communities of a lot of our audience, the guy goes to the girl's apartment to pick her up and her baby sister runs across the room in droopy diapers, her father interrogates the guy, and her mother sizes him up. We would go on dates to eat at the Olive Garden. On *The Bachelor*, he'd take his date to an empty five-star restaurant where the entire waitstaff catered to the two of them. On our dating shows, we'd go to restaurants where there were other people. The cast members were in real places, surrounded by real people. We didn't sanitize our story lines. The prospective dates for our singles had baggage; they had exes, sometimes kids and parents to take care of. As we used to say, we brought the real world of dating and romance to the "flyover" states.

We served an audience who had been roughed up a bit too or who just needed to laugh. And we did it *consistently* through casting choices that brought together the most unlikely medleys of celebrities. That cast in season three of *Surreal Life* was brimming over with authentic personalities. There was Brigitte Nielsen, the Danish model of Amazonian/Viking stature and ex-wife of Sylvester Stallone, with her wild, sunny personality. And there was Charo, a nonstop quip machine, if you could understand her thick Spanish accent (which we ended up having to subtitle). She said my favorite line of hers as she arrived in the *Surreal Life* mansion: "The first impression I get when I walk into this house is Liberace with diarrhea, 1940."

Then there was the guy who became a game changer for us, first brought to our attention by our intrepid casting director, Laurie Muslow. His name? William Drayton Jr., a former member of Public Enemy, a rap group he founded with Chuck D., who hyped himself as the greatest hype man in the history of hip-hop, who had been known for wearing eccentric hats, oversized glasses, and a clock around his neck when he rapped onstage. Back in his heyday, he had gone by the name of Flavor Flav or just Flav—as he introduced himself to me and Mark when he finally arrived for a meeting with us at our office in Hollywood.

He was late, it turned out, because he didn't have an ID, and security wouldn't let him on the lot. No ID, no driver's license. He didn't even have a wallet. Once we got him through security and into the office, Flav came alive and started bouncing off the walls. Up until that moment, I wasn't sure what to expect, having no idea where he was in his life or his career, which had peaked in the early nineties. But it honestly didn't matter. Flavor Flav was a real-life cartoon character. Mark and I lost it, laughing our heads off. No matter what Flav said, we cracked up—at how he said it, what he said, his phrasing, and his endearing mannerisms.

Then Flav became serious, insisting he play us a song from a new album he was working on. The music was less than so-so. It was horrible. The lyrics went something like "I'm gonna love you. I'm gonna love you har-hard." But we couldn't help being entertained by his innocence, how he genuinely liked listening to his own stuff and just assumed we'd be impressed, how he really believed this was going to be his next big hit record and break him out of his slump.

We loved Flav. He was crazy, real, and a nonstop laugh track. And it turned out that he was basically homeless, living on a friend's couch in Studio City, as broke as could be. He had just gotten out of Rikers Island after serving time for not paying something like four hundred parking tickets. Not his first stint in jail, either. Hence, the stiff sentence for unpaid parking tickets. We never found out how, without a dime, he got himself to LA from New York. But here he was, ready for *Surreal Life*. We made him an offer and gave him a cleanup—or car wash, as we called it—meaning a haircut, a shave, and new clothes. If we had any reservations about him, he overcame them by saying, "You put me on your show, and whatever you ask of me, I'll work harder than anyone else you've got." And we put him on the show.

We were impressed on the first day of shooting when Flav arrived—wearing the new clothes he'd picked out, which were in keeping with what he had always worn—at how insane his energy levels were. He was in his late forties or early fifties by then, but he was like a kid. One of the first things he did was meet Brigitte Nielsen and he was instantly enthralled and attracted to her. The two of them together, just visually, were almost a sight gag. She was like over six feet tall and he's 5'7". The top of his head was barely up to her chest. But Flavor Flav, acting like a man who had a magic touch with women, went right ahead and said something flirty to her. What did she do? She playfully slapped him. And what did he do? Without hesitation, he playfully slapped her right back. At that moment, Brigitte looked at Flav and said, "I love you."

That was just the first day. The two began their special relationship then and there, one that would spark immediate word of mouth for the show and that we could have never seen coming. Flavor Flav was the main player in making *Surreal Life* the major hit that it became that season. He delivered on his promise to work hard and then some. In the process, he always wanted to make sure we were happy with what he was giving us. As his producer on the set, I became the coach on the sidelines of what he treated as the most important game of his life. Every day during breaks, we'd huddle up and talk. He listened to every word when I'd tell him what was working or not working.

Since reality TV is a producer's medium, we wear many hats on the set. My job was to plant the seeds by giving Flav (and others) feedback and suggestions without writing dialogue or directing the action as it was happening. If Flav was coming off overly combative and fighting with another cast member, I'd say, "You know, if you keep picking fights, it makes you look like you're an ass. What would be interesting, and better for you, is if you were able to apologize and maybe talk about making peace. Can you have that conversation?"

Flav would listen and go for it. If I set up a dinner, suggesting, "I'd love for you to gather everyone at the table and then offer to make a toast," he'd take it a step further to make it even bigger, more impactful, and more entertaining. In that instance, he stood up, raised his glass, and proclaimed, "Hear ye, hear ye, hear ye, Flavor Flav has something to say." With everyone's attention, he proceeded to do this lengthy rhyming rap that built to a sincere apology. And it worked.

But then, because Flav had taken it even further, so did I. On the next break, I told him, "That's what I'm talking about! Great job. Don't you want to know if your apology was accepted?" Of course he did. So then, the next step was for him to try to get five minutes alone with the offended party and ask. Bingo. The results were charming, even poignant, always funny.

We knew Flav would connect with a new generation of fans and be a draw for old-school rap/hip-hop fans. But we had no clue that he would merit two new series of his own. The first one, *Strange Love*, came about as a completely off-the-wall idea that I pitched before we wrapped production on that season's *Surreal Life*.

We had all obviously seen the budding relationship between Brigitte and Flavor Flav. We could see that it wasn't only feigned for the cameras. Flav was saying things like "Brigitte, you're my cup of tea," and "I could really fall for you." Brigitte was saying things like "You know why I love spending time with you? Because there's a lot more there underneath what meets the eyes." But even if it was real, the assumption was that it would all come to an end like a summer romance—or a reality TV show fling. That's when I thought how amazing it would be if they had a chance to continue the relationship and see if Flavor Flav could truly land Brigitte Nielsen.

Moving quickly, I had my art department team find a picture of a lavish multitiered wedding cake with a bride-and-groom cake topper on it. Then we changed the topper by photoshopping a picture of Flav's head on the groom in the tuxedo and Brigitte's head on the bride dressed in a wedding gown. We made the groom look really short and the bride really tall. Then I take the picture and carry it into the office of VH1 executive Jeff Olde—recently brought on board by Brian to oversee our projects (and to become VH1's senior vice president of series production and programming)—and I say, "Flavor Flav tries to get Brigitte Nielsen to marry him in two weeks, as he follows her around the world."

Oh, man, I'm not sure how long the laughter went on after that. All I know is that they bought the show *Strange Love* in the room that same day and ordered ten episodes (one hour each) to begin shooting in Italy (where Brigitte lived at the time) as soon as possible. So not only were we now gearing up for season four of *Surreal Life*, but we had a second series to make happen.

Not enough can be said about the role that Brian Graden played in championing our creative stamp. A pop culture guru, he is a genius and a competitor in this business who took a chance on our invention of reality sitcom and celebreality all the way to the top, ultimately giving VH1 a brand identity and a massive following. Brian was one of the few executives I encountered at his level who believed, first and foremost, in talent—not just in front of the camera but, perhaps even more, behind it. Jeff Olde was similar to Brian in terms of executive temperament, vision, and belief in talent. Jeff was a massive contributor to all our shows. And his biggest contribution was empowering my partner, Mark, and me to pursue our authentic passions—our comedy, our story lines, and our characters. Jeff supported us 100 percent, as was the case when he joined the team as we traveled to Milan to shoot *Strange Love.*

Brian and Jeff were game changers in their own right and taught me so much about executive leadership when it came to problem solving at the higher levels.

Ever since the third season of *Surreal Life* had aired and fans had gone nuts for the show, we'd watched constant commentary on Internet message boards (before Twitter, et cetera) that focused on the relationship between Flavor Flav and Brigitte Nielsen. In fact, for a long time afterward, wherever I went, the number one question asked of me was "Was Flav's pursuit of Brigitte real?"

My answer? It's always been the same. It was 100 percent real for Flavor Flav. It was not real for Brigitte Nielsen. But we didn't know that at the time. Not until we arrived to prep our shoot at her house in Milan did we have our first clue.

We were shocked to find that she had her live-in fiancé in the house. Brigitte had no qualms introducing this younger European handsome dude as such and then saying, "OK, so what are we going to shoot?"

I had to be the bearer of bad news that, given this revelation, the show was probably not going to happen. It wasn't the first and certainly not the last time that I'd be challenged to think of a way to salvage an opportunity about to go up in flames. To be clear, sometimes flameouts can't be salvaged. Nor should you try to make something good out of circumstances that have gone sour when someone has misrepresented themselves. But whatever your position may be as an executive or leader, you have to expect some challenges to be thrown at you, especially with major projects. And it's your job to adapt to problems as they occur and not be flustered or thrown. As you stay calm and focus on the big picture, solutions will begin to materialize. A reaction to avoid is the one where you try to undo what's happened. That's not real. Yes, by letting go of what was supposed to happen, you can make a change or even an improvement toward a better outcome. You can choose to pivot—as people say when things really aren't going well—to a new direction. Sometimes you have to cut your losses before they deepen. Above all, you can't spin it.

Telling her the truth, I said, "Brigitte, this is not going to work. We are shooting a show about you and Flav—it has to be real."

"Real? Of course it's real."

"No, Flavor Flav is coming here to hopefully be with you and start a relationship with you."

Brigitte Nielsen then looked at me as if I was insane and said, "Are you kidding me? I have a fiancé. Why would I be with Flav?"

Holy shit! That was even worse. But instead of just canceling everything, I went to plan B to buy some time by finding somewhere else to shoot. Obviously, we couldn't stay at her place or in Milan. Instead, we'd have to rent a villa somewhere and pretend like it was hers. Why? For there to be a semblance of reality, Flav had to at least think he was coming to her house to court her. We found a villa that was on Lake Como in the Italian Alps, part of the Bellagio, and all I could do was encourage Brigitte to play along until I figured it out. The whole premise had been blown, and I was still trying to figure out if something real, though unlikely, could possibly happen.

This was not sitcom reality, made all the more apparent when Flav arrived and we started shooting. How ironic. We were in one of the most romantic settings in the world, but there wasn't much connection at all—because it wasn't real for Brigitte.

The shoot had been scheduled to go on for twenty to twenty-five days. Shortly after getting started, two days along, Jeff Olde from VH1 catches up with us at the villa on Lake Como. He watches from the control center on the monitors as we're all observing the misfire. Just not happening.

Jeff watches, takes notes, and says little. After a few hours, he comes to me and Mark and says that he's going to step out and look around the town. We nod and then he says, "This is off, right?" We admit that it is. Then he asks the obvious—why it's not looking like the way we described how it was going to be.

We have to tell him the truth—that we just learned Brigitte has a fiancé and probably duped us to book the show. And yes, there's no real connection even though we were sure there was at one point.

He takes all this in and then says he now has a grasp of the situation. He suggests that Mark and I will have to figure out what we want to do. He then hands us a yellow Post-it note that says, "Special or nothing." That's his recommendation—to shut this ten-episode series down right now and turn the project into a really good two-hour special about Flav and Brigitte out on the town in Milan for a good time and some laughs. Or pack up and go home. But before making the final say, he goes on, "You guys decide. You've got to find out if there's really something there or not." We agree to do that and meet in the morning to let him know how to proceed.

We take a break, set up lodging for the crew for the night, and then book a hotel for ourselves, Mark Cronin, Ben Samek, and me. It's across the lake from the villa, as that's all we can find. In this interval, I admit to the two of them, "It's up to Flav, I guess." We talk about it further and realize that there's not much else to do. We can't make Brigitte want to be with Flavor Flav romantically if that's not what she wants.

Then I go back to the set and shut the show down for the night. I take all the cameras out of the room and tell Brigitte and Flav that it isn't going well and we don't know why but it's up to them to figure it out. Before I leave, I have a private word with Flav, like a coach with his most valued team member. "Hey, man, you have one night. You have one night to see if she's going to fall for you. You have one night to make it happen—for her to be with you. I'll come talk to you in the morning."

I will never forget how despondent Mark, Ben, and I were as we crossed the lake to our hotel at sunset. The backdrop to that moment was unbelievably beautiful, and we couldn't enjoy it. This was our life, our work, the reality of our dreams come true, right? And we were about to lose this series, which had so much promise. You could not have chosen a more picturesque setting in the world, and we were completely miserable.

The next morning we got up, crossed back across the lake to the villa, and knocked on the door. Nobody answered. We knocked again. Nothing. Finally, just before we were about to leave, the door opened, and it was Flavor Flav in a robe, his usual buoyant self and he led us to Brigitte Nielsen—who was still in bed. He went back and took her hand and she told us, "I love this man. I want to be with this guy."

It was as real as real can get. That was it. We reported to Jeff Olde, he gave us the green light, and we shot the rest of the series. None of us asked what happened. Brigitte never knew that we almost canceled the show. My hunch is that Flav wooed her and worked his magic, they made love, and that was it. She wanted to be with him.

They had a real romance. Brigitte fell in love with Flav. For real. The chemistry we had seen on the show wasn't faked or temporary. It was authentic. It was a wild ride. Once Brigitte told Flav about her fiancé, we were able to bring him in as part of the conflict and later edit those scenes to come before the Lake Como romance really kicked off. By the time we'd finished in Italy and followed the couple to New York for a huge Public Enemy concert, Brigitte had chosen Flav over the other guy.

At the end of the season, after lots of ups and downs, Flav was close to convincing Brigitte to move to Las Vegas to have a child with him. Great cliff-hanger, right? Nobody had ever seen anything like it. The two were just so improbable together. And they might have even lasted another season or made it as an actual married couple, but something happened in the months when we were editing the show to entice Brigitte to go back to her fiancé after all.

The details were murky, but a lot of this drama was playing out off camera during that time. In fact, when the show began to air, their relationship was more or less over. *Strange Love* was already a huge hit so, to keep it real, I quickly shot a new ending to acknowledge the breakup, and accepted that the one season was going to be it for this baby.

The rewards of authenticity go far beyond show business and apply to everyone. When you find your authentic voice, people tend to listen. When you speak and act based on a clear point of view—rather than being a yes person or a copycat—you create a platform from which to create other opportunities.

THINK LIKE A CELEBRITY

When you pause to consider where most dreams begin, usually you'll note that most start when you're young with that universal longing for fame and fortune—not necessarily in that order. Maybe your first dream starts with the desire to do something meaningful with your life in a way that makes you special. And then there's the longing to love and be loved. Stars who captivate our imagination appear to be living the dream we wish we could have. Of course, the myth is that celebrities get to have all the money, fame, and love they want, right? That's why an unscripted story line that centers on a pop culture icon's tumultuous, funny, and even dysfunctional search for love can be so watchable—because we feel better knowing they have the same struggles we do. That's why, once we wrapped *Strange Love*, we knew it was not the end of the inimitable Flav on VH1. And it wasn't the end of us creating series about the famous and not so famous in their search for love or money or, yes, fame.

Celebreality took off not only as it humanized the stars we may have once put up on a pedestal, but it also helped us everyday humans feel a little bit more like celebrities ourselves.

Along these lines, my feeling is that we can all think more like pop culture icons by expecting that we can make our own dreams come true. The operative word is "expectation." Celebrities usually expect to make the most of every opportunity. Why shouldn't you too?

My way of expecting success after we moved on from *Strange Love* was to double-down on the search for more opportunities in the form of good ideas. Where could I expect them to come from? Well, the best ideas don't come out of thin air—as every entrepreneur, executive, innovator, and thought leader should know. The best ideas, including the innovation of this genre called Celebreality, come from paying attention, from listening and watching, and from being constantly curious. If you want to be a creative developer of great ideas, become a fan of other creators' ideas. Learn what makes ideas marketable and successful by being a consumer of developed content. As you learn to tune your instincts to be able to hear an idea's potential when it first comes across your radar, then bring in your other senses to gather stories, wisdom, humor, insights, and characters that are all in abundance around you. Think like a celebrity idea gatherer and expect to find your gold.

You can also follow the impact of ideas and stories on your consumer or end user to find out what does and doesn't work in your presentations. For example, what caught my attention as soon as *Strange Love* went off the air was how the online traffic for those message boards just blew up. Women and men wanted Flavor Flav to know they were with him, posting heartfelt messages like "Forget her, Flav!" and "You're better than the other guy, Flav!" Tens of thousands of fans—total strangers—became invested in his love life. Crazy!

Flav took it hard. He came to see me, and as he sat in my office, just the two of us, man to man, he poured out his heart. I listened and let him vent. He kept repeating the fact that we all knew: "It's over. It's really over." Boy meets girl; boy gets girl; boy loses girl. He sounded like a man who had only found love once in his life.

Finally, I stopped him and said, "Hey, man, you're gonna be fine.

You're gonna find the right girl, Flav." How could I convince him? Then it dawned on me! This was the most obvious idea that would have never come to me if I hadn't been sitting there listening to his love troubles. "Not only are you gonna find the right girl, Flav," I went on, "but, in fact, you know what? You know what's crazy? Have you ever seen *The Bachelor*, Flav?"

"No." He shrugged, all downcast.

"Dude, I'm gonna find you a girlfriend. You're going to be *The Bachelor*!" He had no concept of what I meant, so I explained that the show was about a guy who gets to meet all of these women and he gets to be with the hottest girl.

Flav could only give me a dubious look and say, "Word? C'mon, Cris. You know no girl's gonna pick me."

"No, no, no, Flav, *you* are the bachelor. You do the picking."

"Word?"

Absolutely, I promised him. I pitched it to him, calling it "The Black-chelor" and proposed the Flavor Flav version of the Big Kahuna of all dating shows—twenty girls, plus a competition to get Flav to pick one of them, with eliminations and everything.

Mark Cronin loved it too and this time, without rushing, we put our time into developing the format and getting it ready to pitch to VH1. Only this time, they didn't green-light the series right away. What very few people know is that we quietly shot a pilot over one weekend where we hired eight young women to actually vie for Flav's approval. We had to do the pilot after the first question out of the mouth of someone at VH1 was "Who would want to date Flavor Flav?"

Our pilot answered that question. It was bawdy and funny, and Flav was the maestro, the ultimate hype man for why he could be an eligible bachelor. We did setups with dates and little contests. It worked. We took in the tape and VH1 green-lit the series. We didn't end up calling it "The Black-chelor." Everyone thought that was offensive. It was, of course, and intentionally so. But we recognized that we were pushing the envelope and being as politically incorrect as we could be. Besides it was satire. But we settled on *Flavor of Love*.

We were greatly criticized for incorrectness. Mark and I took a lot of flak, with our peers asking us, "Why would you dress him like a jester and feed him fried chicken and play on stereotypes?" The truth is we let Flav be Flav. We never asked him to wear anything other than what he picked out and how he dressed himself. We tried to feed him different things not because we had issues with fried chicken but just for variety. He ate what he ate. In fact, later on, he would open up a fried-chicken restaurant as an opportunity to continue to grow his career and finances. As a real-life cartoon character and pop culture icon, Flavor Flav didn't need any enhancement. In building our episodes, we did spend time with him in story development so that we could use his quirks, like giving all the contestants nicknames—which became iconic pieces of pop culture. There was Smiley, Black, Serious, Hoopz, and Deelishis. To name a few. Many of the contestants would emerge with renown and reality shows of their own. Yes, our opportunities gave birth to other opportunities.

Mark Cronin was a mastermind at coming up with hilarious props for the episode devices. Short of including a rubber chicken, we went all out. OK, we might have actually used a rubber chicken at one point. There was the time, for example, when Flav was going to have a lobster dinner (Mark's idea) and then, pushing it to the limit, Mark had the idea of finding, literally, a forty-five-pound lobster. So there was Flav, who was 135 pounds, only ninety pounds heavier than the lobster!

Then, when the butler—the white butler Flav could never understand—delivered the lobster to the table, claws sticking out and nobody to crack the shell, it was a comedy sketch in the making. We didn't comment on it or prep anyone. Flav would react, and it would be brilliant.

Flavor of Love would go on to have three seasons. It was an entertainment phenomenon. The first episode drew some five hundred thousand viewers. That was abysmal. But it kept growing exponentially with every week, and nine million people watched the finale the first season. The second season finale was the highest-rated nonsports television event on cable for all of 2006. We honored our audience just as celebrities pay attention to their fans by developing content that was clearly resonating as our successes grew.

We had some misses, for sure, but we were also like the party that was open to whoever wanted to hang out and laugh with us. Celebreality was a gift that kept on giving, and I have to give credit to the celebrities who helped define the genre. We didn't make them or remake them. The power of *Surreal Life* and all of our shows was that we were able to reintroduce these pop culture icons to a whole new audience. Flavor Flav was the prime example. At one point, I sat down and watched these old documentaries on Flav and Public Enemy. Nothing had changed. Everything was the same: his expressions, the clock he wore, the way he dressed, the corny but funny jokes. Nothing had changed from back in the day. Just everybody missed it or forgot it.

Besides reintroducing celebrities to a new audience, celebreality was a new way to make a living for a whole hell of a lot of folks we cast. Look at Flav. When he came to us, he hadn't worked in a while and didn't seem to have any prospects. In three years, he was not only a household name—getting his debts squared away—but he was driving a mother ship of a platform on which to look for love. The irony of all ironies is that he ended up not marrying any of the winners of *Flavor of Love*. He apparently had embraced his persona as a bachelor. Or black-chelor.

Flav's sayings became part of the lexicon. He was impersonated on *Saturday Night Live*. He had high school kids who weren't even born when he was in his prime suddenly walking around, doing lines like "Flavah Flaaaaav!" and "Yeaehhh, boyeee!" He had merchandising with his clocks and glasses. *Flavor of Love* was a monster viral hit before that was a thing. It changed pop culture. Flav reclaimed his image and brand and was back again, able to create the reality of his dreams like all his fans.

The same thing happened for other celebrities who relaunched their careers from *Surreal Life*, as well as from shows produced by others becoming hip to celebreality. We still owned our niche, but I couldn't ignore that we had quickly gone from almost not selling our crazy idea that became *Surreal Life* to within a few years having everybody and anybody trying to get in on the celebreality game. We saw the rapid change in the reaction to our casting efforts.

From the start, casting had become a sport to Mark Cronin and me. We loved the chase and the challenge of going after celebrities who still wouldn't give us the time of day. For example, we weren't well received by the management for Verne Troyer (Mini-Me from the Austin Powers movies). Like him they were also little people who yelled at us about exploiting and mocking them, but ultimately they said yes. And he was hilarious on the show. We went to Christopher Knight—formerly known as Peter Brady from *The Brady Bunch*—and implored him to come on *Surreal Life*. Our pitch to him was that if he did the show, thereafter he would only be known as Christopher Knight. He only agreed at the last minute. Sure enough, he did the show and reclaimed his true identity, and no one has called him Peter Brady ever since. Well, not quite. We did another show for him and Adrianne Curry, winner of *America's Next Top Model*, after the two of them met and developed a romance on *Surreal Life*. Their show followed the romantic development of their relationship and was called *My Fair Brady*. They did get married as a result of the show, although they would later divorce. But he was known either way as Christopher Knight.

We made casting mistakes. For our fifth season of *Surreal Life*, Brian Graden decided that the best celeb we could hire would be José Canseco. He was in the news, readying to testify in front of Congress about steroid use in baseball—the first player to talk and not well-loved in sports circles. Mark and I met with him and saw right away that he would be holy hell on the set. He wasn't a nice guy, and that was putting it mildly. His reputation was bad, and his manners were even worse.

Brian and the VH1 team didn't care. We went back and forth. Their point was that there was going to be a groundswell of attention, and everyone would tune in, even if Canseco was an asshole on the show. They held the strings on this one, and José Canseco came on board as one of the highest-paid cast members we ever had. He was a pain from start to wrap and not worth it ratings-wise either.

Other than a few misses, though, we continued to attract pop culture figures who cared about making the show a success for everyone. Most of our casting choices were deliberate, but every now and then we stumbled onto someone perfect we hadn't even considered. That happened toward the end of *Flavor of Love*'s three-season run when we decided to build a new *of Love* show; as opposed to a hip-hop dating show, we wanted to try the rock 'n' roll version.

We loved the idea and came up with Tommy Lee of Mötley Crüe, who had previously been married to Pamela Anderson. We almost closed the deal with Tommy Lee, but then it fell through. We met with all kinds of rockers, but nobody had it all. We were going nowhere until a suggestion came up for Bret Michaels from Poison. He seemed fine from afar, but it wasn't until he walked in for our meeting that I saw what a star he could be. He was hard-core rock 'n' roll and also incredibly articulate. More than anything, it was apparent right off the bat that Bret Michaels had a fantastic sense of humor.

One moment, Bret was like a smart businessman and regular guy. The next, he was this edgy rocker from Poison. We had found our celebrity for *Rock of Love*. Then we had to figure out the story line. Unlike Flav, who was looking for true love, Bret was a ladies' man— by any account and in true rock 'n' roll fashion—who probably had no desire to end up with any one woman. But for the show, and we pushed this, the premise was that he needed to settle down now. And we were going to find him sixteen candidates so that he could choose the right one for him.

Everything was a go. Then I noticed a pattern that started to occur on the first day of shooting as I watched from the control room. Each time a girl was introduced, Bret was charming, and he would go up and say, "Hey, what's your name? Where are you from?" And she'd answer, give her name, and say, perhaps, "Florida."

Bret would say, "Oh, Florida's great." Then he'd add that he knew that because he had played such and such an arena in Jacksonville. Each time he met a girl and she told him where she was from, he would name the arena in her town, and that was it. And then he would move on.

There was no banter, no flirtation. There was this weird awkwardness.

So I call for a time-out and pull Bret aside, and I say, "Hey, is everything OK?"

"Yeah, it's great, it's great. Everything's good for you? Is it going well?"

Oh, no, he thinks it's going well—I think. Then I say, breaking the bad news to him, "Not really, Bret. It's not actually. I know you're not married, but you've been around. I mean, you like girls, right?" He gives me an offended look, so I explain, "It's just it looks like you're uncomfortable. But you've been around a lot of women?"

He assures me that, of course, he has been around a lot of women.

"Great! We need to watch you do your thing. Just think like you're on a date with these girls."

Then Bret Michaels says, "I haven't been on a date since I was thirteen years old." He pauses and shrugs, confiding, "Since I was sixteen, I'd meet a girl, I'd get laid, and I'd probably never talk to them again. I've been doing that for the last twenty-five years."

Thus began my tutorial for Bret in how to talk to a woman, how to be curious about where they were from, how many siblings they had, what their hobbies were. And at some point he was going to have to sit down and have a meal with them on a date. He was incredulous. "Yeah," I said, "you have to date them, take them out for a meal and a night on the town." It was a foreign concept to him.

We couldn't let that backstory be part of the show because even with the crude comedy, we tried not to fully alienate women in the audience. When it came to storytelling on these dating shows, celebrities and all, I had to keep reminding the story team and our producers that nothing was more important than watching a guy or a girl fall in love or fight for love in the end. No matter how crazy the antics became, we couldn't lose sight of or take the focus off what made viewers tune in to watch—the act of falling in love, the emotion, the attraction, and the problems. We were doing a comedy, yes, but it was a romantic comedy and still a love story in the end.

Thankfully, Bret Michaels was a quick study. He became a dating pro. I was his love guru, and he went to work. To be on the safe side, I set him up with an earpiece in his ear so I could feed him questions to ask on his dates. "What do you do for a living?" "What's your favorite movie?" "Do you like to dance?" This was stuff I doubt he cared about at all. But he took it all the way.

Was it pure reality? No. But something winning happened in front of the cameras. We did it for three seasons, and he became the ideal date. His only complaint was eating in all the restaurants. He was healthy and couldn't eat all that stuff, so he would have to fake the eating. Other times, he didn't fake it and got mad that he was gaining weight. Yep, dating can be fattening.

Rock of Love was another phenomenal hit. After three seasons of the same bachelor trying to find love, I realized that we had come to the point that no one cared if he found the right woman or not. They were just entertained by the show. They loved Bret Michaels too and had this new intimate connection to him that elevated his profile all the more. Just like Flav, he was the only star who could have done his show justice as he did.

Today, as I recall these stories and look back to the formative years of celebreality and all the events that set it into orbit, I'm most amazed at how the definition of stardom has changed since then. In Hollywood, if you ask anyone the difference between Angelina Jolie and Kim Kardashian, that's a joke. One's a bona fide actress and star, and the other boasts a sex tape and a reality show. But in most places outside of Hollywood, Kim Kardashian might be a bigger star. That is also the nature of tabloid excitement over Kim and Kanye and the ability we have now for celebrities to harness social media to become more famous just for being famous.

Having a reality show these days is not only acceptable but sometimes enviable. It should be noted that the Kardashians and all the housewives and the Snookis, they didn't just grab attention because they had the means of getting a show. There's something about them that made them special, that touched a nerve. I don't know all the celebreality stars who are dominating different forms of media these days. But I believe they all have that special something and that their dream was to be famous and they expected success and made it a reality. You don't become a multimillion-dollar brand without having something different to offer. You don't reach that level without vision and a plan to play the game your way.

I'm proud of the opportunities that celebreality has created. Look at how these celebrities have sought to own their success by taking advantage of a reality-show platform. They have multimillion-dollar businesses. They have book deals and recording contracts, endorsements, and production companies.

They don't apologize for those opportunities. They run with them and bet on themselves. And, something that I began to recognize in this explosive expansion of my dream, and that you can borrow for your motivation, they continually lift the bar and reach higher—continuing to hustle tomorrow more than today.

nine

Every Day I'm Hustling: *The Art and Business of Storytelling*

Stories constitute the single most powerful weapon in a leader's arsenal.

—Dr. Howard Gardner,
author, professor, Harvard University

Whenever I'm asked about how to survive in a tumultuous arena like the entertainment industry, the answer goes back to how I grew up and learned to outhustle and outwork the competition. Even as the head of my own company or running a division of a global corporation, I still know that in order for us to be trailblazers—living the *principle that you have to create your own rules in order to conquer your turf*—hustle is still the name of the game. You don't stop hustling because you've reached a certain level of success. You do raise the stakes for yourself so that you remain relevant.

In my business, I do that by continuing to be an avid consumer of stories—listening, reading, watching, and paying attention to what's out there. Stories in all forms are an endless source of fascination to me. In fact, as much as I love working in the field of television, what I love most is being a practitioner in both the art and commerce of storytelling.

Here in the twenty-first century, at a time when ideas are considered the number one currency of the marketplace, I believe that everyone—no matter what your hustle—can benefit from understanding how ideas are communicated through stories.

THE STORYTELLER IN YOU

Even if you don't work in a field like the entertainment industry that relies on storytelling as its main offering, everyone needs to command the basics of marketing—which is nothing more than storytelling. So, whether you're marketing yourself, your business, a project, an event, or a cause, honing your storytelling skills will be to your advantage. Consider the points made by Hollywood producer Peter Guber in *HR Magazine* in 2008:

> *The ability to articulate your story or that of your company is crucial to almost every phase of enterprise management. A great salesperson knows how to tell a story in which the product is the hero. An effective CEO uses an emotional narrative about the company's mission to attract investors and partners, to set lofty goals, and to inspire employees. Sometimes a well-crafted story can even transform a seemingly hopeless situation into an unexpected triumph.*

I believe there is a natural storyteller in each of us. Storytelling is in our human DNA. Think about the cavemen creating stories by drawing on a wall. Think about ancient religions and the stories employed to explain the universe. Think about the Bible. For as long as the human race has been on this planet, we've been figuring out different ways to tell stories. We tell stories to connect to one another and to our ancestors, even though the modes of storytelling have evolved dramatically over time.

As a lifelong learner—not to mention as the son of two educators—I am an ongoing student of how stories are shaped and how they shape the public's imagination. From the basics of how to develop story structure with beginnings, middles, and ends, to the nuances of story archetypes, I've observed storytelling in everything. It's in our memories, in advertising, in books, movies, music, pictures, cartoons, YouTube videos, blogs, politics, public speaking, and stand-up comedy. We look at art and our brains immediately ask—*What story does it tell?* We meet someone and ask—*What's your story?*

Some people are naturally great storytellers. They understand timing, surprise, suspense, and how to read a room. They know how to hook you and not let you go. They know when to be understated, when to be intense, and when to be over-the-top. The best jokes are stories. The best sales pitches are stories. If you listen to the best salespeople, you don't even know they are selling you. They're just telling you a story. Often, whenever you sell anything, you're really selling yourself. So the story you tell about yourself may be the difference between making the sale or not.

Let's take the classic job-interview setting. In seeking an entry-level job or looking to change career paths, what story you tell about yourself will no doubt vary depending on who is doing the hiring and what that person is looking for. Even though your résumé should tell a story about your career experience, I will let you know that only 5 percent of interviewees I've met get hired based on the résumé. The other 95 percent who get hired are those who can answer the questions that tell me who you are—with examples and story illustrations.

When I conduct an interview, the three storytelling skills I like to see are *enthusiasm, engagement,* and *focus.* Enthusiasm as a storyteller and communicator reveals your interests and your passion. If you're just making small talk, that's not as compelling as if you're talking about how much you learned from a tough challenge or why you love coming from a small town. Enthusiasm—or passion—gives you an aura of confidence and presence. Always start with enthusiasm. Engagement can be twofold. It's how you listen and adapt to questions being asked of you and how you respond with your own level of curiosity. Engagement also shows your authentic point of view. Focus as a storyteller helps you stay concise while sticking to a theme or message. What you choose to focus on when you talk about yourself also tells a story about your internal motivator—what drives you. Are you more interested in the money, perks and hours, or the opportunity to continue on a path that you care deeply about?

Of course, if you want to know what kind of storytelling I like to hear from candidates for employment in my business, you can always grab my interest when you let me know how you consume stories regularly. How much TV do you watch? What shows do you like? Why? Why do you think they work or not? The best stories tell me about where you grew up, about your background, even about influential storytellers in your upbringing and education. What's your connection to culture? I'm looking to find out what are the things you believe or don't believe in terms of the future of television as an art form. Through the course of the interview I'll look for the value you might bring to our company in terms of reading, writing, and storytelling. And key to your story is to let me know where you look for your dream to take you. What is your ambition? What's your long game in this business?

The interviews that fall short for me are the sort of shotgun conversations where you come in and are all over the place. In the entertainment industry, shotgun storytelling might go something like this: "My goals? Well, I like directing. I'm good at it. But I've written some things, nothing that you've probably heard of, although writing is a strength. So is producing. At my last job, I worked closely with a producer, and I would consider producing."

That person has just come in and named all the jobs in the entertainment business. I've also had candidates say things, in order to qualify for a job, that weren't true about their interests and experience. First of all, the truth usually has a way of rising to the surface. Second, the truth makes for a winning story.

If you are interviewing for a job in research, say, but your dream is to produce documentary features, it's refreshing for you to be up front about your vision going forward. If you can get excited about doing the job being offered as a means to your future goals, it's a win-win. Ambition is golden—especially with a work ethic to back it up. When I meet with job candidates who entertain and inspire me with stories about where they come from, where they are today, and where they envision themselves going forward, I can't help but want to be part of that journey.

Storytelling is powerful not only in selling or communicating to others but also in how you inspire and motivate yourself. The story you tell yourself about the results of your hard work—good or bad—is the one that determines whether you ultimately own your own success. If you blame others or your industry for not giving you a break, that is not ownership. By the same token, if you are successful at something, you can claim it and also be willing to acknowledge the contributions of others.

Storytelling gives you the power to make sense of your struggles and your failures. After all, the road to success is littered with stories of icons who failed miserably early in their journeys, only to roar back to life in incredibly successful incarnations. Oprah was once told she was unfit for TV. Steve Jobs got fired from his own company. We all know how those stories wound up.

Individuals who own their success, no matter where they are in their journey, are among the first to share the ups *and* the downs with others. They're willing to share some of the credit for their success with others and share guidance with others so they too can learn how it might be done. And one of the most powerful ways to share success is to be willing to share your story—to say, *Hey, I can do this. Here's how I did it and how you can be successful too.*

Not everyone gets this. In listening to accounts from some of my successful peers, I sometimes hear that they don't really own their success. In the world of reality television, for example, there are producers and executives who are among the first to downplay and disparage the very shows that made them the richest—by apologizing for selling the stories that gave them their success. You can't do that. You can't be in the hustle and then look down at the hustle at the same time.

Let me encourage you to own all parts of your story. As you embrace your inner storyteller, you own your success, in part, by putting perceived failures into the context of lessons learned for overcoming the odds. Instead of telling the story of how you took a risk that didn't pan out, you can follow the story line that shows how you learned what you needed to know for the next go-around. The story of your success will be all the more rewarding if you choose to own the mistakes, disappointments and losses that you overcame.

My suggestion is that when you employ vision to see where you're going, why not ask yourself what success story you'd like to tell others once you get there? The only limits are those of your imagination.

SO YOU THINK YOU CAN PITCH

Every sales and marketing person should know the fundamentals of pitching. Every entrepreneur should be able to pitch—no, not necessarily at TV-show pitching level, but at least enough to tell a succinct story of what you're building. Even if your area of interest doesn't require you to pitch, you would still do well to learn some of the tricks of the trade. If you're good at pitching, you can always get better. In fact, those of us who pitch stories for a living are always upping our game.

In the everyday hustle of pitching stories for what I do, there is no reason to separate the art from the business. A good story sells itself. To make sure I've got a good story before I even develop the pitch, I like to study the storytelling that has worked in classic television episodes or in hit movies. Those archetypes jump out at you. They begin with a premise or a promise, a question or a quest that keeps you on the edge of your seat as you wait to find out what's going to happen next and how it's going to all turn out in the end. My challenge then is to translate those elements into a reality television context.

The story you pitch has to have a beginning, a middle, and an end. You need to have a hook that makes the story unique; it doesn't duplicate or copy something that's already out there. You need to develop details to make your story inviting. A common mistake is to try to pitch a thought about a kind of show you'd like to see or a backdrop for a show. A thought is not even an idea. You can have a thought about a show that's set on a deserted tropical island. But that's not a story. However, when you add the details of asking what happens when sixteen fit, attractive individuals get stranded on this island and have to survive, then you have the start of a story. When you add the hook that the sixteen people will be separated into two groups—let's call them "tribes"—and that they have to depend on each other, at first, as they compete in challenges with the other tribe to earn the rewards of food and housing, but then, when they lose a challenge they have to get rid of one of their own tribe members, ultimately competing against each other with everyone for himself or herself, you have a story like none other. When you add the ending to this story by borrowing from a classic like *Lord of the Flies* so that only one person is left standing at the end, you have a hit show called *Survivor.*

When it comes to pitching preferences, I'm the first to say that you need to be concise, speak clearly and not too fast (yeah, I still work on that), and make lots of eye contact. You don't need to be in the room for an hour. Thirty minutes is plenty of time to break the ice, perhaps with a personal anecdote that cues up your pitch, tell the main points of the story, present any visuals you've brought along, and then open up for questions. Eye contact helps you read the room and make sure your audience is with you. That's why brevity is important. Busy executives always appreciate brevity. The saying that "less is more" is one to remember for your pitch. The best part of the pitch is often when you allow your audience to ask questions. Instead of taking a question as an objection, use it as a sign that the executive or listener is becoming invested in your story.

When you prepare to pitch your idea, rather than creating a script that you have to follow, create an outline for your presentation that you can even jot down on an index card. By all means develop some good lines for yourself that might get a laugh or two or get everyone's attention. Build your pitch around the questions of why your idea is needed or perhaps what problem or void it will address. What makes it different from similar efforts that haven't done well? What makes it like something else that has been successful but maybe even better? What makes you the best person to execute the idea?

Sometimes I think of a pitch as being both the opening and closing arguments of a lawyer to a jury—with a break in the middle to show evidence, i.e., a sizzle reel or PowerPoint. In my approach, that means starting broad and narrowing to make my close. We recently sold a format from the United Kingdom to CBS that built on the broad statement about stories dominating the news—detectives hunting down fugitives and people trying to disappear from the authorities. At a time when we're all on the grid and able to be tracked more easily than ever before, here's the question: Could you truly disappear from the authorities in this day and age? With all the social media, closed-circuit television, cell phone tracking devices, and GPS systems built into your car and all your electronics, can you truly go off grid?

Everyone wants to know: Could you disappear? And for how long? Those are the questions our show was going to answer. We would identify twelve people, regular, everyday Americans, fed up with Big Brother and fed up with being spied on, who think they can genuinely disappear. We would put a team together of renowned experts—ex-CIA agents and ex–Homeland Security agents—who would search for these twelve people. We'll call them the fugitives. We'll call the team that's out to track them down the hunters. We'll give the fugitives twenty-eight days to see if they can hide from our hunters. And we'll call the show *Hunted*.

When you pitch your story or idea, whether it's a TV series, a product, or yourself, the response you get will often come down to the value that your unique commodity brings to the buyer and also to the value that you add as the person who is going to execute the idea you've just pitched. Just because you pitch a great story or a fantastic idea doesn't mean you are the best person to develop it—unless you have a proven track record.

In my business, that happens a lot, even with professionals whose agents have set up a meeting for them to pitch a story that they don't own or a project that they don't have any experience or expertise to offer for getting it made. A common mistake, for example, would be to pitch a series that followed the daughters of President Obama as they go about their lives, escorted by the Secret Service, going to school and doing homework and having to get help from their dad on things like math that he can't answer. A great premise with lots of storytelling potential, right?

But did they know President Obama? Did they have access to the Secret Service detail? Had they made a show like that? No, not at all. Just pitching the idea doesn't prove your value to getting the show made—which would not be easy in the least even for someone with a track record. Now, if you pitch a scavenger hunt around the world and you've been a producer of a show like *Amazing Race*, you add value to helping bring your idea to life. If you don't have that experience, my advice for a newcomer is to develop the hell out of a masterful presentation, maybe create your own pilot, and then pitch it, showing the value you bring as the storyteller. Another approach is to attain a degree of ownership in your idea or story before you pitch it to others. Someone might come in and say, "I have secured the exclusive rights from the US Navy to develop a reality competition with them. I'm not sure what the idea is, but I've got their full consent and cooperation." That gives me an incentive to say, "You have the rights. We'll figure out the format. Let's make a deal."

That's my point. The bottom line we all learn when we are in the hustle of both pitching and buying stories is that sometimes the make-or-break piece of the equation is finding the right collaborator. If you talk someone into buying into your idea and they don't work with you on it, you will face an uphill battle. On the flip side, when you tell a story that someone else can see and help shape, you can then choose to join forces and achieve results that will only improve the odds of success for all.

FINDING YOUR BRAND

In a storytelling industry like the entertainment business, there's a popular saying, first coined by Viacom's Chairman of the Board Sumner Redstone, that content is king. It's a truth worth considering for every business. In 1996 Bill Gates also put the saying into usage in the tech world by predicting that in the coming years, he expected content to drive most of the money made on the Internet. When you think of everything that's come into being in the digital world, it's all content driven—from the pictures, posts, and videos we share, to the social networks, blogs, and search engines designed to sift though data to find that content.

We can all agree that content really is king. Even though the platform of how and where we watch may change, the importance of the story content doesn't. We can't predict how far the new platforms will take us and whether, as some say, TV will be a relic of the past or what mode of delivery will gain the most traction—from subscription-based television to Netflix-type streaming to Hulu and YouTube to connecting online or through your video game systems. Those are just different ways to distribute content.

Whether it's played on an iPhone or in the back of a taxicab or on a screen in the men's room urinal, I'm confident that content will continue to matter. Fortunately, because my hustle is always going to be involved in different phases of developing, selling, and making content, I'm confident in my job security. Not only because I have expertise in content but also because of something else that is as important in my view, and that is culture.

After all, how does your content become significant? How do you move the needle so that your content registers on the public radar?

Culture. Content and culture are good bedfellows. Not long ago, I had this conversation with Pitbull, who observed that when music is culturally connected, whatever the genre, the content can then push the needle in terms of influencing social consumption and attitudes. Reality TV pushed the needle when Mary-Ellis Bunim and Jonathan Murray put it on MTV. Celebreality pushed the needle that mattered in popular culture. Content that reflects culture is compelling if you've grown up in that culture and never been represented in entertainment before.

What my creative partnership with Mark Cronin did was to honor that underrepresented culture. And we gave our viewers content that told their stories, and in turn made VH1 the number one cable channel—with an audience that arrived in droves and is mostly still hanging out.

In the process, we naturally developed the secret sauce of our storytelling brand. That's a topic I hear entrepreneurs asking about all the time—how do I find my brand? The answer is to spend time developing the story you're using to tell the world who you are, what you do, and how you do it. Your brand should also reflect your understanding of culture and your market.

As I think back to the insane amount of successful content that 51 Minds had in production in the years between 2004 and 2008, I know we upped the ante by taking our cues from culture—and from our loyal audience. We became the most prolific purveyor of unscripted content on cable television. The pace was unbelievable. I ran two sets at the same time. Sleep was optional.

We had become such essential earners for VH1 that we gained the reputation for being able to take just about any crazy idea, develop it with the same comedy styling that had become our mainstay, and cast it with must-see characters—celebrities who were already famous in some way or real people turned reality stars—and then come out with another winner.

We were like mad scientists in our laboratory, pushing the limits of celebreality, our brand, into old and new forms. Since *Fear* was a format I'd produced and clearly knew very well, that became the model for a show we developed called *Celebrity Paranormal Project*. Instead of casting kids to investigate haunted locations, we cast a mix of actors, comedians, models, athletes, and reality stars to go in and monitor paranormal activity in condemned sanatoriums across America that were known to be "severely haunted."

One of our most memorable celebrities on that show was Gary Busey, the Oscar-nominated movie actor who had been in a terrible motorcycle accident and had his whole brain rebuilt after that. Gary alleged that he had died on the operating table and had come back after dying. So he told us from the start that he was highly attuned to the presence of spirits and ghosts.

Though I had shot at several supposedly haunted locations, I feel safe to say that aside from some creepy moments, no ghosts showed up. Well, when we walked into that abandoned sanatorium in Kentucky where we had been informed that many deaths took place because of tuberculosis, Gary Busey's paranormal sensors suddenly went haywire, and he had us all convinced the entire place was freaking filled with tortured ghosts!

The rest of the cast was terrified. Busey wasn't just telling us what had happened in this place; he was hearing voices, having conversations with the dead, and sounding both insane and knowledgeable. In fact, he was so immersed in his reality that those of us in production were looking at one another and whispering, "What's going on? Is this real? Not real?"

Whatever the answer, Gary Busey really believed he was there to monitor the paranormal activity. He genuinely believed that he had been to the other side once because of his motorcycle accident and that experience therefore gave him the power to see dead people. And there was no doubt in his mind that he was seeing ghosts in this sanatorium.

The show did well enough for a first season but didn't have the staying power of our comedy blockbusters. *Surreal Life* was the gift that kept on giving. In addition to its own seasons, we finally did a competition format called *Surreal Life: Fame Games*. It was kind of a no-brainer; we brought back the biggest personalities from our different casts and pitted them against one another in various challenge competitions. Our dating shows, *Flavor of Love* and *Rock of Love*, also had characters and story lines that bred shows. After Tiffany Pollard (nickname "New York") became a hit on *Flavor of Love*, we went on to do three seasons with her—*I Love New York*, *New York Goes to Hollywood*, and *New York Goes to Work*. Similarly, *Daisy of Love* was a dating show spin-off for a runner-up from *Rock of Love*.

To an extent, we nearly fell victim to our own success, because we could never successfully veer from our raucous brand of comedy, which had put us on the map. Plus, going against our brand would not have been smart, especially with the advent of *Dancing with the Stars*. After that show premiered in 2005, celebreality became a staple of network television, a mainstream phenomenon. We knew that to stay alive we had to protect our niche in comedy and continue to be different from the rest of the pack.

Highbrow we weren't. Then again, satiric storytelling often works on two levels—one is totally basement-humor foolishness, and the other is so smart and witty that it hits your brain in that flash as you get the joke. Did we poke fun at others? Hell, yeah. We were on cable. The more scathing, the better. Nobody was spared.

I remember how nasty the media critics were about *America's Most*

Smartest Model. And that was one of my favorite shows. Just in the title itself. Doing some of his best work ever, Mark Cronin ran with the funny premise from Ben Stiller's *Zoolander* that already spoofed high-fashion models, then played havoc with elements from *America's Next Top Model.* Amping up the stereotypes that models aren't supersmart and that the better looking they are, the dumber they might also be, we set out to prove that theory and have fun with the possibilities. The humor even bordered on highbrow—you have to be arch to get that the joke was in the title—and the show was one of the wittiest on our production slate. As President of MTV Networks at the time, Brian Graden called it his favorite show.

Ultimately, even though Mark and I both gave it our all in trying to make the show a hit, the format didn't work and the show lasted only one season. However, I learned an interesting lesson from the process. Sometimes you have to let even your best ideas and stories go, even though they might develop into full-fledged hits if given the time and proper enrichment. There is a myth in the industry of storytelling that you may only have one big earth-moving idea. Too often people think they will live or die based on the success of their one idea. They pour all their energies into that one project, and when it doesn't go or isn't well received, they fall apart. You have to get past that. Your ideas can't be so precious that your well-being depends on getting praise and winning awards for them.

That was a lesson I learned from the criticism we got for *Flavor of Love.* We got killed for casting women who, according to the press, were too "ghetto." That was when the new president of VH1, Michael Hirschorn, gave us the idea for *Flavor of Love Girls: Charm School.* It would be great, he suggested, to counter all the flak by giving our *Flavor of Love* contestants a chance to develop social graces, etiquette, and manners and show they really did have class. Mo'Nique was the perfect host, and we built another hilarious challenge format. One of the highlights was a visit to none other than my alma matter, Cal State Fullerton, where *Charm School* teams had to learn the principles of debate from the college debaters and then compete in debates against one another. In another episode, our cast members competed on teams to raise the most money for a charity drive. The show itself charmed the hell out of the critics and was a smash. Guess what. After *Rock of Love* took off, we built a show for those contestants and called it *Rock of Love: Charm School.*

For the most part, I let criticism roll off my back. But as our shows became more popular and more pervasive in pop culture, I was attuned to their impact. In fact, I'll never forget a truly eye-opening response I received after previewing the first episode of *Flavor of Love* for a close friend and colleague of mine. Will Griffin—Ivy League educated with law and business degrees from Harvard, African-American, and one of the smartest guys I know in the entertainment business—was running the television division for Russell Simmons when we met. In later years, after he had moved on from that position to start his own consulting business, I would hire him as a consultant to help advise me on the expansion of my operations at the time. Will is a real champion and someone whose opinions I deeply respect.

But I wasn't sure how to react when he called me up and got to the point. "Cris," he said, "you are going to set the black race back twenty years with this show." He took a breath, and before I could say anything, he added, "But I'm going to tell you right now that this is some of the best and funniest television I have ever seen."

Wow. Was he serious?

Oh yeah. Will went on. "I have now watched it twice, and I laughed even harder the second time. You have a major hit on your hands."

After we hung up, I had to really search my soul. Flavor Flav was always a cartoon character to me who made fun of himself and by extension made fun of the bigots who created the stereotypes in the first place. If you look at the same kind of humor on display in, say, *South Park*, you could accuse that show of setting back everyone in the human race. So, on one hand, I had no problem owning the entertainment value of a show that used comedy to make people laugh and perhaps to feel uncomfortable enough to get mad. On the other hand, I didn't want to only tell those kinds of stories.

The situation was not uncommon for anyone in a creative or entrepreneurial role when you have an identifiable brand that has performed well. Some might even say—*Hey, why change? If it ain't broke* . . . Not surprisingly, whenever Mark and I would meet with the executives from MTV/VH1, Brian Graden and Jeff Olde, they were keenly interested in us delivering more of the same that was our stock-in-trade. Putting myself in their shoes, I understood. But that didn't mean I was feeling fulfilled as a storyteller.

My solution was to go back to the basics of story hustling—by adding projects to my plate that wouldn't take away from the commitments that were working but would give me a change of pace and allow me to diversify and grow. Whenever you need to change up your game, you shouldn't be constrained by the brand or reputation you've established for yourself. Don't forget where you've come from and the lessons you've learned, but bank on your instincts to take you to new heights. By embracing an idea or project that's new and challenging, you get back in the learning curve that fuels your passion. And it's one more way that you get to write the rules of your own success story.

WHERE YOU FIND GREAT STORIES

When you're ready for a challenge or a change and looking for your next inspiration, you will discover that the greatest stories or ideas often turn up in the least likely places or are staring at you right in the face. They are really all around you. When you find them, they might look like nothing, and only you can see what they can become and only you can be the one to polish them so that later on everyone will say they were diamonds in the rough.

Sometimes you focus on the kind of story you'd like to uncover, and sure enough it pops into view. That's sort of what happened for me when I decided that I wanted to work on some stories of transformation. As it so happened, I learned from my agents at CAA that Jamie Foxx, an Oscar-winning film star, wanted to get his foot into reality television and had a show he was trying to develop along those lines. Not unlike the premise of *Charm School* for ladies, Jamie had an idea of a finishing school for gangsters—that would explore the possibility of taking a group of thugs, basically, and attempting to turn them into gentlemen. Jamie had already sold the idea to MTV, calling it *From G's to Gents*, and now he was meeting with various production companies to choose one to help flesh the idea out, build the format, and make the show.

As we sat down to meet, Jamie described who these cast members might be. He explained, "I want to take the guys that come from single homes, who might have been in juvie, who didn't have many options. I want to take the guys who didn't have a dad to tell them how to tie a tie, you know?"

"I do," I answered. I told him that he was talking about many of the guys from the neighborhood where I'd grown up.

He told me more about how he grew up, the positives and the

obstacles that had shaped his dreams. Then I talked about El Monte and how the memories of where I came from were always a part of the storytelling I was most passionate about.

When he decided he wanted me to develop the show, I know that the kinds of stories I'd been doing on VH1 weren't the main selling point. Certainly, he could see that I had a track record and could execute and deliver. But I think what made him choose to work with me was in getting to know my story, even from one meeting. After that, I went to work. Aside from the title, there was nothing—not a host or a setting or a semblance of format. For the host, we cast Fonzworth Bentley, an actor/rapper/dancer, not to mention a producer and author on subject matter of interest to the modern-day gentleman. The show was authentic, entertaining, and also emotional. We told stories that touched a cultural nerve and yielded a big hit for MTV—for three seasons.

The other project that really let me stretch as a storyteller came about after I read an article in *Source* magazine, the insider's guide to hip-hop, which is a music and culture that has always spoken to me. Again, staying in tune and reading as much as I can are parts of my job. The moment I saw the cover of the magazine with its picture of a producer named Irv Gotti draped in an American flag, I was captivated and had to read Irv's story—from starting a rap label called Murder Inc., home to artists like DMX, Ja Rule, and Ashanti, and also helping discover Jay Z, to suddenly having the federal government come after him out of the blue one day. The feds raided his business—because, they said, he was alleged to have ties to a really dangerous gangster who was already in prison for life—and accused Irv of numerous criminal activities that included money laundering, racketeering, selling drugs, and a list of other offenses. With no evidence to support the allegations, the government filed charges against him, his brother, and the label.

It's widely known that when a case like this goes to trial, the government has a 98 percent conviction rate. That's why innocent defendants are often talked into cutting a deal. But Irv fought the charges every step of the way. It took him a year and put him out of business and cost him every penny to his name to defend himself. After a year, he was found not guilty on all counts. But now he had to start over.

This was a phenomenal story that made me want to follow the journey of how he would be able to build his life and dream back after being forced to start over again. The first person I contacted to help introduce me to Irv was Russell Simmons, cofounder of Def Jam and known as the most important businessman in the history of rap and hip-hop. Russell and I had shot a pilot together with rapper Trick Daddy and had some other ideas we'd been discussing.

After Russell made the introduction, I set up a meeting at my office in Hollywood. Irv Gotti, in town from the East Coast on other business, shows up in old-school g style, with about eight people in tow. A true hip-hop posse. He walks in, a light-skinned African-American with a shaved head and a disarming almost baby face when he smiles that can become dead serious in an instant, tied together by his megasized persona. He comes into my office, full swag, the big boss, the whole thing.

Irv sits down and says, "Now, what the fuck is it you want from me?" I'm starting to answer when he says, "Man, I'm gonna be honest with you, Cris. I took this meeting for one reason—'cause Russell asked me to and . . ." I think he's about to say because of *Flavor of Love*, which is a monster hit. But no. On the contrary, Irv says he isn't going to work with me because, in his view, our shows "clowned" black people. That's about the end of it until he adds, "I'll tell you what you can do for me. You can get me Hoopz's phone number."

Hoopz was the nickname given by Flav to one of the girls on the show. So apparently Irv loves the show and watches it but thinks I'm reinforcing a negative stereotype. I listen to all this bravado and look around at his guys in their white T-shirts: big guys, textbook thugs. I'm thinking—*Oh, my God, this is a disaster.* But I say, "All right, um, listen, man. Let me tell you what I think is interesting." And I start telling him about his story, as I see it and why he should do a project and what I'd do.

He gets quiet. He leans forward. By the end of the meeting, he shrugs and says, "OK, I'm interested." He's about to go back on tour while getting Murder Inc. back together, and he's going out briefly with Ja Rule and DMX in a tour bus. "You know what, Cris? You're right. This would make a great TV show. We're gonna get on that bus. And let me tell you, man, when we tour, it's fucking crazy. We party like fucking gods." He goes on and describes what he means.

This isn't what I have in mind. I just tell him, "Yeah, that's not going to be a show, man."

"Nah, it's gonna be great! It's gonna be good TV." After further discussion he backs off, saying, "I don't think I'm going to do reality TV. Murder Inc. is coming back together."

With that, he grabs his posse and leaves. The next thing I did was to sit down immediately and send him an e-mail about what he'd been through—all the injustices and everything that could be part of a show that would speak on behalf of others and the injustices they had suffered and how I believed it would be a shame if in the next chapter of his life he didn't take advantage of telling that story and show how he was going to get his life back.

Five minutes after I sent the e-mail, he called to say, "All right, listen, man. I'm in. I'm game to explore this."

From there, I was able to go and meet him in New York and then went up to Connecticut to meet his wife, Debbie, and his kids. The two were in the process of getting divorced but were a team as parents and in what they had been through together. The story was even more phenomenal than I had known. After that, I met his brother and his parents. There was no question in my mind that this family story—an American story—was the show.

It was about resilience and redemption. We would ask if this man could get beyond how his business and family had been destroyed, how he and his wife had become estranged, and what the struggles were for his two young boys and his daughter, who loved their dad more than anything but had to watch him almost go to prison and lose every penny. More important than putting his business back together, the question at the heart of the story was whether he could put his family back together.

I made a convincing and emotional pitch but Irv wasn't seeing it at first. Then I pitched it to VH1. They were wary. Instead of a green light, they gave me $350,000 to shoot a pilot, not a lot of money for the scope of the show.

But the bigger problem about that was Irv wouldn't sign his deal. He said, "You shoot that pilot. I'll look at it. If I like it, I'll do the show and then I'll sign your contract. If I don't, I'm out."

VH1 countered that they wouldn't do it unless we could guarantee that Irv would do it and that he'd do it at the rate they were asking for, if the series did get picked up. So I guaranteed VH1. Rather than have Irv sign the contract, I took a $350,000 gamble and proceeded to shoot the pilot. That was a classic moment of me betting on myself and my ability to tell Irv's story right. If I was wrong, I would be out a lot of money and time. But listening to my passion and purpose, I felt this was what I had to do.

Everything came to a head one day after I had shot an interview with one of Irv's sons, who was around thirteen years old at the time. The conversation was real, as in a documentary, and as the son asked his mom if she and Irv were going to get divorced and as he asked why she wouldn't let his dad move back into the house, I filmed that moment. Instead of stopping, I kept pushing for this truthful question to come out because it was the elephant in the room that nobody was addressing. That night Irv found out about the scene from a distraught Debbie and the next day he showed up during filming and went ballistic, telling me, "This shit is fucking done. It's over. You crossed the line! You motherfucker . . ." He just went off. His point was that he wanted his kids protected and their issues kept off the table. As I recall, he threatened to come after me with a baseball bat to my head.

I cleared the house. Irv calmed down, and I said, "I made you a promise that we were going to cover this as honestly as possible and I was going to tell your story. And in the end, let me edit it. If you don't like it, that scene is out. I'm not even telling the network about what I've shot so they can't hold us to it."

When I finished the edit, Irv flew out to Los Angeles. I didn't say anything ahead of time when we went to screen the pilot together, just the two of us, except that I thought it conveyed a balanced message. When we came to the scene with his son, he tensed up and then just nodded but held back his emotions until the end. Afterward, he started to cry as he said, "It's beautiful. I love it."

We then showed the pilot to VH1, and the show was green-lit on the spot. *Gotti's Way* went on to be a great and meaningful series. We did three seasons, and Debbie—who everyone was rooting for— became a huge star.

And Irv Gotti, who had reclaimed his family and his life and had rebuilt his business so that he could once again own his success, was about to give me the most important advice on the most critical crossroads of my career.

The experience of telling a different kind of story fed my vision for the future. Today my passion is to tell more stories that tap the direction of popular culture in ways that elevate communities and society in general. One of my newest passions is a show that tells the story of how veterans returning from multiple tours of service overseas—who have had trouble finding work here at home—can now be leaders in helping our nation rebuild its crumbling infrastructure, demonstrating their expertise on these massive projects that we always describe as "military operations."

Another story I can't wait to tell is something on a very large scale. Ever since I arrived at my current post, one of my goals has been to reinvent Endemol's massive hit, *Extreme Home Makeover*. But they had done it so well and had set the bar so high, efforts to create anything new always fell short. Then, after seeing a sizzle reel for an online show called *Blank Spaces* from our digital group, Endemol Beyond, it hit me that we'd been looking at it all wrong. We didn't need to remake homes. What we needed to do was remake community spaces! In looking at neighborhoods hurt after businesses close or buildings are torn down, we could give them makeovers—using walls for murals to be painted by artists and empty lots for community gardens. The show would also create opportunities for people who live in the community to thrive in the new businesses that we can create. This is what's happening in popular culture anyway, so why shouldn't that story be told?

This is the best part of my reality. No matter how many challenges are on my plate, I still get to wake up every day and look forward to a new idea and a new story to tell.

Why not ask yourself what you love best about your daily hustle? If you can't quite answer that yet, open yourself to the ideas that are there right in front of you, asking to be put to good use.

ten

Know When and When Not to Leave Money on the Table

The biggest risk is not taking any risk. . . . In a world that's changing really quickly, the only strategy that is guaranteed to fail is not taking risks.

—MARK ZUCKERBERG,
cofounder and CEO of Facebook

Of all the principles we've looked at so far, perhaps the most important success principle I can emphasize is that of *choosing to take on the mantle of leadership*. Of course, leadership is meaningful throughout your journey of turning dreams into reality. It's also a key ingredient that separates them that do and them that don't. Leadership requires many of the capacities that drive other principles—belief, courage, vision, commitment, resourcefulness, instincts, patience, the ability to motivate and inspire others, and, as always, a relentless work ethic.

Going the distance is the test of leadership. The farther and higher you go, the tougher the terrain, where there's no trail to follow but the one you are creating not just for you but the rest of your team. At the core of leadership is that rare capacity to articulate purpose that lifts you and everyone around you.

The money part of it, as you've seen so far, was never the motivation for me. But building a company of substance and value that could compete and win, against the odds, of course, that meant something. Seeing our company thrive was empowering, exciting, and fulfilling. Still, I will tell you straight up that in April 2007 when the question was first raised, the idea of selling the company was not and had never been a goal or a dream.

Not for me, not in the least. I was thirty-four years old, and the thought of selling was pretty foreign to my way of thinking. The truth is that although we're all responsible for creating opportunities, sometimes opportunities come to us, and we have to decide what to do about them.

THE ART OF PATIENCE IN A DEAL

The idea to acquire 51 Minds started with Ron Milkes, head of mergers and acquisitions for Endemol North America, a division of a global TV corporation based in the Netherlands. Endemol was the name given to a merger of two companies belonging to Joop van den Ende and John de Mol, the two who created *Big Brother*. When the founders moved on after becoming billionaires from the sale of their company, Endemol, to a consortium of banks and investment firms, a board of directors took over. David Goldberg, the chair and CEO of Endemol North America, was responsible for expanding the corporation's footprint here in the United States and beyond. Under David's leadership, they were actively looking to acquire production companies.

During the scouting process, Ron brought David a copy of the *Los Angeles Times* business section with an article on us that was entitled "The Kings of Dubious TV":

... another day in the frantic world of unscripted television for Cronin and Abrego, who in the last few years have emerged as one of TV's hottest producing teams. . . . With a steadily growing fan base, the shows have turned VH1 and the so-called celebreality brand into a cable powerhouse.

Shortly after that, Endemol reached out to Mark Cronin's attorney, as a point person for both Mark and myself. Then David and Ron set up a lunch, mainly to get to know us and discuss our work and our direction. We didn't read much into it. We did know that they were taking meetings with a select few production companies. Unlike most production companies contracted by the studios, networks, and cable outlets to create and produce their shows, we were in the minority that did own our content, making it valuable for syndication, licensing abroad, and exploiting online in shorter entertainment pieces. Actually, we owned more content than we had time to count, and that put us in this attractive category.

The brilliance of Mark Cronin at that first meeting was to just do what he always did—to make jokes and have everyone cracking up. Everybody seemed to get along great. Before long Endemol took the next steps in pursuing us. My reaction initially was one of curiosity.

This was during the absolute busiest I'd ever been, with a schedule that was so bananas, all I could do was keep my nose to the grindstone. My brain had only so much bandwidth, and it was devoted to figuring out how to keep everybody on the team, some 250 now working for us, on top of their game. When I wasn't jumping back and forth between our sets in Los Angeles, I was flying off to Hawaii or New Jersey to oversee our shoots there.

Mark and I had always done well divvying up the production workload, and this time period was no different. The added demands for me were now that we were hitting on all cylinders, some of our celebrities suddenly became full-time jobs. Sometimes I thought of myself as a firefighter rather than a TV producer, running around putting out the celebrity fires lit every day at our various productions. I was also still driving the creative team, heading up all the development for pitching new shows.

There was little time to enjoy the perks of success outside of work. Not that I was complaining because it was my choice. But my schedule was creating strife at home, not surprisingly, and it wasn't going to be fixed by earning, or even spending, more money. And meanwhile, little had changed in terms of my lifestyle. I wore jeans, sneakers, and a black T-shirt to work every day. My family was still in the same house we'd been in for a while, the second one we'd owned, and I was still driving the same car, nice but not flashy. At least, I wasn't still driving the red Toyota pickup!

These choices had to do with my leadership style—to be an example to everyone on the team that I was in this because I wanted to make exciting television, not for the perks. Obviously, I expected a lot from everybody, believing that every single person—from the camera assistants and post-PAs on up—mattered to the whole. The atmosphere I sought to create was one in which everybody who was with me in the trenches pushed harder because they didn't want to disappoint me, not because they were afraid that they'd get fired for falling short. As a leader, I held myself accountable for any shortcomings. My number two guy, Ben Samek, was a leader in his own right, and if anyone fell short in his area, that was on him.

Those concerns were my priorities. So when Endemol started making moves to take a closer look at us, I sort of thought there was a deal to be made for us to sell our library of content. However, before they could assess the value of the company, we had to do a thorough organization of our books. We were operationally organized, but we had grown so quickly in such a short amount of time that we had years of paperwork and logbooks to review and put into reports so that we could even do an assessment of our worth. The other housekeeping challenge was to log our archives of footage—close to five hundred episodes of television. We owned every last bit of it, which gave me confidence that we'd be able to sell it. During this assessment period, I was gung ho, telling Mark, "Hey, whatever you can get for the library, I'm down."

That would have been a no-brainer. Mark had been going strong for many years before our success and might have seen this as an opportunity to slow down. That wasn't where I was at all. But that difference was not a point of contention whatsoever. It was a given that we had built all of this together, so my attitude was that if we could sell the library, split the proceeds fifty-fifty, we'd live a modern-day version of *All's Well That Ends Well*. And that's when we hear unexpected news from Endemol.

We are informed that the library, while great, is not so valuable. The problem is that the bulk of our shows won't do anything internationally. Therefore, because they've already been shown domestically and because their international sales team doesn't see potential for exploiting the library in new markets, the evaluation is not what any of us hoped it would be

None of this bothered me. From my point of view, we had already been paid for the shows and we had a ton of new content in the pipeline, so I said, in effect, "Whatever you can offer for the library, we'll consider it."

Did they have an offer? Yes, but as they explained, they wanted us to understand that it was in two parts, combined. They proceeded to put a nominal sum on the table for the purchase of the library. Before we could even consider the offer, they then let us know that what they really wanted was to buy the entire company. As David Goldberg put it, "The real investment here is to buy your future. We want you guys."

The terms, we were told, included the offer of an employment contract for what would be the next six years. And the money they offered, added to what was on the table already, was in the vicinity of $100 million.

Mark and I and our representatives sit there in shock. As soon as the Endemol team leaves, Mark jokes and makes a comment to the effect of "Well, that's a nice starting place."

I don't say anything yet, maybe because it's not real to me or too crazy to believe, but as I drive home that night, I begin to mull over what this offer means.

Yes, the huge amount was amazing. Incredible. Unbelievable. Some might even say this was akin to winning the lottery. Not at all. That would always infuriate me to hear. After all, the offer reflected the unbelievable game-changing amount of work that had put us on the map to make us so valuable. It was not the $265 million that Microsoft paid Tony Hsieh, the young entrepreneur who created the online advertising service LinkExchange, nor the nearly $1 billion that Amazon would soon pay to acquire Zappos, the online shoe store that Hsieh had built as CEO and key investor. For the acquisition of a media company, the offer was in the zone of the going rate. It wasn't what offers would later be at the height of the gold rush for reality TV production companies—like the $360 million paid for 80 percent of Leftfield Entertainment (*Pawn Stars*).

But, to be fair, it was beyond the realm of anything I had expected. Only for me, something felt wrong. I couldn't do it. I'd never, ever wanted to take a job for the money. Selling the company with the understanding that it wouldn't be ours after six years went against many of the principles that had fueled my success. How was I supposed to go against what I'd always done, and that was betting on myself?

When I called my parents and told them the offer, I remember my mother not being able to speak. It was that hard to fathom. My mother's main input was for me to do what I knew was best. Was this deal leading me further along toward my goals? Was this the direction that I felt was right? As I talked it out, I heard myself getting to the bottom of my concern. At first, when we were approached about selling the library, I had no problems parting with the past. Mark and I had killed it together, and the two of us had worked so hard to make all of it possible. But to sell the company, the future, and be tied to Mark Cronin's future—when we were at different places in our focus and in our lives—that was too much risk I couldn't control.

Mark flipped out. Understandably. But once he saw that I wasn't going to change my mind, he took a different tack. That's part of why we were such a great team—because we were both relentlessly persuasive. Besides that, again, he is really smart, and he is a skilled deal maker and negotiator. Mark's comedy never got in the way of his ability to be business-minded in looking for different angles and running numbers in advantageous ways. His goal thus became to devise alternatives that would make us both happy in the end. All he kept saying to me was "Look, you just can't tell anybody you're out. Don't say you can't do it. Let's figure it out. Is there a deal that works?"

"No," I'd repeat, "I don't think there is." Of course, I told him if there was a way for him to make a deal just for his part, then he could sell. But I couldn't.

Nothing worked for both of us. The day finally came when Endemol wanted our answer. Our agents and lawyers responded by saying that Mark's answer was yes, that he wanted to make a deal, and my answer was no. Any hope that we could do this separately went out the door when Endemol told our representatives, "We're going to make a deal for both Cronin and Abrego or nothing."

Mark was devastated. But I couldn't sell. Was I still shell-shocked from the dissolution of the Brass Ring partnership? Not totally. But somehow I equated selling what Mark and I had developed as setting us up for another difficult partnership chapter. Although the Brass Ring dissolution was behind me, there was actually more drama to come—as I would soon learn.

Intellectually, Mark Cronin understood my reservations about selling. But he was also crushed, as he had his own plans and goals. I think that this was where a degree of animosity kicked in between us. Clearly, to him, he had a right to be angry that I had blown the deal of a lifetime. Clearly, to me, I had a right to be wary of the risk to everything I had worked hard to build by taking a deal that hinged on our future productivity together.

The atmosphere was not toxic by any means, but it was contentious. My focus was on working and just keeping on at keeping on. I wanted to move forward.

But guess what. Endemol came back with a sweetened offer. They bettered the money by about 30 percent. But still, I could not say yes to a job for money. I had to control my destiny; that was the risk of putting my fate in the hands of any entity but myself. Endemol soon upped the ante again. Inasmuch as I kept saying, "No, I'm sorry. This isn't going to work," I also gained an immense respect and appreciation for the Endemol team and especially for David Goldberg. He was someone who set the bar high—with his business acumen, his passion for content and for culture, his ability to mentor and lead, and his global vision.

Each time Endemol raised the money, and I said no, I and everyone else assumed that we were done. Then, in the fall of 2007, this news broke in *Variety*:

Endemol USA is acquiring a controlling interest in producer Charlie Corwin's Gotham-based Original Media—a move that gives the reality powerhouse a presence in the feature film and scripted TV businesses.

. . . Total value of the deal is estimated to be in the ballpark of $50 million. . . .

One could have assumed that Endemol had achieved their goal of diversifying their portfolio. But in early 2008 they came back with renewed interest. They offered a formula to address my concerns about the future division of labor between Mark and myself. By no means a foolproof solution, it was an improvement from where they had been before.

Putting myself in Endemol's shoes, I understood why they wanted and needed 51 Minds—because they had no presence in cable. They did the big broadcast shows, adding most recently hits like *Wipeout* and *Extreme Home Makeover*. With their expertise, they were actually too big to do cable, and so the strategy in buying us would give them presence and know-how they lacked. Smart. But I couldn't quite see what a deal gave us in terms of the opportunity to go beyond what we already did. Would this let us develop and sell for big broadcast network media? Would it open doors to developing scripted material? Would a deal lock us in forever to doing the same content and even close doors in the future?

It all came to a head when I was on my way to one of our sets in Van Nuys, *New York Goes to Work*, when my phone started going nuts with one call coming in after another, and the only one I picked up was from my agent, Michael Camacho, who began, "Hey, listen . . . Cris, turn off your phone."

I never turned off my phone. There was way too much going on, and I had to be reachable. But I turned it off. Better, I took the battery out and went back to set. Everything had been well delegated and was running smoothly. On the way home, I turned my phone on, and it was full of messages, with everyone asking for me to call back. When I walked into the house, Adriana was up waiting. That was unusual. Even more unusual was that she had been getting non-stop calls too—from my business and personal attorneys.

Everyone had the same message: "Cris, this is real now. This offer is not going to change your life. It's going to change your kids' kids' lives."

The offer had doubled from where we had started. The terms involved a payout over time, not all at once, with protections and contingencies. Even though I had not intended to use patience as leverage to up the money, somehow refusing to go for a deal that wasn't right for me had gotten us twice the offer from where we started.

Everyone was so dramatic. The pressure was unbelievable.

Patience is more than a virtue in deal making. It's a survival skill. When you cultivate patience, it's a risk you take that the other party may walk away. But if you go against your better instincts, you may risk locking yourself into the wrong deal. You can listen to advice, but ultimately on any deal that's going to influence the future of your dream, it's got to be your call.

RISK BY ANY OTHER NAME

Now there's good news and bad news. The good news is that I have to fly out to New York to go to work with Irv Gotti on our second season of *Gotti's Way*. That means I can buy time. The bad news is that now I'm just sitting on this powder keg.

Toward the end of the shoot, Irv invites me to go with him to a

basketball game—for the New Jersey Nets as they were still known—
and we're riding in the van when I tell him what is going on. All
along I've been keeping him abreast of the developments, and he has
never told me what to do.

Finally, he's heard enough and tells me that I need to listen to
him. Then, in his highly colorful way of talking, Irv recounts the tale
of when he was on top of the world and how his ego was out of control and he was making so many millions, and getting paid a million
dollars to record albums for the likes of Jennifer Lopez. He's telling
me about how many offers of untold millions he turned down whenever any major label tried to buy his company. He kept turning down
all these chances he was given to sell his company and to go to work
at higher levels in the music business. Why? Because, he says, "I was
like you. I kept saying that I am going to always bet on myself." And
then everything came crashing down, and the offers were gone. "I
had my chance, all that money on the table, and I didn't do it. Man,
you never know what's gonna happen. You gotta take that money off
the table now. In this business, you've gotta know when."

"How is that not selling out?"

Irv tells me, "You're not selling out, and you're still betting on
yourself because the reason why you're getting that offer is because
you created that opportunity for them to even offer you that. I'm not
gonna tell you that you're stupid not to take it. You do what you gotta
do. But if you're smart, and I know you are, you will make this deal."

The great thing about getting advice from Irv Gotti was that he
had no agenda. And so I was listening hard to this hip-hop mogul
who'd had it all, only to lose it through no fault of his own, and then
was forced to start all over again to rebuild his life and fortune.

Making sure that his message got through to me, Irv finished our
talk by telling me the story of the man who waited for help from God
in New Orleans when the flood happened after Katrina. The water

was rising up to the man's doorstep, and the last fire truck made it out to his house. When the rescue guys told him to jump in, the man said, "I'm good. I'm gonna ride this out by myself. God's gonna provide." Then, after the waters rose to cover the house and the man was on his roof, rescue boats made it out to him in the night and told him to jump on board, but he said, "Nope, I'm here waiting on the Lord. He'll provide for me." Before long the water was up to his chest, but luckily a helicopter flew by and dropped a ladder down. The man waved them off, saying, "No, thanks. God will provide. I'm good."

And so the helicopter flew away, the water rose, and the man drowned. So when he gets to heaven and arrives at Saint Peter's Gate, the first thing he says when he met God is "Lord, I waited for you to provide."

And then God says to him, "Hey, I sent you a fire truck, a boat, and a helicopter. What else were you waiting for?"

Irv's point was "Yeah, God could have brought you this. You know what that means? That means this is yo' shit, man. This is yo' thing. You brought this deal and made it happen, by betting on yourself." In his view, the smart risk was to take the deal and build the next success from there, as I had always done in the past. The shortsighted risk was to ignore an opportunity that wouldn't repeat itself. Or as Irv said, "They offer you that kinda money 'cause you brought it, you made this, and you did this, so why the fuck won't you take it?"

Irv Gotti was right. I had left so much money on the table for others before. It was time to take the money off the table.

I flew home the next day and said yes. Everyone who had been trying to make the deal was beyond happy. Even though the magnitude of it hadn't yet hit me, the relief I felt was overwhelming. Someone even joked that I should be credited with the timing that led to doubling the money. Like it was all by design. And come to think of it, maybe it was.

CHOOSING REALITY FOR LIFE

In the aftermath of closing the big deal, I learned many unprecedented life lessons. The one I can share most readily is that once I had said yes, the next step was to give it my all and make it a massive success for everyone involved. It was like getting to a mountaintop and looking over to see that the next peak to climb was hidden in the clouds. I was still playing the long game.

The timing could not have been more opportune. If we had waited until later that year, we would have never been able to sell during the global economic meltdown of late 2008 and 2009. We would have missed the window. David Goldberg had risked more than anyone on behalf of Endemol, and he had done so with tenacity and purpose like I'd never seen up close. And as much as I would have liked to have kept everything lower profile, for every kind of reason, I knew that Endemol was going to run with the story of the sale in every outlet, like this piece in *Variety*:

> *In a deal valued at upward of $200 million, Endemol USA has acquired Cris Abrego and Mark Cronin's 51 Minds Entertainment, the reality factory that perfected the celebreality genre with nonscripted comedies such as* Flavor of Love, I Love New York, *and* The Surreal Life. . . .
>
> *Endemol is taking a 51% interest in 51 Minds, with options to acquire a greater stake in the company at a later date. The $200 million figure doesn't represent the actual purchase price but rather the potential value of the deal if a host of financial targets are met over the next few years.*

After the paperwork was completed and we settled into a postsale rhythm, Mark and I did not see eye to eye on the division of labor and how the formula for compensation with those differences should work. He was ready to wind down; I wasn't. It was always going to be tough, as I had worried before making the deal. Still, on a personal level, we could both look back at what we'd accomplished together and know that we had come, we had seen, and we had conquered.

With Brass Ring, I had chosen to work with a friend who was not the right partner for me. As for the partnership with Mark Cronin, he was absolutely the right partner for as long and as far as we had come in the short time that we had. So that was an upgrade of the lessons on partnering with others. Even so, sometimes as goals and dreams evolve, the partnership runs its course.

In August of 2009, however, I was not feeling so philosophical when we hit our first major crisis in 51 Minds Entertainment's tenure under Endemol. "Crisis" is not really the word. Combine catastrophe with a horrific tragedy, and there was no one to respond but me.

At the time we had a VH1 show called *I Love Money*, a competition format that was in its third season. One of the contestants on that show was a man by the name of Ryan Jenkins. He had previously been on one of our other shows, *Megan Wants a Millionaire*, starring Megan Hauserman, a *Rock of Love* reality-made celeb. In early August, Jenkins won *I Love Money*, collected his honorarium check, and left the show on his own, then went to Las Vegas, where he married a woman and, a short time later, took her to another state and murdered her.

Jenkins not only murdered the woman, but in an attempt to cover up his crime and conceal her identity, he cut off her fingertips and pulled out her teeth, then stuffed her into a suitcase that he dumped in a trash bin before fleeing the country. Jenkins was Canadian, so the police launched an international manhunt to locate him. It was a nightmare.

Viacom, the parent company of VH1, was in a full panic, it was a PR debacle, and Jenkins was on the run, leading the manhunt to Canada. He stole a car and a boat and crossed the border before checking into a motel, and just as police closed in and cornered him, he hanged himself.

Viacom immediately issued a press release saying that they had nothing to do with the shows, which were made by 51 Minds, a third-party production company, and that they were just the end user. They then proceeded to cancel everything we had in production and development with them. Aside from a handful of other outlets, VH1 had been the platform for everything we made. So 51 Minds instantly bottomed out. The company almost imploded.

This meant that after emerging from the financial collapse of the previous year without being hurt, we had our own crash a year later, and I had to go out to sell like never before in order to rebuild if not save 51 Minds. Now I had to add to our lineups on places like Discovery and the History Channel, where we had sold shows before. And, of course, I had to start flying to media capitals like New York to go out and meet new buyers, hoping to establish relationships that would bring new vendors.

This was one of the most sobering challenges of my career. I had to go into these rooms and swallow the medicine on behalf of 51 Minds, a company that was mostly known for madcap comedy reality, and on behalf of Endemol, our new majority owner, and whoever else.

But over the next several months, I made the rounds and got the ball rolling again, eventually selling shows to new vendors like CMT (*Redneck Island, Top Secret Recipe*) and E Television (*Bridalplasty*) and rekindling our relationship with a new slate for VH1 (*TI & Tiny, Mario Lopez: Saved by the Baby, La La's Full Court Life*, and many more). By the time I was ready to step away from 51 Minds and let someone else run it—as one option in my contract allowed—I had brought the company back to almost 80 percent of where we had been before the crash. Again, the ability to sell and be an earner kept me alive. What was different was learning to run the company as if it was mine, but with the interests of Endemol at stake.

While all of this was unfolding, there was a new complication that had seemed to come out of left field. Rick Telles and his lawyers had found language buried in the legal paperwork we'd used to end our partnership that they argued said that, even though we were ex-partners, we still had certain fiduciary responsibilities to one another. And they were using that legal language as a basis for his claim to every franchise that had spun off from *Surreal Life*.

Initially, they filed the suit claiming that Rick was owed $50 million—including supposedly half of my half of the reported proceeds for the sale of 51 Minds to Endemol. They traced the purported fiduciary lineage through that third season of *Surreal Life* when Flava Flav got his own shows, *Strange Love* and then *Flavor of Love*, and then they literally diagrammed a tree that showed almost every show on our slate up to that time that was three or four generations removed but still a branch from the original tree.

Rick had already made millions of dollars on *Surreal Life*. I toughened up to fight and finally got a great lawyer to represent me—at great expense. But because of the legal paperwork we had signed as part of the business divorce, this was going to go to arbitration, no matter what, where the arbitrators (sometimes retired judges) tend to decide these cases often just by splitting the baby down the middle, agreeing with part of what each side contends.

The depositions and the hearings were insult upon injury. No different from any lawsuit. Rick's lawyers read every e-mail I'd ever sent him, trying to twist everything to mean whatever they wanted it to do. Rick wouldn't even look at me when I went into the hearing room. The case dragged on forever. Three years later, in February

2012, I was in Paris for work and sitting in a café within sight of the Eiffel Tower when I got the phone call that the arbitrator had ruled. Instead of the $50 million and co-ownership of all those shows, the arbitrator had split the difference and, when all was said and done, Rick was awarded roughly $8 million.

In the scheme of things, it was not the worst outcome. But I couldn't shake what I saw as unfair—that this was money that he would get for shows, not because he had done any work on them, but because of a legal technicality, after five years of my having killed myself to build those shows. This development ate at me because it felt like an instance of someone taking advantage of someone else's work—mine. On principle, I resented how anybody in a business like Hollywood could come along and take credit and demand payment for work they didn't do. On principle, I never wanted to be in a position for anyone to take advantage of me again or be party to anyone else treating a gesture of kindness as weakness.

The eye-opening lesson didn't come until about a year later after I'd been sitting on all that anger the whole time. I should have known better. Just as I'd learned to keep my cool in wrestling as well as in business, I knew that giving in to anger is when you make mistakes, when your judgment can be clouded. But I couldn't get past it. That is, until one day when I was having lunch with Gary Benz, a long-time colleague since my early days with Brass Ring and a great friend. When I admitted to Gary how mad I still was, he gave me frank advice. "Cris, you gotta let it go," he said. "This is killing you. It's like you're drinking the poison, hoping he dies."

And it hit me. *Boom.* I got it. All this time, I had been drinking the poison of resentment, of righteous indignation, hoping Rick would get his—when in fact it was killing me. That was all I needed to hear. I said, "I'm done."

I was good. I let it go. How massive was the load that had been lifted? I couldn't even measure it. All I knew was that the path had been cleared ahead. It was a test of character and leadership.

The lesson no doubt has many applications for all of us. The biggest risk is letting go of the power you give someone else to control your destiny. No matter how justified you may feel in pointing out that someone or something has wronged you or limited your dreams, let that go. Sometimes righteous indignation can fire you up and make you want to fight harder. But in the end, resentment can blind you and detract from the vision that lets you see your greater purpose. Feel whatever you feel and then move on. Own your power and purpose—whether it's as an entrepreneur, executive, freelancer, employee, or simply as someone with big dreams. Because once you claim ownership, your success or failure is only up to you. And that is the most powerful feeling in the world. Trust me on this, and welcome to reality.

eleven

Live Your Full-Court Life: *Embracing What Makes You Different*

I encourage people to embrace whatever it is that makes them different. Not being like everybody, setting your own trends, being your own person, that's what makes you cool.

—On being unique, LA LA ANTHONY,
actress, author, star of *La La's Full Court Life*

The all-important principle of owning the mantle of leadership, as we've been discussing, is directly related to the principle of *taking on a mission that is bigger than you*. For many, no matter what field you're in, there is a natural growth that happens as you move closer toward your highest goals. In the process, as you expand your horizons and broaden your goals, that sense of mission may come to you as a by-product of owning your success. It often comes with a desire not only to motivate and create opportunities for others on your team but also for others you may not even know. The leadership journey is ultimately about making a difference in the world. When you choose to take on a mission that does make a difference for others, you then unleash your own problem-solving and unique talents to actually make the world better. To reach that fullest expression of your potential, your challenge is to take the time to accept, explore, and embrace that which sets you apart.

ARE YOU A MARTIAN?

The real world doesn't always teach us to accept the things that make us different. But every now and then, we have an experience that lets us consider the advantages. Such was the case for me a few years after the sale of my company when I got a weird call on Christmas Day. The number was unfamiliar, but, thinking it might be an emergency, I picked up.

The call was from none other than P. Diddy, aka Sean Combs, aka Puff Daddy, et cetera. He got right down to business, telling me, "I would love to find a way to meet up with you, man. What you've been doing is amazing. We gotta figure out how to work together. Let's meet."

I said, sure we should meet sometime. We were both due for travel, so we agreed to stay in touch by text. After a few texts, he checked in with me when I happened to be in Miami on business.

P. DIDDY: Any chance you can meet up soon?

ME: In Miami. Back to LA at the end of the week.

P. DIDDY: I'm in Miami.

Turns out, he has a house there, and next thing I know, I'm on my way to the address he texted: 1 Star Island. Along for the ride and to enjoy the sights with me is my cousin Christian Sarabia, who has been on my team since our early days with *Surreal Life* and who has risen up through the ranks to become part of the leadership of 51 Minds. As someone that I've had the opportunity to mentor, Christian would be named president of the company a few years after this trip, and I'm glad he was able to hear the conversation that was about to happen.

P. Diddy's house at 1 Star Island, valued at something like $40 million and previously owned by music mogul Tommy Mottola, is a white Spanish-style villa on the water, hidden from sight by lush tropical landscaping. Breathtaking. Christian and I, in awe, walk up to the main door and knock. Right away it opens and P. Diddy is standing there. First thing he says to me is, "Oh, my God, I can't believe it's you."

I smile and greet our host, look over to Christian, as if to say—*is this even happening?*

P. Diddy/Sean then asks us, if we don't mind, to please take off our shoes. The floor is this beautiful dark wood imported from Africa, and he proceeds to tell us the crazy history of this wood as we walk through the epic house barefoot and outside to a resort-sized swimming pool. Beyond it is the bay, where a yacht and several Jet Skis are waiting for whoever wants to go for a ride. It's P. Diddy living the life, complete with a Jacuzzi and voluptuous women in bikinis just hanging out and chilled champagne at the ready.

Finally, after the tour, we go inside, sit, and begin to talk about television, where it's been and where I think it's headed.

That's when P. Diddy again says how he can't believe he's talking to me. "Man," he goes, "you're a Martian."

"Excuse me?"

"You're a Martian. Like me." Not sure what he means, I nod. But then he leans in and asks, "How do I become you?"

There is a confusing moment as I'm still unclear as to what he's asking. Obviously, he wants to expand his horizons into areas that I know about. Even so, my first response is to tell him I don't think he wants to be me. "'Cause I'm sitting here on Star Island with you.

Whereas, if you were me, you would be home in the San Fernando Valley with three young kids, running to Home Depot and back." Not to put down my quiet life away from work, but I was pretty sure he wouldn't trade places, if given the choice. Neither would I.

We all laughed. And after that, he said, "No, but you are unique. And you are a Martian."

As we continued to talk, I realized that one of the things that made him a Martian, as he put it, was that he didn't really have an agenda or a particular project that he wanted to push. He just was insatiably curious. He genuinely wanted to know more about the television industry and the changes that were going to be coming down the pike. He just liked getting to know people who were unique and who had specialized knowledge he could learn from.

After a while, I began to see P. Diddy's larger point that having big vision could be seen as an alien trait—not only the hyperfocus needed to make ambitious plans and dreams happen, but the unique ability to visualize the whole playing field at once and into the future.

When we left to drive back to our hotel, I asked Christian if he saw me as a Martian. Yep, he pretty much did.

Well, after years of thinking it was just me who was wired differently, I was relieved to know that I wasn't alone. But I also realized that I had put so much focus on where I was going and what I wanted to accomplish that I hadn't spent enough time cultivating self-awareness of my differences. Why was that important? First, with better self-understanding of what makes me tick and what makes me unique, I could better harness the capacities of being different. And, what's more, as a parent, mentor, and business leader, I wanted to be able to identify those unique capacities in others and empower those individuals to embrace their differences.

I know that not everybody is a Martian—what Malcolm Gladwell describes in his book *Outliers* as someone whose success is so far outside the norm, like a snowstorm in mid-July, that it can't be explained by talent or ability. But what if we each have an inner Martian or outlier that can be tapped occasionally to push us to the next level in our journey to success? In fact, Gladwell's premise is that if you want to understand an outlier, you have to look less at that person and more at the influences that surround that person: his or her family, culture, community, and experience.

When you look at your own differences, most likely they have to do with influences that make you who you are—not just your personality traits but the values that motivate you. That's *Motivation Lesson #12*: Recognize the *values* that define you, not anyone else. It's an exercise in self-awareness, often skipped by many a successful person. By accepting the premise that you're not like everybody else—and why should you be?—you're given the freedom to explore the less obvious facets of your potential. Have you limited yourself? What are the best differences about you that maybe you could take time to embrace more fully? And the big question for all of us, how can these discoveries help you expand your dreams and goals?

If these questions are ones you haven't thought about much, you can start the process of answering them with pen and paper or on a blank document page on your computer or mobile device. Ask yourself in what ways you are absolutely unique in your entire neighborhood and on your street and in your household. It's probably not one thing that will set you apart but a combination of your background, your experiences and expertise, your record of accomplishment, and most of all your point of view and your values. As you recap what those unique traits are, you might want to highlight five of them that most define you. Now ask yourself if you are putting those traits to use as part of the reality you seek to create.

You will find that this kind of self-awareness will also come in handy the next time you face a turning point or a big decision about where your mission should take you next. In my case, these kinds of questions were very helpful in the fall of 2013 when I came to yet another major crossroads.

If I chose to go one way, building on where I had come from, I could finally slow down and savor the success I'd achieved, make up for lost time, and get to do all the things that I'd missed over the past several years. If I chose to go the other way, I would be catapulted up to a daunting level of responsibility, with crazy and complex demands I'd never juggled all at the same time before.

The choice was an outlier in itself. The backstory was that in the fall of 2013, Endemol North America's CEO, David Goldberg, was suddenly on his way out, after not being able to reach terms to stay on. Shortly thereafter David would move on to run and grow Banijay North America, an international media group, in his stellar fashion. In the five years that he had been my boss, he was a true mentor. He believed in my potential and took me under his wing for no other reason than that he could. David would include me in dinners and meetings unrelated to my running of 51 Minds. He introduced me to associates at higher levels of the media world and enabled me to cultivate relationships outside my scope of contact. He valued what I did, eventually tasking me to develop and help oversee an Endemol network show (*Does Someone Have to Go?*) for FOX. Before working with Dave, I would never have considered running a division of an international corporation as something I'd want to do. But after seeing him operate at the highest level of our industry—with his unique understanding of the global marketplace and the shifting media landscape—I did start to wonder if maybe one day that too could be me.

To my surprise, "one day" came much sooner than later. A month after the announcement of David's upcoming departure, as I approached year six in my agreement with Endemol, I was given the option to stay on as the head of 51 Minds Entertainment but without ownership, now that they would be fully acquiring the company. We could agree on a salary, and I could continue to be creative, just without any stake. Or, because of my track record in bringing 51 Minds back from trouble to growth over the last almost six years, the higher-ups came up with a novel offer—a position as cochair and co-CEO of Endemol North America, a job to be shared with Charlie Corwin (whose company Original Media had been acquired shortly before us). The contract would be for four years.

The deliberation was brutal. When I thought about what it had taken me to get to that point, what I had asked of myself and my family for a relentless fifteen years, what I had sacrificed and what I had missed, I had to ask myself why I would do it again. Not for the money or the perks. That was never and could never be a reason.

Self-awareness led me to the answer and the decision. Could I see myself getting comfortable by sticking to what I knew, coasting along, taking time off? The joke was that if I decided to open up a little gardening business, I'd probably have twenty customers by tomorrow. Still, deep down I realized there was no reason that I couldn't take the co-CEO job and also commit to carving out more time for my family.

Why would I take this job? From the start, my dream was to work in television, and this was the opportunity to elevate the game and do it at the highest level—creating opportunities for a new generation of storytellers in every aspect of TV and media, in digital, on an international level. With a platform of that scope, I could truly do more to make a difference for others. Not only would this be a way of bringing more diversity into the storytelling and talent on our shows, but I could also promote more diversity in the field of entertainment in general. The possibilities were unlimited. Endemol would soon merge with Shine to become the Endemol Shine Group, a leading global powerhouse that would put me and my co-CEO at the helm of Endemol Shine North America with a roster of shows unlike any other producer and distributor of content in the world—in both unscripted and scripted. We would be able to expand our reach into untapped markets, including growing our presence in South America. We would be at the forefront of developing online content, short form, and televised live events, building brands and harnessing the star power of names like Pitbull, Mr. Worldwide himself. We'd be collaborating with digital pioneers such as Michelle Phan, soon to be known as the Oprah of the Internet, with ICON, an online lifestyle network of her own and a billion viewers built in at launch.

In deliberating over my decision, I thought about the future Cris Abregos out there and about anyone with a dream, anyone who didn't come from privilege or connection, and even those who did but who had lost faith in their own possibilities. I had been raised to set an example and so, of course, I thought about Latino kids and others growing up in neighborhoods where most people don't see beyond the end of their streets—kids for whom there wasn't anyone like me letting it be known that the dream of making it to CEO could be a reality. Yes, I thought about Carlos, gone as of this writing for twenty-five years. I still thought about him every day, the promise made not to forget him, and to carry his memory with me into every new adventure and challenge.

For all those reasons, I decided to take the job. Or maybe I had to take it because I really am a Martian.

LEAVE IT ON THE FIELD

In exploring and embracing what makes you different and how your values determine your decisions, you may come up with a list of priorities that you have in fact been neglecting. If your goal is to live a more fully realized life, there is no reason that you can't now give more attention to those priorities. That was brought home to me after undergoing a super-extensive physical that was part of the terms of the sale of my company. Endemol had to be sure that they weren't going to spend all that money only for me to croak.

The physical cost eight thousand dollars in order to get it all done in one day. When the results came in, as I reported to my mother, "The doctor told me everything was great, but I need to lose weight."

She promptly said, "*Ay*, I could have told you that for free." That's Tina Abrego, always telling it like it is.

As soon as I chose to make my health a priority, all the principles for turning dreams into reality applied to weight loss and to creating a tough daily regimen for myself that has been transformational. By making my health and fitness an integral part of my schedule, I realized how important that one hour of the day was to gain perspective on all parts of my work and life. One of the things that I've realized is how my intensity at work can take a toll not just on me but on everyone around me. That perspective has led me to a greater understanding of why I continue to push with a level of intensity that makes everything high priority. Interestingly enough, I've come to the conclusion that a part of that mentality comes from being a survivor and from not being able to let go of the struggle that once helped me overcome obstacles.

A true revelation, I had to face up to the fact that it was time to ease up on the struggle. That has been a crucial lesson in owning my success. At work, my ability to delegate to the leaders in all our departments—like my cousin Christian, who is now President of 51 Minds, and Ben Samek, now COO of Endemol Shine North America—has freed me to get up every day and be the motivator-in-chief that I love most about my job. My cochair and co-CEO, Charlie Corwin, and I have a great protocol for taking charge of our respective areas. We communicate openly about all facets of the operation and collaborate on the big picture, fine-tuning the corporate goals for all our stakeholders.

This process of clarifying your values and priorities can help you whenever you're stuck or at a crossroads—whether you're starting out or reinventing yourself or you own your own company or you are a CEO kicking yourself into another gear. Setting your priorities can be as simple as having a conversation with yourself about what aspects of your dream matter most and what actions you will take to make that a reality.

Setting priorities may also remind you of other parts of your life that matter. Family has always been a priority for me, and recently, I've gained greater self-awareness from overdue conversations with my father about his approach to parenting. When we talked, he made it clear that part of my intensity had to do with his decision to make sure that my brother and I learned to fight—as he had been forced to learn to survive when he was growing up.

In fact, I did learn how not to be fearful, how not to cry, how to be tough, how not to be intimidated. Yet the fight instilled in me was not true to who I was. I'm a sensitive guy. You can't be a storyteller and not be sensitive. But as I now understood, I didn't have to always have that edge. I could rewrite the rules for myself and give myself permission to evolve, to part ways with the struggle and the fight.

As a result of these conversations, I've also come to see that the values that matter most to me are those that both my parents still embody—especially their commitment to increasing educational opportunities for young people who lack the resources to pursue their academic dreams. As a matter of fact, that commitment is what led me to conceive of the Carlos Hernandez Jr. Memorial Scholarship so that deserving scholar athletes at Mountain View High School in El

Monte could be supported through the scholarship fund to take their journeys to top institutions of higher learning. When I brought it up, my parents were all for it. My mother agreed to help me set up the foundation and oversee the process of identifying the candidates at Mountain View High School. She has also helped me do things like donate air mileage to our recipients in order to make sure those who are chosen have all the resources needed—not just to attend Harvard and Georgetown and universities far away but to avoid the culture shock and challenges of adapting to the reality of their dreams once they get there.

The gift of being able to do as a family for other families has been the epitome of what it means to have a big dream become my reality. When I meet the scholarship recipients, I am always inspired by how they are able to see beyond the end of their street, against much tougher odds than I faced. They've already learned the truth about winning that I learned from my parents—who each put their own different spin on it.

My mother is the epitome of someone who believes actions speak louder than words. Winning, according to her, is revealed by actions, not by touting your accomplishments. That's part of her sense of privacy too, and her mantra is that you should focus on moving forward and making tomorrow better.

Back in high school, my father passed on a crucial piece of advice that I think sums up the most important lesson about what it takes to win at anything. The lesson came after a football game back in my junior year. It was our first year to make it to the playoffs, and we traveled to El Cajon in really cold weather to play the number one team in our division. It might have only been forty degrees but we thought it was freezing. Guys on our team were wearing long sleeves under our pads, even gloves and beanies under our helmets. Suddenly the El

Cajon team ran onto the field, wearing no shirts under their pads, like this was nothing. They were huge, muscle-bound, and fierce—like a team in the NFL. They went on to punish us, 65 to 0—a basketball game score. I was out of my mind, doing everything and anything, playing seven different positions, throwing my body everywhere I could to make something happen to change the tone of this ass kicking. I even resorted to cheating—grabbing face masks, you name it. When I got to the locker room, I was still angry and humiliated yet was startled to see a lot of our players openly crying. Why? I found that confusing.

Because of where my family lived, the coaches let me ride home with Dad, rather than go on the bus, and as he and I drove along, he said nothing. That too was confusing. Why wasn't he giving me his usual critique?

"Are you upset?" I asked.

"Not at all." More confusion. He said matter-of-factly, "You played your ass off out there."

"I did everything I could." He nodded, having seen. Then I admitted, "There were a lot of guys crying in the locker room. I don't know why I didn't feel like crying."

"Of course you weren't crying. You did everything you could to win. Why would you cry? You left it all on the field."

I had never heard that expression before. Was there anything more that I could have done? Nope.

My father said, "Those guys didn't play as hard as they could have, and they didn't leave it on the field. And that's why they feel bad, because they can't go back and do it over again."

Those are the best measures I can offer to you for living your full-court life. Did you leave it all on the field with actions that speak louder than words? Actually, in passing on the values of leadership to our three kids, Adriana and I keep those lessons very much in the forefront of motivating each of them—as different as they are from one another.

They know all about creating opportunity, about owning their success, and making their dreams reality. And they probably do think their dad is a Martian.

It's elementary—just make each day count in the reality game. And as you assess where you are and how far you've traveled, even if it's just to get to the point of believing in the reality of your dream, give yourself the boost of looking back at everything you've accomplished and weathered—especially the toughest moments and most intimidating challenges—and claim the victory that you deserve for rising to each occasion and leaving it on the field.

The question I'm most often asked is *what I want to do next*. The better question is *how I want to live next*. I'm excited to challenge the next generation of practitioners in the art and business of storytelling to shape television of the future. When I hear colleagues say that the end is near for TV, I don't listen. That's their fear. This is the most exciting time to be an influencer and disrupter in my industry, especially with the rise of multicultural communities enriching the global conversation.

Success to me now is appreciating and loving the ride. How about that? I've written this book about how to *attain* that success. The next one will probably be about how to *maintain* that success. In the meantime, as we say on TV, please stay tuned!

Still Climbing

When I first decided to reopen the box that I found up on a back shelf in a closet in my house, taped up tight with warnings not to open it, I thought that there would be things in there that I'd forgotten. Who did I want to prevent from breaking the seal and opening it up? Me. I don't know what I thought would happen by opening it up, but nothing did. If anything, the decision to open the box and write about the accident and talk about those events was liberating. A load was lifted. Neither my parents nor Adriana had known about the box or the journal. The conversations we had were cathartic.

Strangely enough I had remembered the contents exactly as they were—the shorts I'd been wearing, the accident report, the court transcripts, the articles about accident survivors who felt they needed forgiveness. When I reread the entries in the journal, they matched the memories that I had played and replayed for years. Opening up the box and going through it made me realize how haunted I had been, especially in the spring each year during the months leading up to the anniversary of when the accident happened.

The question arose at last if it was guilt that had been keeping me from feeling truly successful. There could be some truth to that. No, the accident wasn't my fault. But a part of me was stuck in the past, always asking why I couldn't have prevented it. Illogical, I know. Yet there it is.

Sometimes I have sensed Carlos trying to get a message to me to cut myself some slack. There was definitely something uncanny about the encounter with the two *cholo* guys in the cemetery that afternoon shortly after his death, the ones who told me that I had to change so that Carlos wouldn't have died in vain. The mystery remained that I'd been to the cemetery many times yet never seen them again and never found their brother's grave again.

There was another memorable encounter I wanted to include here that happened back in that period right before I took the new job at the helm of our division of Endemol Shine, when things were getting crazy as I was trying to bring back business for 51 Minds. For a short period, I had felt lost in my job. It was an unfamiliar feeling, just a sense of being lost in my direction.

At that point, I hadn't been out to the cemetery in maybe seven years. I had actually initiated the plan to create the memorial scholarship fund in Carlos's name but his sister, Christine, had shut it down. I didn't feel the need to have her permission, but I had hoped to have the family's blessing; instead I was going to do it without them. That may have been on my mind one afternoon when I just got up and left work, went and got into my new car—that I would have loved to have shown Ghost—and decided to go for a drive. Once on the road, I headed out to Montebello and stopped to buy a coffee and some flowers.

When I got to the spot where I was certain Carlos was buried, once again I couldn't find the plot. This time, I knew there was a gravestone. I'd visited it many times. But it was nowhere to be found. I walked around in circles, trying to orient myself, without any luck.

After a bit, I notice this older Mexican guy up on the hill, leaning out of his car, watching me. *Strange,* I think. Or am I just imagining it? After walking around again and still not finding the gravestone, I'm about to get back in the car and try a different area when he approaches and asks in Spanish who I'm looking for. I answer, *"Uno amigo."*

Then in English, he goes, "Who are you looking for, a grave site?"

"Yes, I am." I have the feeling that he doesn't believe me.

He peers at me closely, asking, "Are you lost?"

He put into words exactly where I was in my life. In my mind, I answered—*Yeah, I am lost.* Out loud I said that I'd give it another try.

The man suggested that if I went to the office and gave the date of death, the people there would give me a map with a grid.

After thanking him, I nodded and went to my car, hiding my shame. I felt so low. I had forgotten Carlos. I had promised that I wouldn't, and now I couldn't even find his grave. Once I got to the office, the people there looked up the plot number and showed me the map with a grid. I had been in the wrong section. So I drove back and found the overgrown section where Carlos was buried, and at last I located his grave, placed the flowers in the holder, and sat down a little ways back from his grave. I was hanging out with Carlos, drinking my coffee, listening to Morrissey and the Smiths on my phone.

All of a sudden, I see this older, small woman, dressed in a longer skirt, as she approaches Carlos's grave and sits down to pull up a lot of the grass that is around him. After pulling up most of the grass, she takes the flowers out of the holder and holds them as if she's going to get up and walk away with them.

At that point, I stand and say, "Excuse me, ma'am. . . . I'm sorry. I just put those there."

"Oh," she says, "I'm just cleaning it up." With that, she replaces the flowers and begins to leave.

In a flash, I'm almost sure that the woman is Carlos's mother. My body goes cold. But it's been so many years that I can't recognize her. Of course it's her. Or is it? I can't recall her from the funeral, even though I know she was there. It was a blur.

Before the woman leaves, she turns back to me and asks, "Did you know him?"

After a pause: "Yeah, I knew him."

"How did you know him?"

Inside I'm in knots, telling myself—*Don't tell her. She doesn't know you. She doesn't recognize you.* I decide that I'll lie and not tell her anything. Better yet, I decide to leave. "Well," I begin, "I better be going."

She nods and then asks, "You're Cris Abrego, aren't you?"

My heart almost stops. Chills go up and down my whole body. I want nothing more than to say, "No, I'm not." Instead I nod and say quietly, "Yes."

"Do you remember me?"

Not 100 percent sure, I just say, "No."

Then she tells me, "I'm Carlos's mom."

I say something polite and then, "Oh, I'm sorry. I'm going to get going so you can have your time." I start to walk briskly away.

Carlos's mother calls after me, "Hey, hang on. Come back."

I stop and turn back.

"Can I ask you one thing?" she asks.

"Sure."

She says, "Can I give you a hug?"

And I went back to her, and she gave me a long hug. As she did, she said, "I forgive you."

She asked if I had kids, and we spoke for about five minutes longer. When I said again that I needed to get going, she added that she knew that Christine had been saying no to setting up the scholarship fund, but as far as she was concerned, "You have my permission and my blessing. I'm really proud that you would do that. And I want you to do that."

And so the next month, the scholarship was up and running. And Carlos's mother came to the first scholarship presentation and met the recipients, and we made it a reality.

I leave you with that story because her message felt miraculous to me, easing the pain of the loss that lived inside many who were touched by Carlos and also letting me believe that forgiveness is possible. It is God's work that we give ourselves permission and blessings to make a difference for others. I happen to believe that Carlos sends me people from time to time, whether they're angels or not angels; they appear for all of us to send the message that all of our loved ones who are no longer with us are still counting on us—on me and on you—to do our best and make the most of what we've been given, to keep on climbing, loving what we do, learning what we can, and just being good to one another.

Committing to Your Twenty-Year Plan

E ven though I've made this point throughout *Make It Reality*, it bears repeating that the choice is yours to get going toward the destination of your dreams. It's really up to you to come up with your own road rules. As you've no doubt concluded, no one else is waiting to pave the road for you. This is your moment, the time to create your own path. In doing so, if you believe in yourself and your dreams, embrace your vision and what makes you different, and have the courage to bet on yourself, the destination will be greater than you ever imagined.

COMMIT TO THE LONG GAME AND PRACTICE SUCCESS ON A DAILY BASIS

How do you officially get started or reboot a game plan that hasn't been working? The first step is to make the commitment in as con-

crete a way as possible. It's hard to see into the future and to anticipate all the changes that will happen outside of your control. But
even if you don't yet have the complete vision to see where possibilities might lead you, don't let that scare you or prevent you from getting started. Be emboldened simply by making the commitment.

Lots of people choose to commit to their dreams with official
declarations. You can do it for yourself on paper or by making a vision board with a visual depiction of your ultimate dream at the top
so you can look at it every day. Or you can do it by sharing your decision with family and friends in person or through social media. What
really counts, as I've said all along, is to give yourself permission to
dream. If you don't yet have an idea of a field of interest or potential
direction that engages your passion and your sense of purpose, feel
free to reread earlier chapters that challenge you to think about what
you love to do, what you're good at, what sparks your interest and
curiosity, and what values matter to you in making a commitment to
turning your dream into a reality.

Something powerful happens when you put the word out to others or just to yourself, or when you elect to come up with a specific
Statement of Intention. It could be something along the lines of
"One day I'm going to work in _____ (your field of interest)
and will distinguish myself by _____ (for example, mastering your lane or being known as an innovator, et cetera . . .)."

As important as that Statement of Intention is, can you follow it
up with a game plan that you begin today, perhaps with a Statement
of Conviction and Action? This is where you make the commitment
to the long game and to the actions you will take on a daily basis.
What is it about your Intention that gives you a sense of priority and
that you can treat as an article of faith, almost like a religion? Your
Statement of Conviction and Action describes why you believe in

yourself, what resources you bring to your purpose, and what you're willing to do to take action on a daily basis as you pursue your Intention. Your "why" can be as simple as "I'm motivated to pursue my path because I believe in my assets and resources that include _____ (list attributes you already have that empower you) and my ability to take specific action by _____ (how you intend to train for success) on a daily basis."

THE FOUR PHASES OF THE TWENTY-YEAR PLAN

If you are really starting out, I recommend that you imagine a journey that is as crazy, broad, big, and ambitious as you dare. As long as you recall the general stages of creating your reality over the long haul—the long game—you can begin to shape your reality in the present, even changing your prospects for success in the immediate future.

What follows is a brainstorming tool for coming up with a first draft for your Twenty-Year Plan. Again, your plan may take you longer than twenty years or nowhere near as long. You may be starting at Phase Two or Phase Three, depending on where you are in your life and career already. You may need to complete your college education or return to school before you really get going. No matter where you fit in, the key is to continually fine-tune and flesh out your goals in realistic ways that are relevant to the general stages: Phase 1 (Learning to Navigate), Phase 2 (Determining Your Direction), Phase 3 (Achieving Mastery of Your Lane or as an Entrepreneur), Phase 4 (Expanding and Growing Your Dream, Adding Value for the World).

Questions to Inspire Your Game Plan

Learning to Navigate, Mastering the Lay of the Land

- What are your three top strengths that will serve you as you learn every aspect of your chosen field?

- What is a weakness you seek to overcome?

- Who is your mentor or adviser or inspiration?

- What obstacles stand in your way? How can you challenge yourself?

- What resources do you have or hope to have to overcome those obstacles and meet those challenges? What life lessons give you confidence to beat the odds?

- As you gain mastery and practical knowledge of your field, how can you continue to embrace your role as a student?

- As you attain success at your current level, what can you do to master the responsibilities of someone at a higher level?

Determining Your Direction, Refining Your Goals

After spending time honing your knowledge and skills in your chosen arena, you get to the point where you're ready to look at your overarching dream with more specificity. In my case, the dream was to one day work in television. But after five years of learning the lay of the land, I was able to focus in on a specific lane for myself: to become an executive producer. As you refocus your dream and your ideal destination, begin to map out your A to B steps for getting there. Questions that you can ask yourself now and when you get to that point are:

- Now that you've chosen your dream direction, what are the most ambitious goals you can set for yourself over the next few years?

- What are the more "realistic" and reachable goals you can set for yourself over the next few years?

- What ideas, projects, practices, assets, or other resources do you have that will let you create opportunities for yourself starting right now?

- What are the steps and positions you need to reach on your way to your ultimate destination?

- What are your main drivers? What are your distractions? What are your excuses?

- What makes you a standout at what you do?

- What are your specific time deadlines to meet your most tangible goals?

PHASE 3:

Mastering Your Lane, Building Your Brand or Business

If you are at this phase or looking down the road to shape your plans, you have hopefully figured out the "what" and the "why" of your dream. It's now time to put to use every lesson you've learned so far to build your reality—by focusing more on your "where" and "when" and with "whom" and, of course, "how." The questions below can be applied whether you are working for someone else or are building your own business, career, or platform. That makes you an entrepreneur.

- When you assess how far you've come from where you started, what makes you feel the most proud?

- What lessons have you learned from mistakes, missteps, and failures that motivate you to succeed now?

- What principles for success have been most useful in guiding you so far?

- Who do you consider to be the main members of your team? What strengths of advice, help, and support do they offer you in building your reality?

- What communication resources do you need to convey your reality to others?

- What do you consider to be the peak of success you hope to attain in five years?

- What milestones do you plan on reaching on your way to that peak? When do you plan on reaching them?

- What actionable steps must you take to meet your milestones?

- How would you like to improve as a leader?

PHASE 4:
Growing Your Dream, Adding Value to the World

If you are at a point in your journey where you are asking yourself not just how to attain success, but how to maintain it, you are probably ready to grow and expand your dream. You've reached a level of accomplishment through struggle and hard work, and now it's time to recharge, perhaps with a new energy source, or even to change the game and not just for you but also to add value for others by making your dream even bigger than yourself. You may want to consider the following questions that can help you assess where you are and how to move forward for this next leg of the journey:

- What sparks the same fire that once empowered you to overcome challenges? How do you feed that drive now that you have reached tough goals? What gets you inspired every day?

- How can your success make a difference for others?

- What values describe both you and what you offer to the marketplace as a successful individual and/or company?

- What areas of your life have you perhaps neglected or had to sacrifice? How do you plan to achieve more balance?

- What creative problem-solving abilities serve you on a daily basis?

- How are you challenging yourself as an influencer, innovator, disrupter, or risk taker as you raise the bar going forward?

- What learning goals currently inspire and motivate you?

- Who are the stakeholders you hope to benefit in all you do?

- In growing your dream to add value to the world, how would you most like to be remembered for the reality you attained?

Finally, you can always draft a pitch-style log line for the reality you now envision for yourself and your journey. Let it fire up your imagination. Let it feed your hunger. Let it excite you every night when you go to sleep and every day when you get up. Then throw out all the rules, and go take the ride of your life. The road is yours to make real.

Remember the Success Principles

- Bet on yourself.
- Find what you love to do and choose to do it for a living.
- Employ vision (see what no one else can).
- Cultivate an unstoppable work ethic.
- Prepare for each and every shot by training like a professional athlete.
- Embrace your passion and your purpose.
- Create opportunities for yourself because no one hands them to you.
- Write your own rules for success.
- Be willing to change the game.
- Believe in a mission that's bigger than yourself.
- Above all, take on the mantle of leadership.

Armed with These Motivational Lessons, You Have Everything You Need to Make Your Dreams Reality!

#1. PASSION can reveal the path to your dream.

#2. With FOCUS, you can achieve your goals, that is, as long as you have the stamina to outwork, outhustle, and outdeliver everyone else.

#3. Employ VISION by finding examples of someone like you who has achieved their dreams.

#4. When you play the long game, vision and COURAGE will take you out of your comfort zone and help you to overcome obstacles and set goals for yourself.

#5. SELF-MOTIVATION comes from balancing rewards with the lessons you learn from criticism and high expectations of yourself.

#6. RESOURCEFULNESS is a leadership trait needed for every team. Know what resources you offer in terms of innovation, creativity, and problem solving.

#7. If you can fall in love with the GROWTH that comes from struggle, and if you choose to feel that you're richer for what you've learned and discovered, you will find the means for experiencing daily success.

#8. RISK and ORIGINALITY let you change the game. Not everyone is going to get it or get you. But if you really believe, chances are that somebody else will too.

#9. When you INSTIGATE your own opportunities, success will breed more success. Those results can then be leveraged.

#10. Only you are the AUTHORITY on your game. You write the rules of your own success.

#11. AUTHENTICITY is the cornerstone of reality. The truth is a hit.

#12. SELF-AWARENESS lets you grow your dream and inspire others. Embrace the values that define you, not anyone else.

acknowledgments

If I've learned anything from the daunting work involved in writing a book like this one, it's how similar the process is to transforming your dream into reality. This last year has truly been a journey, and I know it's one that I couldn't have completed on my own.

Big thanks must go to Celebra publisher Ray Garcia for having the vision that inspired the journey in the first place. Thank you, Ray, for tricking me into thinking this could be easy! And Jennifer Schuster, our intrepid editor, thank you for taking that vision a step further and for pushing and guiding me and the rest of the team to not only execute our big ideas but to make them jump off the page. To everyone at Celebra/Penguin Random House and to our sales associates, *mil gracias* for raising your game on behalf of *Make It Reality*. A massive thank-you to Mim Eichler Rivas—you truly are an amazing storyteller, and I'm honored to have shared this journey with you.

Thank you to the team at CAA, especially Simon Green and Christy Haubegger, who were passionate about making sure I had the best possible book home. Christy, I'm fortunate to be working with you *and* to have the privilege to call you a friend. Thank you for everything and mainly for helping me to change the tape that plays in my head.

I owe a lasting debt of gratitude to a handful of special individuals whose encouragement and support have been meaningful throughout my life and career. My eternal thanks go to Sy and Tina—or Dad and Mom, as I like to refer to them. Mom, thank you for always believing in me and for never making me feel like my differences were ever something that would hold me back, and more importantly for putting up with Dad all these years! Dad, I know your life wasn't easy growing up, but thank you for being the man you were then when I was growing up and the man you are today. You continue to set the bar!

To my brother, Steve, it's been a wild ride, and I'm glad you're a part of it.

To my *tía* Oliva, my second mom, *muchisimas gracias por todo, Tía*! And for always supporting me, caring for me, and above all for always praying for me.

To Uncle Sammy, my first teacher in comedy, for truly teaching me the art of timing.

To my EL MONTE DOGS, where do I start? Danny "Dog" Hernandez, thanks for your honesty, loyalty, and more importantly for never allowing me to take myself too serious.

To Sal Garcia, thank you for taking the time to read the book, multiple times, and for giving me honest feedback, and more importantly for you and your family.

To Casey "Catman" Diaz, you epitomize the word "loyalty."

To Brian Reyes, thank you for housing me, back in the day after I got my first job in TV and quickly found out it didn't pay shit!! I always remember our talks at the kitchen table in Palm Springs, both of us talking about our dreams; you would say you were going to be chief of police, and I would say I was going to run my own production company!! *Ha, like that's ever going to happen!* Oh, wait. . . .

Thank you, Pam Barkas. Yup, you were *that* teacher—the one who made a difference in my life. Thank you for your belief in me and even more for inspiring me to write stories. Plus, you were the first white lady I met who was nice to me!

To Adam "the Gooch" Delgado, thank you for being in my corner and for letting me know that feeling scared is different from being scared.

To Frank Alonzo, thank you for teaching me that even when things get incredibly tense and the stakes are high, there's always room for a joke and a laugh.

George Herrera, I don't know where you are or if I ever said this to you, but thank you. Putting me on "project best" as a counselor after my accident truly set me in the right direction.

Many of the positive lessons I learned about success could not have been attained without the contributions of key colleagues along the way. Mark Cronin, I start that list with you—because as funny and smart as you are, you were also a great mentor and partner who taught me to fight for our creative beliefs, and more importantly, you introduced me to Mastro's Steakhouse!! Keith Cox, I am forever in your debt. You taught me the truth about recognizing great ideas as the true gold of our industry.

To all of my colleagues who are or were part of the MTV/VH1 universe, thank you for the inspiration of your talents and vision. There are not enough words to convey my gratitude to Brian Graden and Jeff Olde for your leadership and your brilliance.

The trajectory of my life and success would have been very different had it not been for Tim Hincks and David Goldberg, two individuals who first opened the door to my new home at Endemol

Shine. Tim, thank you for giving me the opportunity to do what I love at its highest level, and David, thank you for getting me ready for it.

Big thanks to all of my Endemol Shine colleagues here and around the world. Thank you so much to all of you who have cheered me on in this book-writing process—with sincere appreciation to Danita Ruiz, who has worked triple time to make sure that I'd meet the deadlines.

Special acknowledgments go out to everyone at Team 51 MINDS. Thanks for giving beyond what each of you even knew was possible. Thank you for letting me push you and for pushing right back. That's how we keep winning.

My warmest gratitude is due to the artists and individuals who have generously given of themselves on behalf of *Make It Reality*. Shout-outs to Pitbull, Steve Harvey, Eva Longoria, Chris Gardner, Will Griffin, George Lopez, La La Anthony, Ryan Seacrest, Irv Gotti, TI, Mario Lopez, Flavor Flav, and Bret Michaels. Thank you all for your inspiration.

Jon Murray, thank you for your generosity of time in reading a draft or two of this work. Your praise means the world to me.

Finally, I'd like to extend my sincere appreciation to some individuals whose influence makes a difference every single day.

To Charlie Corwin, thank you for your support with the book, and I'm always grateful for your candor.

To my attorney and friend Jeanne Newman, you truly have changed my business and in turn changed my life. Thank you for all our talk. What I love so much is that I forget you're actually an attorney.

To Christian Sarabia, thank you for proving that if you follow the steps, this book does work! Ha. Thank you for always having my back. We have been in some battles, but no matter how bad it got, I knew that I could look over my shoulder and you would be right there. I know you don't like that I tell people you're my cousin, but it's because I'm so proud of you and the leader you have become.

To Ben Samek, "thank you" doesn't cover it, but I will say it anyway. Thank you for your tireless work ethic, your continued commitment, your unwavering loyalty, and above all your belief in me. I hope you're ready for what's next.

And last but not least, let me acknowledge Adriana—thank you for your patience and help in not just making this book a reality but making my dreams a reality! To our kids—Mateo, Eva, and Benicio—even though this book has no dragons, princesses, or rockets in it, I hope you guys enjoy and are proud of it, and that, more importantly, I hopefully left it on the field.